Horrifying Children

Horrifying Children

Hauntology and the Legacy of Children's Television

Lauren Stephenson, Robert Edgar and John Marland

BLOOMSBURY ACADEMIC
NEW YORK • LONDON • OXFORD • NEW DELHI • SYDNEY

BLOOMSBURY ACADEMIC
Bloomsbury Publishing Inc
1385 Broadway, New York, NY 10018, USA
50 Bedford Square, London, WC1B 3DP, UK
29 Earlsfort Terrace, Dublin 2, Ireland

BLOOMSBURY, BLOOMSBURY ACADEMIC and the Diana logo are trademarks of
Bloomsbury Publishing Plc

First published in the United States of America 2024

Cover design: Eleanor Rose
Cover images: Doll photograph © Robert Edgar; Supplementary image © Getty Images

Bloomsbury Publishing Inc does not have any control over, or responsibility for, any
third-party websites referred to or in this book. All internet addresses given in this
book were correct at the time of going to press. The author and publisher regret any
inconvenience caused if addresses have changed or sites have ceased to exist,
but can accept no responsibility for any such changes.

A catalog record for this book is available from the Library of Congress.

ISBN: HB: 978-1-5013-9056-2
ePDF: 978-1-5013-9054-8
eBook: 978-1-5013-9055-5

Typeset by Newgen KnowledgeWorks Pvt. Ltd., Chennai, India

To find out more about our authors and books visit www.bloomsbury.com
and sign up for our newsletters.

This volume is dedicated to all of the enthusiasts who collect, catalogue and curate television programmes, comics, toys and other treasures from our past.

The editors would like to dedicate this book to:
Lauren: Her grandparents, Ann and Jack, who patiently endured hours of Goosebumps *every summer, and bought her most (if not all) of her* Point Horror *collection.*
Robert: His mum and dad (Jenny and Fred) for allowing him to use their attic as his personal archive of 1970s and 1980s ephemera. He would also like to thank his brother, Stewart, for sharing his toys. He would also like to dedicate this to his partner, Julia. And, as always, for M and the memory of her childhood.
John: His children, John Joseph and Marian Rose. Horrified, perhaps, but never horrifying.

CONTENTS

Part One   Hauntings and Spectres

Part Two   Memory, Process and Practice

FIGURES

CONTRIBUTORS

Hollie Adams is a secondary-school teacher based in the UK. Hollie is an independent researcher with interests in pedagogy, children's fiction and eco-horror.

Fernando Gabriel Pagnoni Berns is Professor of Audiovisual Thought (Cinema and Literature) and teaches undergraduate seminars on international horror cinema at the University of Buenos Aires, Argentina. He is the director of the horror film research group 'Grite', and has published chapters in the books *The Films of Delmer Daves* (2022), *Doubles and Hybrids in Latin American Gothic* (2021), *Gender and Environment in Science Fiction* (2018), *Critical Insights: Alfred Hitchcock* (2016), *Dreamscapes in Italian Cinema* (2015) and *To See the* Saw *Movies: Essays on Torture Porn and Post-9/11 Horror* (2013), among many others. He has written a book about the Spanish television series, *Historias para no Dormir* (2020), and has edited a book to celebrate the bicentenary of Frankenstein (2019).

Fiona Cameron is Lecturer in Creative Writing at Bangor University, North Wales. Her most recent poetry collections are *She May Be Radon* (2021) and *Bendigo* (2015). Her recent work has appeared in *Poetry Wales*, *Strix Magazine* and *Horror Across Borders*. She is currently writing and researching a poetry/memoir project which explores deep time and the 'opening of the field' in a specific six-acre rural location on the Wirral peninsula.

Jez Conolly is co-editor, with Caroline Whelan, of three books in the World Film Locations series – *Liverpool* (2013), *Dublin* (2012) and *Reykjavik* (2012). He wrote regularly for *The Big Picture* magazine and website, and currently contributes articles for *Beneficial Shock!* magazine as well as numerous other cinema books and journals. He is the author of three monographs offering detailed analyses of John Carpenter's *The Thing*, the 1945 Ealing Studios portmanteau horror film *Dead of Night* and the 1966 John Frankenheimer film *Seconds*. His new essay on *The Thing* will appear in *Scarred for Life, Volume 3*. Jez is former Head of Student Engagement with the University of Bristol Library Services, UK, having recently retired to live in Scotland with his wife and two bears.

Miranda Corcoran is Lecturer in 21st Century Literature at University College Cork, Ireland. She is the author of *Witchcraft and Adolescence in American Popular Culture: Teen Witches* (2022) and the co-editor (with Steve Gronert Ellerhoff) of *Exploring the Horror of Supernatural Fiction: Ray Bradbury's Elliott Family* (2020).

Flannán Delaney lives on the banks of the River Lee with their partner, a flatmate and two cats. They spend much of their free time trying to stave off the end of the world.

Robert Edgar is Professor of Writing and Popular Culture in the York Centre for Writing at York St John University, UK. He has published on *Venue Stories* (2023), the *Routledge Companion to Folk Horror* (2023), *Adaptation for Scriptwriters* (2019), *Science Fiction for Survival* (2019), *Music, Memory and Memoir* (2019), *The Arena Concert* (2015), *The Music Documentary* (2013), *The Language of Film* (2010; 2015), *Screenwriting* (2009) and *Directing Fiction* (2009). He is also co-editor of the forthcoming volume, *Alan Garner: The Work of Time*. Robert is a member of the York Centre for Writing, and he is the co-convener of the Music Memoir Research Group and the Hauntology and Spectrality Research Group. He is a member of the York St John Unit for Satire and he works on the Terra Two Project.

Benjamin Halligan is the director of Doctoral College of the University of Wolverhampton, UK. His publications include *Hotbeds of Licentiousness: The British Glamour Film and the Permissive Society* (2022); *Desires for Reality: Radicalism and Revolution in Western European Film* (2017) and *Michael Reeves* (2003). He has co-edited the following books: *Diva: Feminism and Fierceness from Pop to Hip-Hop* (2023); *Adult Themes: British Cinema and the X-Rating in the Long 1960s* (2023); *Politics of the Many: Contemporary Radical Thought and the Crisis of Agency* (2021); *Stories We Could Tell: Putting Words to American Popular Music* (2018); *The Arena Concert: Music, Media and Mass Entertainment* (2016); *Resonances: Noise and Contemporary Music*; *The Music Documentary: Acid Rock to Electropop* (2013); *Reverberations: The Philosophy, Aesthetics and Politics of Noise* (2012) and *Mark E. Smith and The Fall: Art, Music and Politics* (2010).

Max Hart is an archivist and independent researcher living in Chicago, Illinois. In 2019, they received a Bachelor's of Arts in Visual and Critical

Studies from the School of the Art Institute of Chicago, United States. Born out of an interest in performance art and queer theory, their undergraduate research focused on the relationship between commercial children's media and emerging sociopolitical metanarratives at the turn of the twenty-first century in the United States. Their thesis, *An Adult Nightmare: Garbage Pail Kids and the Fear of the Queer Child*, utilizes the controversy surrounding the popular children's trading cards to bring the problematic of a 'queer child' into conversation with the work of queer theorist Lee Edelman. Currently, they work as a video archivist at the non-profit Media Burn Archive in Chicago, and are rekindling a studio practice. Their current research interests revolve around the importance of play, childishness and monstrosity to the philosophy of Georges Bataille.

Alexander Hartley is a graduate student at Harvard University, United States, originally from the UK. He researches the movement of terms and ideas between the realms of law, politics and culture in the English, French and German-speaking worlds. His dissertation examines the relationship between British and French colonial copyright law and modernist ideas of authorship. His other writing has addressed Samuel Beckett and Bertolt Brecht's lawsuits, the American midcentury policy and poetry of 'urban renewal' and ideas of 'tolerance' in late critical theory.

Wayne Johnson is Senior Lecturer in Film Studies and Media and Communication at York St John University, UK. He has published on religion and popular culture in the UK and the United States, and the representation of New York City in American culture. He is the co-author (with Keith McDonald) of *Contemporary Gothic and Horror Film* (2021). His current areas of research are children's TV Gothic horror as well as the spectral Western. He is co-editor of the forthcoming volume, *Alan Garner: The Work of Time*.

John Marland is Senior Lecturer in Literature at York St John University, UK, where he has both taught and developed undergraduate courses in literature and film. He has published on *Thomas Hardy and the Folk Horror Tradition* (2023), *Adaptation for Scriptwriters* (2019), *The Language of Film* (2010; 2015) and *Screenwriting* (2009). He is co-editor of the forthcoming publication, *Alan Garner: The Work of Time*.

Keith McDonald is Senior Lecturer in Film Studies and Media and Communication at York St John University, UK, and holds a PhD from Birkbeck College, University of London, UK. He is the co-author of *Contemporary Gothic and Horror Film: Transnational Perspectives* (2021) with Wayne Johnson and *Guillermo del Toro: Film as Alchemic Art* (2014) with Roger Clark. He is currently involved in teaching and writing about hauntology and popular media on a number of projects and is co-writing a book on the Gothic and supernatural in the Western film genre. Other interests include pedagogy, transnational media and fan culture as online activism.

Jackson Phoenix Nash is an associate lecturer at the Open University in the School of Arts and Humanities. He completed his PhD in gender studies at the University of Sussex in 2019 with a focus on transgender YA literature. He is a fellow of the Lambda Literary Foundation Writer's Retreat for Emerging LGBTQ Voices in the YA workshop, and his fiction and poetry have appeared in over thirty publications. His debut poetry pamphlet will be published by Little Betty in 2024. Jackson identifies as a queer trans man.

Stella Miriam Pryce is a PhD researcher and ESRC scholar in Children's Literature at the University of Cambridge, UK. Her thesis entitled 'The Spectre of Childhood' bridges the gap between Children's Literature Studies and Spectrality Theory. Specifically, her research examines childhood identity and positions the figure of the child as spectral in British children's fiction. In addition to her academic work, Stella is a keen creative writer and runs her own theatre company.

Michael Schofield is a multi-modal artist and Lecturer in Media Studies at the University of Leeds, UK. His practice-led doctoral thesis (2018) examined the 'hauntology' of rephotography. Since completing his PhD, he has published research on hauntology in the *International Journal of Film and Media Arts* and in his book, *Narrating the City* (2020). His current research into spectrality, memory and media expands its scope to address sound and the moving image. Schofield also makes experimental films, publishing and exhibiting work under the alias Michael C. Coldwell, and he releases hauntological music under the name Conflux Coldwell. His critically acclaimed album CC – AM was described as 'everything hauntology could and should be in 2017' by *The Wire Magazine*. As an academic, he has taught photography and film-making at the University of Leeds, Leeds Arts University, Sheffield Hallam and York St John University, UK.

Merinda Staubli is a PhD candidate at RMIT University in Melbourne, Australia. Her research focuses on children's horror television in Australia in the 1990s and early 2000s. She has previously researched the reach of horror beyond the cinema screen and has published on the potential effects of VR on the horror genre. She is a horror film-maker and her short films have screened at multiple national and international film festivals, including: Monster Fest, A Night of Horror International Film Festival, Ax Wound Film Festival, El Vampirascopio, MidWest WeirdFest, Women in Horror Film Festival, Atlanta Horror Film Festival and Idaho Horror Film Festival. Her film *Helminth* (2017) was awarded 'Best Midnight Short' at Nightmares Film Festival (2018).

Lauren Stephenson is Senior Lecturer in Film Studies and Media and Communication at York St John University, UK. Her research interests include horror cinema (in particular, British, American and New Zealand horror), gender and horror, cinema and social justice and representations of women's friendship on-screen. She has written on the British TV series *Dead Set* (dir. Yann Demange, 2008), the 'Hoodie Horror' film cycle, representations of transplantation in *The Eye* (dir. David Moreau and Xavier Palud, 2008) and women's friendship in *Vicky Cristina Barcelona* (dir. Woody Allen, 2008). She has also written pieces on the film-maker Coralie Fargeat for the *Cut-Throat Women Database* and on Jennifer Kent's *The Nightingale* (2018) for the *Bloody Women* online journal. Most recently, she has written for *The Routledge Companion to Folk Horror* (Edgar & Johnson eds., 2023) on 'Restoring Relics – (Re)-releasing Antrum (2018) and film as Folk Horror'. She is the executive producer of the short film Cost of Living (2022), and the co-founder of the Cinema and Social Justice project at York St. John University, UK.

Elizabeth Tussey is an Appalachian writer and genealogist residing in Coraopolis, Pennsylvania, United States. She is a graduate of the Northeast Ohio MFA Consortium, United States, and her poetry and prose have appeared in *Barn Owl Review*, *Postcolonial Text*, *The Women of Appalachia Project*, *I Thought I Heard a Cardinal Sing* and *The Encyclopedia of LGBTQIA+ Portrayals in American Film*.

Adam Whybray is Lecturer in Film Studies at the University of Suffolk, UK. In 2015, he received his PhD in the Philosophy of Film from the University of Exeter, UK. He previously contributed the chapter '"Well futile": Nathan Barley and Post-Ironic Culture' to James Leggott and Jamie Sexton's 2013 publication, *No Known Cure: The Comedy of Chris Morris,* and has articles published in the journals *Comedy Studies*, *Childhood Remixed* and *Gothic Studies*. He has previously given conference papers on the fairytale games of Stephen Lavelle, Emily Short and Edgar Allan Poe, the 2010 London student protests and the avant-garde band The Residents. In his spare time, he co-hosts *Still Scared*, a podcast on children's horror.

ACKNOWLEDGEMENTS

The editors would like to thank Katie Gallof, Stephanie Grace-Petinos and Alyssa Jordan at Bloomsbury for their ongoing support in the development of this book.

Many thanks to all the participants and attendees at the Horrifying Children conference held at York St John University, first planned for 2020 and resurrected in 2022 following the pandemic. Very special thanks to the keynote speakers, Abi Curtis, Catherine Lester, Richard Littler and Diane A. Rodgers. Our thanks also go to Henry Jenkins for giving us a preview of his latest research. Special thanks go to Stephen Brotherstone, Bob Fischer and Dave Lawrence for their *Scarred for Life* live performance and for their remarkable publications, which were inspiration for this collection.

Our work on Horrifying Children has extended into creative writing and our thanks go to Imogen Peniston and all at Greenteeth Press for their collection, *Horrifying Tales*, which was published to coincide with the planned 2020 conference. With the help of Rob O'Connor and Reaper Press, we had a second collection, *Stories from Under the Bed*, to enjoy/unsettle for the 2022 conference.

The editors would like to thank the staff and students of Film and Media, Creative Writing and Literature in the School of Humanities at York St John University for their support and inspiration.

Introduction: The Edwardian legacy and children's fiction

Lauren Stephenson, Robert Edgar and John Marland

There has been an explosion of interest in the impact of children's television and literature of the late twentieth century. In particular, the 1970s, 1980s and 1990s are seen as decades that shaped a great deal of the contemporary popular-cultural landscape. Television of this period dominated the world of childhood entertainment, drawing freely upon literature and popular culture, and much of it continues to resonate powerfully with the generation of cultural producers (fiction writers, screenwriters, directors, musicians and artists) who grew up watching the weird, the eerie and the occasionally horrific: this seems the essence of twenty-first-century hauntology, although it may not actually be that new.

In these terms this book is not about children's television as it exists now, but rather as it features as a facet of memory for contemporary audiences. The ghostliness of memory, the presence of things absent, is redoubled when what is remembered is immersion in outlandish fictional worlds from which one never completely escaped. The (not so little) box in the corner of the living room produced the narratives that millions of school-aged children held in common. And for many contemporary creatives, late-twentieth-century television remains a haunting dreamscape, at the centre of which sits their childhood self, still shaken and stirred by ideas and images that continue to shape their own work. That so many of these TV series featured porous realities and broken chronologies, blurring the boundaries of past, present and future, only adds to the sense of temporal vertigo explored here.

The 'strange' material to which they were exposed is a formative influence upon the present. Such is the legacy of the television programmes at the core of this collection.

> It doesn't feel as if the 21st century has started yet. We remain trapped in the 20th century ... in 1981, the 1960s seemed much further away than they do today ... cultural time has folded back on itself, and the impression of linear development has given way to a 'strange simultaneity'. The ghost here, is a 'spectre understood not as anything supernatural, but as that which acts without (physically) existing'. (Fisher 2014)

The 'haunting' of adults by what has been seen on the screen is crucial to the phenomenon that Fisher identifies. This book directly addresses that which 'scared us' in the past and remains with us in the present, interrogating a correlation between individual *and* collective cultural memory. The influence of these previous works is evident through the space they continue to occupy in nostalgic discourse, providing haunted frames of reference for child viewers which, as we see in many of the chapters to follow, hold fast as these viewers age and mature. Indeed, the memory of unsettling images and characters often evolves to become shorthand for adults to express their childhood experience and, potentially, a shared generational identity (Lester 2021; 2023).

As Derrida commented, 'I believe that Ghosts are a part of the future' (Coverley 2020) and as Helen Wheatley confirms, 'Television is full of Ghosts' (Wheatley 2020, 69). Television therefore provides an effective liminal space, within which past, present and potential futures can be experienced simultaneously. Wheatley's statement resonates with a broader conception of visual media as haunted space (Sayad 2021; Leeder 2015), one in which the subjects are held in time, existing within a perpetual present. Revisiting these texts then becomes a séance of sorts, where adults seek to commune with past selves and past experiences. However, this book is not simply for adults remembering or reconnecting with their past. The cultural manifestation of these past horrifying representations can be felt in contemporary fiction and witnessed by a new generation. In part this is not necessarily new; the generation who made the programmes that appeared on very modern television screens were themselves young in the very early part of the twentieth century. These Edwardians were themselves replaying experiences they had as children. On British television this can be seen in the BBC adaptations of E. Nesbit's 1904 novel *The Phoenix and the Carpet* in 1976 and John Masefield's 1935 novel *The Box of Delights* in 1984, among many others. However, what is, or rather was, new was the technology that allowed for the simultaneous distribution of these programmes to an audience at the same time. Despite the presence of new technology this was a move from the permanence of the printed word on the page to flickering light on a screen; these were shown and, if missed, they disappeared forever. It was crucial to watch them live only for them to live in memory. This is a form of Dyscronia, where forms of TV replay – literally as well as metaphorically. However, this book is not simply for adults remembering or reconnecting with their childhood. The cultural manifestation of these past horrifying representations is felt in contemporary fiction and witnessed by a new generation. In itself this is nothing new but rather the way cultural production inevitably carries the past into the future:

> [Bagpuss] makes me feel both simultaneously reassured and unsettled. It's filled with old things, lost things, tatty puppets and sadness; folk tales, ships in bottles, abandoned toys and long-ago kings. It's like television made by the ghosts of those Edwardian children themselves. It makes me feel, for want of a better word, haunted. (Fischer 2017)

Fischer continues this with a discussion of his notion of 'lost things'; the idea that in an analogue world where the television in the corner of the room dominated, all we have are fractured memories of what we may have seen as children. The frailties of memory mean that these memories may not be accurate and instead exist as phantasms, however there is the chance that these visual artefacts could be found, slowly degrading in a dusty attic. As new audiences move to 'on-demand' clinically crisp, digital programmes, the idea of the cathode ray tube humming and glowing in the corner of the room seems perhaps even more archaic than an Edwardian bookshelf.

Fischer's idea of 'the Haunted Generation' is important in recognizing the psychological impact of the popular and in providing a counter to common conceptions of nostalgia:

> Pop-Hauntology stems from the melancholic memory of growing up in often quite trying, but oft fondly remembered days, as well as the additional memories of an anticipated future that never came to pass. Our *Tomorrow's World* daydreams may be summed up by the word 'anemoia'. *'Anemoia – noun: Nostalgia for a time you've never known.'* (Koenig, Dictionary of Obscure Sorrows 2012) 'Anemoia' is actually a deliberately 'made-up word', but indeed all words are made-up. With 'anemoia' we know its origin is within *The Dictionary of Obscure Sorrows*, a lyrical art project by John Koenig. Perhaps 'anemoia' will make its way into a more everyday lexicon or spoken language as it defines an actual feeling. One all too common to many children of the Haunted Generation. (Paciorek 2023)

Svetlana Boym (2007) similarly considers nostalgia as an inherently unreliable phenomenon, 'a romance with one's own fantasy' (1). Indeed, Boym traces the etymology of nostalgia back to the seventeenth century,

at which point it was used distinctly within the medical field as a disease
or symptom which could (and should) be cured (1–2). Nostalgia, memory
and past experience combine to create the sense of an unreliable narrator –
we erase, emphasize or otherwise imagine an experience, and so much of
that experience then becomes a fiction of our own making. The chapters
that follow will explore, in many different ways, the slippage between
imagination, text and self.

Finally, this collection not only engages with the thorny notions of
memory and nostalgia, but also intervenes and intersects with the recent
creative and scholarly invocation of the analogue itself; collective fascination
with, and mistrust of, the analogue form has been particularly pronounced
in recent horror film and television, and over the last decade or so we have
seen a growing corpus of analogue horror produced across a wide range of
media. From YouTube (*Marble Hornets* (Wagner 2009), *Mandela Catalogue*
(Kister 2021) *The Backrooms* (Pixels 2022)) to film (*V/H/S* (Bettinelli-Olpin
et al. 2012), *Skinamarink* (Ball 2022)) to TV (podcast adaptation *Archive 81*
(Sonnenshine 2021) and *Yellowjackets* (Lyle and Nickerson 2022–present)),
long-dormant analogue forms are being mined for their potential to evoke
a sense of uncanny familiarity. Analogue modes of TV broadcast and film-
making are being recalled in the digital age as embodied relics of a recent
past. As Stephenson (2023: 175) notes, analogue 'as a medium demonstrates
a "dead" (outmoded) form, whilst its embodiment as a diegetic relic
simultaneously represents a living entity – a tangible body just as susceptible
to harm, manipulation and possession as its human counterpart'. That the
aesthetic feel of the programmes discussed here is actively emulated by
more recent media demonstrates the haunting (and haunted nature) of these
original texts and seems to imply a collective understanding that analogue
serves as effective shorthand for something both homely and, ultimately,
profoundly unsettling.

While all the chapters include discussion of the ideas of 'hauntings', the
book is organized in two parts. The first considers the artefacts of television
themselves as haunted and spectral objects. Initially, Stella Miriam Pryce
considers the haunting effects of the BBC children's television drama *Tom's
Midnight Garden*, a programme which itself draws an Edwardian cultural
past into the 1980s. This is a foundational chapter in providing discussion of
the nature of hauntology and spectrality. This debate continues in Fernando
Gabriel Pagonini Berns's discussion of the adaptation of Alan Garner's
young adult, proto-folk horror novel *The Owl Service*. The function of
fictional texts allowing for an explanation of the inherent trauma of youth is
explored in subsequent chapters. This begins with Fiona Cameron analysing
the function of 1970s and 1980s drama for female audiences. Merinda
Staubli's analysis debates children's television as an 'uncanny mirror'. The
impact of forms of unsettling television on the construction of youthful
identity, in terms of gender and sexuality, is debated in the next series of

chapters. Max Hart continues this theme to discuss *Garbage Pail Kids* and queer representation. Jackson Nash discusses gender non-conformity and transgender representation in *Round the Twist*.

The function of children's dramas as representing 'coming of age' for its young viewers is significant in the form having a lasting impact on the psyche of its audiences. Miranda Corcoran discusses the domestic space and the trauma inherent therein for the adolescent in a discussion of *Stranger in Our House*. These chapters mark a tonal change in the collection in moving from nostalgia and pop-hauntology into difficult territory. Adam Whybray extends the discussion to the 1990s with an examination of the unsettling effects of *The Demon Headmaster*, discussing the 'suburban eerie' of the two iterations of *The Demon Headmaster* as an expression as neo-liberal folk horror and, in doing so, politicizes the form. The section finishes with Ben Halligan's analysis of Jimmy Savile; an exemplar of how the recent past has taken a darker turn with terrifying revelations. This chapter deals with the broader social context of the 1970s and 1980s and deals with revelations of institutional sexual abuse. That which appeared to be simply haunted turned out to be truly demonic.

Part Two, 'Memory, Process and Practice', more formally integrates memoir and self-reflection as an analytical tool. The inclusion of memoir is an important facet of this book and indeed is a feature of much writing about hauntology and popular culture, as can be seen by the quotations above from noted experts in the field, many of whom come from without the academy and write first and foremost as 'fans'. This has three functions; firstly, it acknowledges the critic is also an active participant in perpetuating the effect of the programmes in question. Many of the writers who have written for the book have been affected in a variety of ways and this forms the basis of their discussion. Secondly the use of memoir breaks with a fantasy of a unified historical perspective. These are programmes that are viewed in a variety of contexts with different and plural perspectives; in these terms there is no singular narrative or perspective which is right. Thirdly this acknowledges the importance of the analogue nature of the period being considered. Some of the material is recorded and available on discs, YouTube and streaming services, but not all is. Memoir allows us access to the half remembered and subjective. Part Two opens with a detailed analysis of memory and hauntological in Michael Schofield's own artistic practice. This opens up debates about the nature of memory and the function of video artefacts as forms of 'memory prosthetics'. Flannán Delaney discusses how the nature of horror provides a mechanism for dealing with societal fears, including the past threat of nuclear annihilation and the more recent fear of the pandemic. Alexander Hartley outlines the presentation of trauma to a young audience through 'killing a cow on television', as an ideological output of the DDR. Elizabeth Tussey's powerful discussion of *Watership Down* and the Kent State shootings outlines the function of television as a method for processing trauma, as far as that is possible given the events discussed therein. The function of the television as an artefact in the home is something that is identified in Wayne Johnson's work, through his reflective analysis of the hauntological impact of the BBC's serialization of the German children's film, *The Singing Ringing Tree* (1957), itself a product of a totalitarian regime. The function of the television as a hypnotic presence in the home is outlined in Jez Conolly's discussion of the haunting effect of watching television as an unwell adolescent. In Keith McDonald's chapter, the theme of adolescence is further explored via a critical analysis of the haunting effects of being witness to programmes that one perhaps shouldn't have seen via a discussion of the original TV mini-series *V* (1984–85). The section concludes with Hollie Adams's detailed and hopeful consideration of the practical outcomes of many of the themes contained in the book with a discussion of how eco-horror can be used as a tool for social change in schools.

References

Boym, Svetlana. 2007. 'Nostalgia and Its Discontents'. *Hedgehog Review* 9, no. 2: 7–18.

Coverley, Merlin. 2020. *Hauntology*. London: Oldcastle.

Fischer, Bob. 2017. 'The Haunted Generation'. *The Fortean Times*, June. https:// hauntedgeneration.co.uk/2019/04/22/thehauntedgeneration/. Accessed 24 September 2023.

Fischer, Bob. 2023. 'The Haunted Feeling: Analogue Memories'. In *The Routledge Companion to Folk Horror*, edited by Robert Edgar and Wayne Johnson, 236–44. London: Routledge.

Fisher, Mark. 2014. *Ghosts of My Life*. London: Zero Books.

Leeder, Murray. 2015. *Cinematic Ghosts: Haunting and Spectrality from Silent Cinema to the Digital Era*. London: Bloomsbury.

Lester, Catherine. 2021. *Horror Films for Children: Fear and Pleasure in American Cinema*. London: Bloomsbury.

Lester, Catherine. (ed.) 2023. *Watership Down: Perspectives on and beyond Violence*. London: Bloomsbury.

Paciorek, Andy. 2023. 'Yesterday's Memories of Tomorrow'. In *The Routledge Companion to Folk Horror*, edited by Robert Edgar and Wayne Johnson, 183–93. London: Routledge.

Sayad, Cecilia. 2021. *The Ghost in the Image: Technology and Reality in the Horror Genre*. Oxford: Oxford University Press.

Stephenson, Lauren. 2023. 'Restoring Relics – (Re)-releasing *Antrum* (2018) and film as Folk Horror'. In *The Routledge Companion to Folk Horror*, edited by Robert Edgar and Wayne Johnson, 173–80. London: Routledge.

Wheatley, Helen. 2020. 'Haunted Television: Trauma and the Specter in the Archive'. *Journal of Cinema and Media Studies* 59: 69–89.

PART ONE

Hauntings and Spectres

1

'What is it like to be dead and a ghost? Oh, do tell me Tom, I've been simply longing to know': Hauntology and spectrality in the 1989 BBC television series *Tom's Midnight Garden*

Stella Miriam Pryce

Ghosts, spirits and spectres play a vital role in the children's television of the 1980s, appearing as creatures of the imagination (*Moondial* 1988), entities possessing child bodies (*Chocky* 1984), otherworldly or supernatural tropes (*The Box of Delights* 1984, *The Chronicles of Narnia* 1988) and anachronistic relics returning to embody forgotten histories (*The Children of Green Knowe* 1986; *The Watch House* 1988). Some such phantoms materialize as disturbing, Gothic figures returned from the dead (*Dramarama* 1983–9; *Ghost in the Water* 1982), while others are benignly comic (*Rentaghost* 1976–84). However, towards the end of the twentieth century, ghosts underwent a transformation where hauntings had the potential to move beyond merely a plot device, cliché or generic trope and, as Maria del Pilar Blanco and Esther Peeren explain, they came to constitute 'influential conceptual metaphors permeating global (popular) culture and academia alike' (2013, 1). This essay will argue that the figurative child played a vital role in this specific metamorphosis in a way that is rarely acknowledged in extant criticism of the period. Through close consideration of the BBC's adaptation of *Tom's Midnight Garden* (1989), I will explore the ways in which childhood takes on the socio-cultural function of spectrality in the series, materializing a contemporary discomfort with the idealized Romantic child through its conflict with modernity, the passage of time and social change.

By the end of the 1980s, when children's television and film had been preoccupied with the other worldly, in ghost stories, fantasy, science fiction and the unexplained, the BBC aired *Tom's Midnight Garden* (1989). The narrative explored a world of time shifts and was steeped in a disorientating sense of nostalgia for the past. This adaptation of Philippa Pearce's Carnegie medal-winning 1958 novel had been adapted for television before, to varying degrees of success. It had a record of popularity with viewers, having initially aired on *Jackanory* voiced by Martin Jarvis, in 1967. It was followed closely by a dramatized three-part series for the educational programme *Merry Go Round* in 1968. It seems the intention was to encourage viewers to read the original text, and by 1988 with the dawn of the new English National Curriculum, and its emphasis on a literary canon, this novel was again worthy of revisiting. The 1974 version, produced by the BBC and directed by Dorothea Brooking, had offered a three-part series which, while far more fleshed out than the 1968 version, proved relatively unpopular, partially due to the extent it strayed unfavourably from the source material in its contemporary setting. However, by 1989, the BBC revivified the story once again, in the hands of Julia Jones, this time as a six-part series which, in the main, aimed to remain far more faithful to the original text.

We meet our protagonist Tom Long (Jeremy Rampling) as he is sent to live with his aunt and uncle to quarantine because his brother is sick with measles. Tom is awoken on his first night at the house, to find that the large grandfather clock in the shared hallway of their block of flats has struck thirteen. Investigating this strange occurrence, Tom finds that, beyond the back door, there is a verdant, Victorian garden to explore. As the story progresses, we come to understand that Tom can only enter the garden at night; in the daytime it is gone, and grey dustbins exist in its place. Tom makes many nocturnal visits to the garden where he befriends a young girl called Hatty, yet as the nights pass, Hatty ages and Tom becomes increasingly spectral too, physically fading away. Until, at the denouement of the series, the garden is gone, and Hatty has grown up into Mrs Bartholomew, an elderly neighbour of his aunt and uncle.

Unlike contemporaneous television series such as *Moondial* (1988) and *The Children of Green Knowe* (1986) which also deal in what Roni Natov has termed 'the dark pastoral', what is particularly noteworthy about *Tom's*

Midnight Garden is that it is Tom, the child protagonist, who takes on the spectral guise of the ghost child here. Unlike other children's television of the period, the series does not hesitate in depicting the 'nightmare world of childhood' directly through the child protagonist at its heart (Natov 2006, 119). This deliberate focus can be identified markedly early on, the first time we meet Tom, only a minute into the first episode, when he is shown hiding in a tree. The camera first focuses only on his mother calling his name, with only the leaves of the tree in the foreground suggesting his presence. The next shot reveals only Tom's hands and the rest of his body remains concealed by the tree. Introducing Tom masked with greenery in this way anticipates the pastoral theme of the wider text certainly, but it also uses the visual possibilities of television to present him as corporeally indistinct from the beginning, spectral through his dichotomous presence and absence on screen. It foreshadows his links with the pastoral as he melds with the greenery like a figure of the Green Man, thus rendering him as a feature that is both spectral and part of a mythological past. In rendering Tom as ghostly here, the viewer is introduced to the wider discourse of haunting which permeates the text. Through Tom, the child is not focalized, rather the child and the highly physical connotations of childhood innocence, play and youth are indistinct and elusive. This theme then continues to operate in the narrative, plot and aesthetics of the rest of the series. Tom is not haunted *by* ghosts, as is demonstrated by his intangible corporeality on screen, it is Tom himself who *is* a ghost. Upon entering the garden, it is Tom whose bodily presence is depicted as vague and indistinct, he moves through doors and nobody, except Hatty, can see him.

Benefiting from an improvement of special effects in television technology, unlike the earlier 1973 adaptation, the BBC made the most of the more fantastic elements of the narrative here. There is an extended sequence, where Tom endeavours to pass through the boundary of a door – we see the house remaining fixed and still as Tom's body becomes increasingly faint, the edges of his hair and shoulders are seen blurring as he struggles. Then, as he explores the garden, he sees numerous people, and waves at each of them, but, one by one, they continuously ignore him, leading him to realize he is invisible to them. It is not until the middle of episode three that it is revealed Hatty could in fact see him all along, while the others could not. Depicting Tom as a ghost here, the series offers one of many 'generic conventions which may be used to categorise a programme as gothic' (Wheatley 2012, 385). Helen Wheatley's analysis situates *Tom's Midnight Garden* within a tradition of children's Gothic that she argues was prevalent in the 1970s and 1980s. Wheatley's account tracks the history of children's television in the period most succinctly and does not need repeating here. However, while Tom's spectrality is, of course, Gothic in its approach, I argue Tom's ghostly status operates rather more specifically in this adaptation as a potent conceptual metaphor of haunting. The association of the child and the ghost, established in the opening scene and pursued through the text, is not coincidental, nor is it solely a convention of Gothic television and its popularity in the 1980s. Rather, Tom's ghostliness is a metaphor that yokes together media for children and the burgeoning discourse of hauntology in the cultural production of this period.

The late 1980s and 1990s 'marked the beginning of heightened interest in ghosts and hauntings' (Weinstock 2013, 62). This period of time has since come to be known as 'the spectral turn', a moment where our cultural awareness of ghosts shifted from Gothic tropes and were reconstituted as powerful conceptual metaphors (del Pilar Blanco and Peeren 2010, vii). As Weinstock suggests, as interstitial figures, ghosts are inherently associated with liminality, neither living nor the dead, neither past nor present. He summarizes, 'The ghost functions as the paradigmatic "shadowy third" … as something from the past that emerges into the present, the phantom calls into question the linearity of history' (Weinstock 2013, 62). What Weinstock is referring to here is Jacques Derrida's notion of 'hauntology', an unsettling of ontology that sees the past returning in the present, like a ghost. First discussed by Derrida in his hugely influential book *Spectres of Marx* (1994), which explores how the dissolution of the Soviet Union was haunted by Marxism, where 'ideas thought to be buried would keep returning, albeit in spectre-like traces' (Riley 2017, 18). It is common in discussions of 'spectralities' as they have come to be known, to locate this burgeoning critical sphere in the discourse of critical theory, particularly through abstract and theoretical treatise. However, these ideas were circulating in wider popular culture too, specifically in the children's television of the period.

At the same time as scholarly attention began being paid to hauntology in wider philosophical thought, so too was the ghost central to children's television, such as in *Tom's Midnight Garden*. Created under the circumstances of post-industrial 1980s British neoliberalism, the programme was born of a time governed by collective haunting, a society plagued by the unrelenting ghost of capitalism (Fisher 2012, 16–24). In this way, the series uses the metaphor of spectrality as a way of unsettling the temporality of childhood which is, in Derridean terms, 'out of joint' (Derrida 1994, 2002). For critics like Mark Fisher, Thatcherism beckoned in an age of 'lost futures', a moment where time itself seemed to halt and culture no longer moved forward, rather what was left became haunted by an unreachable fallacy of futurity (2012, 16). In other words, as Andreas Huyssen defines it, this historical fissure was a 'fundamental crisis in the imagination of alternative futures' where culture had become restricted to the world of ghosts and 'compulsive repetition' (2003, 2). However, despite the critical consensus that hauntology was the pervasive cultural mode of the late 1980s, extant criticism of children's television in this period fails to connect its fundamental relationship with the spectral turn.

Despite the centrality of popular culture in our understanding of social movements or specific historical loci, there has often been a tendency to separate popular explorations of hauntology (such as those expressed in popular film, literature and media) from their theoretical counterparts in critical theory. As del Pilar Blanco and Peeren tell us,

> The haunted spaces of popular culture – and popular culture itself as a ghostly space in the sense that, despite the many volumes seeking to define or exemplify it, remains an elusive, contested concept with blurry boundaries – may seem like an obvious topic, but despite the fact that the ghost's most common appearance at the present time is as a figure of popular culture entertainment in (horror) films, television series, popular fiction, and even country music, this space of the ghost remains remarkably under-theorized. (2010, xii)

However one chooses to term it, 'the spectral turn' or, as Roger Luckhurst defines it, the 'generalised economy of haunting', happening at the end of the twentieth century, theorizes in such general terms that it often obscures the specific aesthetics through which hauntology was suffused in the cultural production of the period in question (2002, 528). Del Pilar Blanco and Peeren highlight this issue as the tendency to forget about 'the specificity of ghosts, the fact that they appear in specific moments and specific locations' (del Pilar Blanco and Peeren 2002, xi). In a rather general sense, the sheer number of ghosts appearing on children's screens in the late 1980s is noteworthy but the cultural emphasis on repetition and return can be seen in less obvious ways too.

For instance, it is unsurprising that the BBC relied heavily on adaptations of early classic children's novels as the basis for a large proportion of their output during this period. As Alison Peirse notes, 'the BBC's lavishly produced adaptations of classic children's novels … are perhaps uniquely synonymous with this decade' (Peirse 2012, 110). These programmes may not all use spectrality as their main mode of storytelling in the way we see reflected in *Tom's Midnight Garden*, yet they certainly are indebted to a cultural emphasis on repetition that 'begins by coming back' (Derrida 1994, 11). The BBC's adaptation of *Tom's Midnight Garden*, however, is far more evidentially indebted to this historical moment and is subsequently tied up with the hauntological impetus of the 1980s. While criticism on this adaptation fails to locate its themes of haunting and spectrality in relation to a wider culture of adaptation and neo-Victorianism, there is an obvious link in the programme's thematic concern with haunting to 'the cultural logic of late capitalism' where the future could not be separated from its emphasis on the past (Jameson 1991, 16).

In the original novel, the plot of *Tom's Midnight Garden* wrestles with the idea of chronology. Childhood is explored as simultaneously Tom's present experience and Hatty's memory. Early in episode four, as Tom and Hatty play in the tree house they have erected, they argue about which of the two of them might be a ghost. Tom asks Hatty, 'what is it like? … what is it like to be dead and a ghost?' Yet, to Tom's confusion, Hatty responds by repeating the question, 'Oh, do tell me Tom, I've simply been longing to know.' This leads to an argument between the pair where Tom insists that he is 'not a ghost!' and Hatty counters that she saw him move 'through the orchard door'. In this particular adaptation, Rampling and his co-star Caroline Waldron exaggerate their indignation with each other, verging on the comic. Yet, what is central to this moment is its ability to succinctly demonstrate the tension between Tom (a contemporary child) and Hatty (a child of the past) as they disagree on whose presence is real and who is merely a spectral invasion upon that reality. The inability for either of the pair to pin down exactly who is real in the garden denotes the hauntology at the heart of the text; neither child is willing to identify as the ghost, implying that they might both be spectres of sorts. What Tom's ghostly presence in the garden and Hatty's invasion of Tom's quotidian post-war childhood reveal is the apparitional nature of childhood itself. Both are haunted by the 'nightmare world of childhood' contained in the garden, the loss of childhood and the implied loss of innocence therein (Natov 2006, 119).

A specific way the text directly speaks to the wider concerns of this period of late-capitalist inertia can be seen in its exploration of a romantic, pastoral childhood depicted through its status as a neo-Victorian text. Michelle J. Smith argues that while 'there are numerous novels set in the Victorian period published after 1901, it is not until the 1960s that a sub-set of these historical fictions begin to reinterpret the past that they depict, and which might rightfully be termed neo-Victorian' (2013, 1). However, while this may be true in a broader sense for Smith when reviewing the literature of the mid-twentieth century, this statement ignores the meta-fictive impetus at the heart of Pearce's *Tom's Midnight Garden* (1958). As Louisa Hadley observes, neo-Victorian fiction is necessarily 'bi-directional … pointing to both the Victorian past and the contemporary present' (Hadley 2010, 15). Furthermore, in so doing, as Dana Shiller specifies, neo-Victorian novels 'adopt a postmodern approach to history … reconstructing the past by questioning what we think we know about history and exploring how the present shapes historical narratives' (Shiller 1997, 558). In doubling time itself, this bidirectional narrative also crucially works in reverse too, encouraging the reader to question what role the historical past has in shaping our understanding of the present. Indeed, it is this relationship that lies at the heart of hauntology and the related criticism in the wake of the spectral turn. One may hesitate to see the obvious link between the setting of *Tom's Midnight Garden* and its hauntological status in the 1980s – the programme is not contemporary to its time of production and moves between two historical spaces, one more recent in the 1950s and the other much later in the Victorian period. However, it is crucial to consider these periods in conjunction in this adaptation to understand what Alison Peirse has termed the programme's 'calculated … broad appeal' (2010, 111).

The 1980s saw a distinct public celebration of Victoriana. During her 1983 election campaign, Mrs Thatcher laid out her desire to return to 'Victorian values', citing her grandmother's hard work, self-reliance, cleanliness, neighbourliness and pride in country as uniquely owing to the Victorian period and as 'perennial values' (Evans 1997, 601). One does not need to work very hard to see the ironic association with the ghostly eternal in her mawkish appraisal. This sentiment is reflected in the television programming of the era. Producing a number of prime-time offerings that returned to the Victorian age in various genre categories, programmes such as ITV's *Cribb* (1980–81) or BBC's *Bleak House* (1985) and *Alice in Wonderland* (1986) proved popular with audiences. Writing specifically about this trend in children's television, Alison Peirse groups together a series of programmes, including *The Box of Delights*, *The Children of Green Knowe*, *Moondial* and *Tom's Midnight Garden*, arguing that 'these programmes, with their country mansions, "received pronunciation", polite children decked out in fitted tweed suits, crumpets toasted over the fire and loyal servants, all presented a nostalgic vision of pre-war Britishness' presumably reflecting the kind of 'perennial values' which Mrs Thatcher had in mind (Peirse 2010, 111). The relationship between these texts and their overtly twee Britishness is well charted in Peirse's analysis. In and of itself, Pearce's original text problematizes the nostalgic vision of Empire-driven, pre-war Britishness. What is particularly interesting to me about this particular adaptation is the way it uses spectrality as metaphor for a version of childhood increasingly lost to the modern age. The account of British childhood that Tom returns to in the garden corresponds with the idealized Romantic view of the child, where Hatty and Tom play innocently in the natural world of the garden, uncorrupted by the outside world. Overtly Rousseauian in its pastoral charm, the garden sentimentalizes playing in tree houses, watching flowers bloom and skating on a glistening wintry river. The treatment of childhood is then, in this regard, evocative of the 'mid-nineteenth-century Euro-American flourishing of children's literature as a golden site for fantasy and play' where childhood is seen as 'less … a period of preparation for adult life than as a time wonderfully separate from it' (Sánchez-Eppler 2021, 40). Of course, this notion of Victorian childhood is simplistic and to categorize the period solely in these terms occludes many of the inequalities that did affect the children of the nineteenth century, yet it is commonly portrayed in this way. However, by the end of the twentieth century, critical discourse surrounding childhood had entirely shifted from such an idealized romantic portrayal. And in the late 1980s, it seemed either dead or lost, where the reality of modern life, marked by rampant poverty, high stakes testing and commercialization had killed 'the sacred pastoral of childhood' (Ibid.). At the time of writing the original narrative, Pearce seemed to anticipate this looming reality, and by the production of BBC's *Tom's Midnight Garden* the theme of haunting aligns with the wider discourse of the spectral turn.

Much like Mark Fisher's argument that contemporary music had to turn to ghosts as all other roads to futurity had died, so too Tom has to be rendered as the ghost here as the very mode of childhood associated with the 1980s 'nostalgia industry' had also ceased to be a reachable reality (Reader 2021, 5). This is also true for the viewer, where television's child audience who we may naturally think of as connected uniquely to potentiality and futurity are offered a narrative bound entirely to the past. In returning to the 1950s through Tom's first-person narration and then through Tom to Hatty's Victorian world, viewers access a compounded retrospective. They are caught in the haunting loop of unreachable childhood innocence, continuously asked to look back, if they want to move forward.

Subtle differences from the original text make a conscious nod towards this lost childhood, and the anachronism portrayed in the series points to the hauntology at the heart of its production. As a 'time-slip narrative', inverting the perhaps more commonly known 'time travel narrative', Tom is sent back into the lost past. As Linda Hall describes 'time-slip stories, … may be defined as fiction with its feet in the present but its head and heart in the past' (Hall 2003, 154). In playing with the limits of linear temporality, the time-slip narrative is inherently both futuristic and anachronistic, exploring the dissonant relationship between past and present. In the 1989 adaptation of this particular time-slip story, Hatty's Victorian past jars particularly unharmoniously with Tom's present in post-war Britain. Far from Peirse's suggestion that in returning to the Victorian era the romantic child is resurrected and celebrated, I would counter that the obvious conflict between the two periods portrayed in the series depicts that it is not a wistful or romantic evocation of lost childhood but a deeply troubling one for the contemporary viewer. A reason for this portrayal perhaps lies in the programme makers' awareness of their viewers as children and not adults. For Tom (much like the children for whom the programme was created), the Victorian period is unfamiliar, discordant with the day-to-day lived experiences of childhood. For Hatty, Tom appears as a strange figment of the future, yet, as the viewer experiences the setting of the series through Tom's eyes, the garden is anachronistic, appearing as a conspicuously old-fashioned mirage, in contrast to Tom's aunt and uncle's 1950s house. As Peter Buse and Andrew Stott suggest, 'anachronism might well be the defining feature of ghosts, now and in the past because haunting by its very structure, implies a deformation of linear temporality' (Buse and Stott 1999, 1).

This temporal distortion is articulated most clearly in the recurrent trope of clothing. In episode four, the series makes a rare diversion from the plot of the novel, with the addition of a scene where Tom and his aunt visit a local museum. He is captivated by a series of mannequins dressed in clothes which he recognizes as similar to those Hatty wears in the garden. He asks, 'When did they wear these things aunt?' to which she replies vaguely, looking to the curatorial material for her answer, 'Victorian times'. The camera then pans very slowly down from the mannequin's head to its feet, as Tom thinks to himself 'Hatty could be a ghost … but she's so real'. In tilting the camera down here, the viewer's perspective is calculatedly focused on the mannequin's clothes, starkly clean and crisp, their sterile whiteness a notable contrast to those Hatty wears which are creased and lived in. This moment is undeniably haunted, as Rebecca Munford asserts, 'touched by bodies that are no longer present, uninhabited clothing has a particularly spectral quality, offering a tangible reminder of the otherwise intangible, absent body' (2016, 123). The absent body in question here for Tom, of course, is Hatty, yet the focus on these clothes as the generic items in a museum also equates them with a historical version of childhood now lost to time for the viewer. Elizabeth Wilson highlights the uncanniness of garments which once had 'an intimate relationship with human beings long since gone to their graves' (Wilson 2003, 1). Clothing is so frequently associated with 'our living, moving selves' that when uninhabited, or in this case, only inhabited by an inanimate sort of doll, then 'hint at something only half understood, sinister, threatening, the atrophy of the body, and the evanescence of life' (Ibid.). Of course, Wilson is speaking broadly about clothes and the absence of an *adult* body, but in the case of children's clothing there is also the implied spectralization of one's own self. To look back at old clothes you have outgrown, is to recognize your own ageing. Thus, in this moment, Tom is haunted by the reality that the garden is as impermanent as the childhood it contains. Hatty, he queries with himself, 'could be a ghost' despite his feeling that she is 'so alive', but it is not only Hatty herself implied in this quotation, but also the wider sense of a lost Victorian childhood and the inevitable passage of time. The implied haunting here is not nostalgic as Pierse suggests; in fact, it is quite the opposite – rather than being tinged with evocative longing, it conjures the gothic connotations of fear, specifically the fear of lost innocence and the imposing certainty of maturation.

In the novel, Tom looks up 'Victorian costume' in an encyclopaedia, in an effort to identify what he has seen in the garden. Yet, by moving this scene to a museum in this adaptation, the viewer is reminded even more potently of the historical distance between Tom and Hatty. There is a notable dissonance in the extended shot here, where the camera's focus on the inanimate object of the mannequin is uncanny in its similarity to Hatty but distinctly separate from her through its lifeless suspension on screen. Those writing about Gothic television have centralized the uncanny as a defining feature that characterizes this programming as distinct from other generic categories (such as 'made-for-television horror' or the broader category of 'telefantasy') (Wheatley 2012, 385). As Wheatley illustrates in her writing on Gothic television, this work draws on Freud's 1919 essay, 'The Uncanny' (Das Unheimliche), which pertains to the disarming feeling that occurs when something familiar or 'heimlich' (homely), to use Freud's language, transforms into a threat and returns to haunt through a paradoxical feeling of familiar unfamiliarity. In this scene, the viewer is confronted with an image that evokes so much of Hatty's corporeality (the style of her hair, the clothes she wears and even the mannequin's friendly smiling expression) yet is eerily lifeless. By presenting her likeness as a mannequin here, we are reminded of her apparitional status, and she remains an anachronism, a child of the distant past, reserved to the historical loci of a museum.

This article has endeavoured to demonstrate that Tom's haunting presence in the garden is bound directly to the loss of the romantic impression of childhood at the end of the twentieth century. Much of the criticism that exists around both the television adaptation that I have discussed here and the original novel from which the programme was adapted is focused on the nostalgic contours of the text, questioning to what extent the story speaks to a contemporary child or to a wistful adult's reflection of their own childhood. Critics such as Heather Montgomery have argued that *Tom's Midnight Garden* is centred on adult nostalgia and melancholy where childhood exemplifies 'things slipping away' to the 'ravages of time' (Montgomery 2009, 204). However, as Tom asserts, he is 'not a ghost … but the orchard door is, that's why I could go through it. The door's a ghost, the garden's a ghost and so are you!' Tom's anachronistic place in the garden exemplifies a bridge between the contemporary and Victorian child, illustrating, as Mouhiba Jamoussi has suggested, that the story operates 'between the child and the adult, the fantastic and the real, and the past and the present' (2019, 1). If nothing else, the mere longevity of the story, leading to several adaptations throughout the course of the twentieth century, evidences its popularity for contemporary children. Yet, considering this adaptation in the context of the time it was created, one cannot ignore the historical location of the ghost as a potent conceptual metaphor emerging during the late 1980s and early 1990s. In situating *Tom's Midnight Garden* alongside the wider discourse of the spectral turn, I have sought to show that, unlike the extant criticism on the 1989 adaptation would suggest, this series was not produced in a bubble but was one of many cultural texts that mobilized the metaphorical ghost to demonstrate that the 1980s were a period of hauntology as opposed to ontology.

References

Alice in Wonderland. 1986. [TV programme; Director: Barry Letts] BBC 1, 5 January.

Blanco, M. D. P., and E. Peeren. 2010. 'Introduction'. In *Popular Ghosts, The Haunted Spaces of Everyday Culture*, edited by M. D. P. Blanco and E. Peeren, ix–xxii. London: Bloomsbury.

Blanco, M. D. P., and E. Peeren. 2013. 'Introduction, Conceptualising Spectralities'. In *The Spectralities Reader, Ghosts and Haunting in Contemporary Cultural Theory*, edited by M. D. P. Blanco and E. Peeren, 1–27. London: Bloomsbury.

Bleak House. 1985. [TV programme; Director: Arthur Hopcraft] BBC 2, 10 April.

Buse, and A. Stott. 1999. 'Introduction, A Future for Haunting'. In *Ghosts, Deconstruction, Psychoanalysis, History*, edited by Peter Buse and Andrew Stott, 1–20. Basingstoke: Palgrave.

Chocky. 1984. [TV programme; Director: Vic Hughes] ITV, 9 January.

Cribb. 1979. [TV programme; Directors: Julian Aymes, Alan Grint, Gordon Flemyng, Oliver Horsbrugh, Bill Gilmour] ITV, 23 December.

Derrida, J. 1994. *Spectres of Marx, The State of the Debt, the Work of Mourning and the New International*, trans. Peggy Kamuf. London: Routledge.

Dramarama. 1983. [TV series; Director: Anna Home] ITV, 12 September.

Evans, S. 1997. 'Thatcher and the Victorians, A Suitable Case for Comparison'. *History* 82, no. 268: 601–20.

Fisher, M. 2012. 'What Is Hauntology?' *Film Quarterly* 66, no. 1: 16–24.

Ghost in the Water. 1982. [Film] Dir. Renny Rye, BBC.

Hadley, Louisa. 2010. *Neo-Victorian Fiction and Historical Narrative, The Victorians and Us*. Houndmills: Palgrave Macmillan.

Hall, L. 2003. '"House and Garden", The Time-Slip Story in the Aftermath of the Second World War'. In *The Presence of the Past in Children's Literature*, edited by A. L. Lucas, 153–8. Westport: Praegar.

Huyssen, A. 2003. *Present Pasts, Urban Palimpsests and the Politics of Memory*, 2–8. Stanford: Stanford University Press.

Jackanory. 1965. [TV programme; Director: Joy Whitcy] BBC 1, 13 December.

Jameson, F. 1991. *Postmodernism, or, the Cultural Logic of Late Capitalism*. Durham, NC: Duke University Press.

Jamoussi, M. 2019. 'Connection and Disconnection in *Tom's Midnight Garden*'. *Arab World English Journal for Translation & Literary Studies* 3, no. 2: 2–13.

Luckhurst, R. 2002. 'The Contemporary London Gothic and the Limits of the "Spectral Turn"'. *Textual Practice* 16, no. 3: 527–46.

Merry Go Round. 1963. [TV programme] BBC 1, 15 January.

Moondial. 1988. [TV programme; Director: Colin Cant] BBC 1, 10 February.

Montgomery, H. 2009. 'Introduction'. In *Children's Literature, Classic Texts and Contemporary Trends*, edited by H. Montgomery and N. Watson, 203–7. New York: Palgrave Macmillan.

Munford, R. 2016. 'Spectral Femininities'. In *Women and the Gothic*, edited by A. Horner and S. Zlosnik, 120–34. Edinburgh: Edinburgh University Press.

Natov, R. 2006. *The Poetics of Childhood*. New York: Routledge.

Pearce, Philippa. 1958. *Tom's Midnight Garden*. Oxford: Oxford University Press.

Peirse, A. 2010. 'A Broken Tradition, British Telefantasy and Children's Television in the 1980s and 1990s'. *Visual Culture in Britain* 11, no. 1: 109–24.

Reader, J. 2021. 'Hauntology, Or the Cultural Logic of Neoliberalism'. MA diss., Canterbury Christ Church University, Canterbury.

Rentaghost. 1976. [TV programme; Director: David Chrichton] BBC 1, 6 January.

Riley, J. A. 2017. 'Hauntology, Ruins, and the Failure of the Future in Andrei Tarkovsky's *Stalker*'. *Journal of Film and Video* 69, no. 1: 18–26.

Sánchez-Eppler, K. 2021. 'Childhood'. In *Keywords for Children's Literature*, Second edition, edited by P. Nel, L. Paul and N. Christensen, 38–41. New York: New York University Press.

Shiller, Dana. 1997. 'The Redemptive Past in the Neo-Victorian Novel'. *Studies in the Novel* 29, no. 4: 538–60.

Smith, M. J. 2013. 'Neo-Victorianism, An Introduction'. *Australasian Journal of Victorian Studies* 18, no. 3: 1–3.

The Box of Delights. 1984. [TV programme; Director: Renny Rye] BBC 1, 21 November.

The Children of Green Knowe. 1986. [TV programme; Director: Colin Cant] BBC 1, 26 November.

The Chronicles of Narnia. 1988. [TV programme; Director: Marilyn Fox] BBC 1, 13 November.

The Watch House. 1988. [TV programme; Director: Ian Keill] BBC 1, 7 December.

Tom's Midnight Garden. 1989. [TV programme; Director: Christine Secombe] BBC 1, 4 January.

Weinstock, J. A. 2013. 'Introduction, the Spectral Turn'. In *The Spectralities Reader, Ghosts and Haunting in Contemporary Cultural Theory*, edited by M. D. P. Blanco and E. Peeren, 1–27. London: Bloomsbury.

Wheatley, H. 2012. 'Uncanny Children, Haunted Houses, Hidden Rooms, Children's Gothic Television in the 1970s and 80s'. *Visual Culture in Britain* 13, no. 3: 383–97.

Wilson, E. 2003. *Adorned in Dreams, Fashion and Modernity*. London: I. B. Tauris.

2

Coming of age in *The Owl Service*: England and the uncertain future

Fernando Gabriel Pagnoni Berns

The Owl Service (ITV, Granada Television, 1969–70) was part of the British cycle of folk horror that unfolded throughout the 1970s. The story centres on three teenagers: upper-class Roger (Francis Wallis) and his stepsister Alison (Gillian Hills) who, together with the son of the housekeeper, Welsh boy Gwyn (Michael Holden), share three weeks in rural Wales. Gwyn and Allison discover a set of very old dinner plates with a floral pattern that can be read as owls as well. The design, however, mysteriously disappears from the plates after the discovery. Soon, Alison is possessed by an inexplicable impulse to form paper owls: her possession includes fits of unexplained fury, when she severely scratches her stepbrother's face at the end of episode one. The half-crazed gardener, Huw (Raymond Llewellyn), hints that the three teenagers are in danger of re-enacting an ancient Welsh pagan folk tale (retold in the eleventh-century book *The Mabinogion*) of Blodeuedd, a woman created from flowers to serve as wife of Lleu Llaw Gyffes, whom she betrays in favour of another man, Gronw Bebyr. Gronw then killed Lleu with a spear and the unfaithful woman is transformed into an owl as punishment. As part of an assembled family, the kids bond uneasily, tensions growing stronger as Alison falls in love with Gwyn, thus provoking Roger's jealousy. Three modern-day teenagers are revisited by a curse, similarly locked into a triangle of desire, class struggles and prefixed social roles that threaten to destroy them all. The folk tale represents a challenge to the logic of linear, progressive time.

The TV version retains the novel's plot but emphasizes the estranged relationship between the teens. Amid supernatural occurrences and a sombre mood, the three teenagers try to understand who they are in this assembled family and what are adults expecting from them. In fact, Alan Garner, the author of the book which the film is based on, playfully blurred the identities of the modern counterparts of the Celtic characters (White 1998, 91). As the only female in the trio, Alison is Blodeuedd's modern counterpart, but there is no clear evidence who Gwyn and Roger mirror in the present time. Is Gwyn (or Roger) the husband or the lover, the killed or the killer? Thus, the story traces a folk horror narrative where teenagers struggle to find their own identities and voices in contemporary England. Meanwhile, the past looms above them all, trying to devour their free will. Concurrent with this identity crisis, the story is a traditional 'coming-of-age' narrative marking the transition from innocence experience, passing through a traumatic shift in self-awareness (Tribunella 2010).

In this chapter, I will make a close reading of this TV series that haunted generations to investigate how the show mixed folk horror with youth anxieties to speak about the overwhelming shadows of both, the past and the future in the British 1970s. With both the past and unrealized futures haunting the present, the coming-of-age narratives of *The Owl Service* can be read through the lens of hauntology, a philosophical perspective focused on investigating times 'out of joint'. As such, the coming-of-age narrative here is not only personal, but a reflection of a British national identity coming to terms with its own loss of destiny.

Folk horror and hauntology

Hauntology is preoccupied with chronological time and how not only past, but also future, haunts the present. This is the circumstance that, according to Mark Fisher, falls under the umbrella of 'hauntology'. Fisher starts his reflection about futurism thinking on music. According to the author, electronic music 'had been synonymous with a sense of the future' (2012, 16); yet, in the past years, this sense of futurism became dissonant, a cliché more than a certain promise. 'Twenty-first-century electronic music had failed to progress beyond what had been recorded in the twentieth century: practically anything produced in the 2000s could have been recorded in the 1990s' (Ibid.). In other words, there is some diminishing of the exciting imagery shaping the future, as the future seems, now, very much like the past but with new, not-that-exciting cultural changes. As Fisher argues, 'what haunts the digital cul-de-sacs of the twenty-first century is not so much the past as all the lost futures that the twentieth century taught us to anticipate' (Ibid.).

Hauntology is, basically, a present stained by past and future, with little in terms of real 'present'. There is a deterioration of how we can imagine the future now, as history has shown us that there is not that much difference between past and the things to come: 'The future is always experienced as a haunting: as a virtuality that already impinges on the present, conditioning expectations and motivating cultural production' (Ibid.). A philosophy born from the 'spectral turn', hauntology 'haunts the present with its absence' with roots in dyschronia or 'time out of joint' (Fisher 2012, 18). Hauntology is not about apocalyptic futures, but about a 'future not yet brought into being' (Wale, Gobodo-Madikizela and Prager 2020, 7). Leaving aside the creation of the internet, there is little existing of what the 1970s and 1980s promised about the new millennium.

This haunting future needs a weak sense of present, a general feeling that both past and future are somehow more 'material' than the ephemeral today. At the shift from the 1960s to 1970s, Great Britain was at a loss about its Britishness and identity. The aftermath of the Second World War brought a new geopolitical map where Great Britain lost some of its privileged role at the hands of a new powerhouse: United States of America. Great Britain became a shadow of its former self, a ghostly revenant of a once-mighty state (Walton 2007, 63). This loss of power brought many broader sociopolitical consequences, including an increasing process of decolonization, beginning in 1945. British decolonization processes in India and Africa collaborated with the diminishing of national power. Without the colonial power, the essence of Britishness became ephemeral and in danger of disappearing altogether.

The imperial status as index of national identity was replaced by the mythic 'swinging London' imaginary, pointing to the city (and, by extension, England), as the heart of modern culture. According to K. J. Donnelly, 1968 was a watershed year in the UK, filled with creativity, experimentation and bold countercultural impulse in sexuality, fashion, film industry and pop music. London seemed the centre of global modernity. It was, however, 'short-lived' (Donnelly 2007, 70), as the turn from the 'psychedelic sixties' to the 1970s dissipated the revolutionary impulse. By 1967, 'the swinging scene had been done to death, and now most people were "heartily sick of it"' (Sandbrook 2006, 301). Already in 1969, 'American finance went home, leaving British film production an impoverished ruin' (Donnelly 2007, 71).

Thus, with the imperial status dead and the countercultural ethos becoming rapidly a relic, Britain faced, maybe for the first time in its modern history, a loss of national identity. Thus, identity should be deffered to the future. But what future Britain offered to the citizens?

From 1959 to 1975, Britain accessed what Jonathan Hogg called a 'realist' (2016, 109) response to the Cold War after two decades of first early and then 'maturing' answers to Red Scares (i.e. the fear of communist infiltration and invasion) and nuclear threat. In 1966, the semi-documentary

The War Game (Peter Watkins), which illustrated, through fictional reports, Britain's possible future after a devastating nuclear war, was released in the country. The effects of nuclear war, according to the film, will not only be a shortage of food resources, but also diseases, terminal patients and, even, human sacrifices performed by the authorities to avoid the prolongation of pain. The documentary was considered downright 'creepy' (Heller-Nicholas 2014, 73; Rees 2004, 60) since the future that *The War Game* posed was too credible within the climate of the British Cold War in the 1960s. When the film finally premiered on television, it did so one day before the re-release of the telefilm *Threads* (Mick Jackson 1984, BBC), a fictional film that set out what was happening in a Britain destroyed by nuclear devastation. Further, ideas of the apocalypse as proposed by *The War Game* would be taken up by a British television miniseries, *Survivors* (BBC, 1975–7), which proposed how the UK should shape itself after a pandemic devastated the world, ending a large part of the human population. The TV series tapped heavily on the horrors of the so-called Winter of Discontent (Pagnoni Berns, Aguilar and Juve 2020) and, like in *The War Game*, included human sacrifices performed by 'good' characters.

Why was Britain so adamant in imagining its future as a horror story? Maybe because its present, ephemeral in sense of identity, looked bleak. The negative aspects of Great Britain in the 1970s were, according to Kenneth O. Morgan, mainly four: (1) conflicts with trade unions and a falling economy, (2) anxieties regarding potential wars, (3) a movement towards extremism and (4) an increase in domestic and social violence. 'Without doubt, each of these revealed a new pattern of internal vulnerability not experienced previously, and a marked contrast with the stable social democracy that the United Kingdom had appeared to be since the Second World War' (Morgan 2019, 2). But as both Dominic Sandbrook (2009) and Tara Martín López (2014) argue, the negative image of the decade was a recreation of a historical reality, a kind of fictional image superimposed on reality. Reading against the grain, the British 1970s were not as bleak as remembered, since human rights, minorities' visibility and feminism all got recognition. Yet, this new set of visibilities marking that 'British citizens come in all shapes, ages, genders and colours' (Julios 2008, 5) was part of the problem. Since the 1970s, Paul Ward argues, there has been a sense of crisis about Britain's national identity, being British 'no longer seen as innate, static and permanent. Indeed, it is seen as under threat' (2004, 1). As Alwyn Turner mentions, Britain is (re) created – and that is how it is remembered – as a horror story: 'Having spent the whole decade [1970s] making its own flesh creep by telling horror stories about how bad things were, steeping itself in a popular culture that frequently verged on the apocalyptic, the nation finally found its nightmares coming true with the winter of discontent in early 1979' (2008, 12).

Certainly, England was entering a historical crossroads where the future seemed so apocalyptic that a national essence had to be recovered, not through imperialist enterprises, but through a return to the country's roots, hand in hand with its folklore and religion. Bob Fischer, writing for *Fortean Times* magazine, explains that 'the geographical specificity of the folkloric can inform unofficial identities that in some sense circumvent formalized history' (2017, 2). That identity was channelled ideologically through a return to old Albion, the latter a reservoir of cultures, images and ideologies that were destroyed by industrialization and modernity and that now returned from the past to resolve the current historical trauma. The return to old England served as a moral lesson where national heritage promised 'momentary experience of utopian gratification in which the grey torpor of everyday life in contemporary Britain lifts and the simpler, more radiant measures of Albion declare themselves again' (Wright 2009, 72). Thus, this cycle known today as 'folk horror', I argue, is a response to and a consequence of the British crisis of identity, a sort of distorted reflection of Great Britain experiencing its 'unfinest hour' (Morgan 2019).

The term 'folk horror' refers to a subgenre of horror fiction characterized by reference to European pagan traditions in rural landscapes. Stories typically involve standing stone circles, the horrifying return of pagan forces, rituals and the apparition of creatures from the invisible world. Rather than cinema, television was the privileged vehicle through which folk horror prospered in the UK through the 1970s. The modest budgets emphasized intimate stories saturated with invisible portents and spiritual mood, while the desolated, open-wide British landscapes offered the uncanny sense of seasonal ritual so important to the genre. 'Furthermore, the long history of British and European engagement with paganism propitiated a return of pagan rites in an era dominated by ecological and religious interest (McFarlane 2007, 199).

Following the end of the First World War, the UK witnessed 'an explosion of interest in the British countryside' (Sheeky Bird 2014, 1). The 'long-running series of British Transport Films produced by the Transport Commission from 1949 onwards' were 'tone poems intended to inspire the public to purchase a ticket to Arcadia Junction and reconnect with the landscape and history that city life obscures' (Young 2010). Children's literature 'was at the forefront of the literary struggle to control and shape understanding of the countryside as a place of quietude' (Sheeky Bird 2014, 1). Thus, not by chance two of the most terrifying British TV shows for children took place in the countryside: *Children of the Stones* (HTV, 1976) and *The Owl Service*, both stories led by young adults facing a cyclical time. The countryside was a perfect site for children's narratives, as it offered a space free (at least, to some extent) from parental surveillance, together with issues of 'escapism and nostalgia' (Sheeky Bird 2014, 2) for a pre-modern Britain. The countryside was the perfect site for folk horror, as the soil, the moors and the lakes were sites of isolation, where the past resonated in millenarian stones and green ancient landscapes (Scovell 2017, 37). Thus, it was only a logical step that children's fiction and folk horror addressed each other via creepy stories of the rural supernatural where the past is fleshed out to the point of asphyxiating the main characters, 'especially the kids on whom the future of the nation depends. Further, the cyclical time privileged by both, *Children of the Stones* and *The Owl Service*, denied the possibility of reaching a future, as progressive linearity is disrupted by the past, the future remaining unrealized and always out of reach.

Revisiting *The Owl Service*: Times out of joint

The first issue when addressing *The Owl Service* is its suitability for children. The series, in fact, fits better in what today has been marketed as 'young adult' fiction. Young adult fiction is sustained on the notions than the teenage years are distinct from childhood or adulthood. Such narratives implicate the young individual's development of self and agency while testing themselves amid extraordinary circumstances (Harrison 2019, 97).

At the time, however, *The Owl Service* was broadcast at the teatime slot (a time zone aimed at kids) and controversy was inevitable. Alan Garner's original novel's status as 'children's fiction' may be in dispute. The covers of the original paperbacks only depict owls or silhouettes resembling owls, presenting no evidence that the books were intended for children (neither the contrary). *The Glasgow Herald* dated 25 November 1967 stated that the book is aimed at children yet 'it is, almost totally, an adult book' (Mitchison 1967, 9) while *The Sydney Morning Herald*, dated 15 October 1978 states the book was written for children but 'adults would probably appreciate it more' (111). Further, Garner's book was one of the American Library Association's 'Notable Children's Books' of 1968.

The series' plot is intricate and slow, far detached from what can be considered children's fiction: easy-to-follow narratives within short lengths and speed of action. Not only had the complex plot suggested adult viewers, but also the subject matter: sexual desire. Alison's bare thighs appear in close-up, and she is shown sunbathing in a skimpy bikini. Further, a scene in episode three shows her slowly undressing while Gwyn (and young audiences at home) watches her through the window. In the first episode, Roger is seen swimming wearing only a pair of very brief shorts. His underwear is briefly flashed when he is examining his foot in a later scene. There is even implied teenage sex when, in episode three, Gwyn and Alison spend the night alone in a small outhouse: the outcome of the night is left in ambiguity.

It may be argued that the only element pointing to 'children's fiction' is the 'coming-of-age' narrative. This narrative comes with a sense of 'immaturity, of incompleteness' (Westfahl 2000, xii), where kids or young people strive 'to achieve adult stature' (Ibid.). Certainly, *The Owl Service* depicts, at its core, three teenagers trying to break with the rule of the past to project a new future in Britain. But, to do so, they must first break prefabricated roles and step into proper identities. As such, the folk horror tropes and the hauntological nature of the TV series served well to connect the show with a time 'out of joint'.

The initial credits of *The Owl Service* point to its folk horror's roots. It depicts a series of images of ominous woods. Hauntology is present as well, as one of the images is depicted through what looks like a camera's lens, thus uniting technology and the pre-modern. Discordant scratching and the revving of a motorbike intrude upon the theme, provoking uneasiness, as two eras seem to collapse together rather than follow a chronological order. A candle casts its light while a pair of hands insinuate a bird, another index of pre-modern (before electric light) times. Each image is backed with the motorbike's engine, thus hindering the reading of a definitive period. The first episode opens with Roger swimming in a river, backed with the luxurious green of the forest; the episode then cuts to his father, Clive (Edwin Richfield) trying to repair his modern car, a new mixture of modernity and the pre-modern coexisting. Clive has recently married Alison's mother, and they are staying in Alison's house.

The action properly begins when Alison calls Gwyn to her room, as she hears a series of scratching noises on the ceiling. There, he finds an old dinner service containing owl decorations. After tracing the design, Alison finds that the pattern on the plates comprises flowers and that when put together the flowers make an owl. She starts, obsessively, to make paper owls from the tracings. When Gwyn finds the plates, an abrupt cut takes viewers to Roger waking up from a siesta after swimming. He seems slightly afraid. The legend starts anew, the modern teenagers doomed to repeat the past rather than following linear time. When Roger wakes up abruptly, he is framed by the camera through a hole in a stone slab. He later caresses the hole with his hands. That hole, will be revealed later, was the one through which Gronw had thrown the spear that killed Lleu, thus hinting to a set of treasons and love triangles starting anew.

It is interesting to note that when Alison hears the scratches in her bedroom, she does not call for her mother (who is mentioned many times through the series, but never seen on screen) neither for her father or step-brother Roger. She calls for Gwyn, the housekeeper's son. As this scene opens the series, it is left ambiguous if she does so because she likes Gwyn better than the rest of her family or because she feels the boy, as the housekeeper's son, must serves her. Through the series, she recurrently explains that Gwyn is the only one to whom she can talk freely. Further in the first episode, Alison loses patience with her step-brother when she shows him the plates, as Roger is unable to distinguish designs of flowers from birds. For Alison, the housekeeper's son is more friend and accomplice than Roger, thus creating new dynamics in the family where class hierarchies are diminished or ignored altogether, but also prefiguring tensions and treasons to come.

Haru Takiuchi argues that 'Alan Garner has attempted to craft a way of writing that allows the voices, values and traditions of the rural working class, not just to be heard, but to be given poetic value. In other words, his writing seeks to incorporate the subordinate aspects of culture into the dominant' (2017, 105). Class structures and hierarchies of power are both sustained and contested through the series, as the different characters share three weeks together. When Gwyn's mother, Nancy (Dorothy Edwards), learns that her son and Alison have found the pattern-lined plates, she climbs to the girl's room and angrily reclaims the service. Alison refuses to give her the plates. When the discussion escalates in intensity and animosity, Alison reminds Nancy her role as housekeeper. The woman is clearly angry but insists, until Alison relinquishes and turns out one of the plates, now empty of colours and drawings: the flowers/owls are mysteriously vanished.

It may be argued, and rightly so, that Alison is so far reproducing class structures and hierarchies when putting Nancy in her 'proper' role as just a housekeeper. It is the adult woman, Nancy, the one breaking the rules of etiquette ordering Alison to give up the plates. Yet, this exchange takes place in the series' first episode, with Alison finding some power in her class upbringing to rebel against adult authority. The scene does not speak so much about class structures (after all, Alison gives the plate to her housekeeper) but of youth rebellion.

The lords and servants' aspect is foregrounded repeatedly through the series. In episode two, Clive listens tolerantly to Huw, standing at the middle of the road, telling his story about an old pagan legend, then nearly knocks the gardener over when he does not respond to Clive honking his car's horn. In the same episode, Alison is dismissive towards Gwyn: 'Give him a lollipop, Roger. He's just like his mother.' In episode three, Clive discovers a note Gwyn has left for Alison in the tray. The father is very disgusted: 'Let's have the coffee served straight, without notes.' So far in the story, Clive has not forbidden his son or stepdaughter to talk or play with Gwyn. It is clearly the subterfuge that annoys Clive, as class boundaries can be broken only under his surveillance. In episode four, Alison regretfully tells Gwyn her mother has forbidden the girl from continuing speaking with the housekeeper's son: 'It's quite in order, Miss. And I'll use the tradesman's entrance in future', Gwyn angrily retorts.

Still, there are nuanced shades in the kids, especially Gwyn, which hint to potential disruptions of prefixed roles and, as such, to potential different futures.

Nancy, having once been heartbroken in class/racial tensions in her rural Welsh community because of a love triangle involving an English middle-class man, left her valley with her baby, Gwyn. Since then, as a working-class single mother, she has endeavoured to improve her son through his education. Not only has she removed Gwyn from their original place, as a way to achieve her ambition to educate Gwyn into a middle-class person, but Nancy also forbids Gwyn to speak Welsh, because she sees Welsh as a labourer's language. (Takiuchi 2017, 156)

Gwyn's background as a working-class boy with a privileged education is played out when Nancy threatens to cut short Gwyn's schooling if he does not stop investigating the dinner service. Equally, Clive subtly threatens Alison with cutting her tennis club membership if she insists on secret meetings with Gwyn. The parental shadow has traced a prefixed path for the kids where there is no real 'newness' but repetition: the kids must follow their parents' steps, thus always giving birth to the same. Even Roger has a job lined up in the family firm that excites him little (episode six). Yet, Gwyn's role within the house is potentially disruptive, as he is now the housekeeper's son but may have a bourgeois job in his future. Or maybe not. It is entirely up to him and his circumstances. Yet, the possibility is there, unrealized at the moment. The assembled family presented by *The Owl Service* maps an England in crisis trying to restructure gender and class guidelines. In episode four, Nancy tells Gwyn of Clive's lack of etiquette when a pear ends up under the table because of Clive's inability to properly cut it up into pieces. Even the adult people are insecure about their social and cultural status in 1960s/1970s Britain.

The Owl Service sits uneasily at the brink of change, as the kids can potentially produce more of the same or change hierarchies. 'Garner's literary ideal involves fusing middle-class and working-class cultures' (Takiuchi 2017, 105) and teenagers, more inclined to break boundaries and disobey mandates, are suitable vehicles of class disruption. Episode two opens with Roger, Alison and Gwyn playing pool, all three laughing loudly, no class boundaries between them. Later in the episode, Roger insists on accompanying Gwyn to the village to buy groceries for his mother, ignoring that the son's housekeeper is ashamed of his position as errands boy. Roger does not see his friend's uneasiness simply because there are not (at the moment) class boundaries for Roger. Episode five opens with Gwyn and Alison talking about their futures and their roles in their families.

It is important to point that the friendship between Roger, Gwyn and Alison starts to turn sour after the ancient legend starts its hold on the young generation. In the first three episodes, the teenagers share moments of laughter and play. This changes after two particular events: first, in episode three, after Alison spends a whole night in her childhood playhouse with Gwyn. Alison is febrile and slightly disoriented. The scene reads as an intimate moment between two teenagers, implying sexual awakening. Thus, Alison starts to change. In *The Owl Service*, however, changes of puberty are synchronized with the supernatural. Through the night, Alison finally finishes her bird tracings, all the plates now empty of images: so she now fully embodies the spirit of old Blodwuedd. Second, after Roger shows Clive the pictures he took with his camera at the forest in episode four, ghostly figures appear in his photographs; one is a man poised to throw a spear and, another one, a man and a motorbike. Roger assures Clive that there was no person in the forest when he took the photographs. The ancient legend is becoming more real as the days go on. By episode six, Roger considers seeing Gwyn crying in public 'absolutely embarrassing' and tells Alison that the boy is 'not one of us. He never will be. He's a yobbo. A clever yobbo.' As the series unfolds, Roger becomes increasingly cruel with Gwyn, with their friendship coming to an end.

In this scenario, Roger, Alison and Gwyn are mere pawns of the past. In episode two, Gwyn is playfully pointing a big spear at Roger, just a game that prefigures the roles that destiny seemingly has for each kid. Later, in episode five, Gwyn throws a spear at the stable roof. No matter how much they try to escape the parental shadow, the past will devour any free will. Amid a discussion between Gwyn and Alison, the girl's face is depicted, via brief inserts, painted as an owl, prefiguring thus the inescapability of her destiny. Episode two ends with a wooden panelling falling away and a mural of Blodeuwedd being revealed. In the same episode, Alison lies on a sun lounger reading the Mabinogion. When Gwyn angrily throws her book away, fluttering birds (or loose pages?) hunt down the boy as he flees, scared. Only minutes later, Alison and Gwyn are friends again. The kids are always getting in and out of their prefabricated roles, as they struggle to find their own voices rather than follow the path of old England. As mentioned, Gwyn is seen twice through the series manipulating a spear, suggesting he is the modern counterpart of Gronw. Yet, in episode one, Roger delicately caresses the hole in the granite slab, the same through which the deadly spear must pass, thus suggesting that Roger is the new Gronw, the one who must kill Lleu (Gwyn?).

Faithful to coming-of-age narratives, the three teenagers try to crawl out from prefixed destinies to create their own paths. This clash with the past is best exemplified by the uneasy relationship the kids have with their parents. Gwyn is disgusted or clearly annoyed when her mother asks for him. Both mother and boy seem to fight every time they share a scene. The boy is clearly trying to crawl out from his mother's gaze, the latter always – literally – observing him from the background. Gwyn is not the only one trying to form an identity of his own. In episode one, Roger reproaches his father for his attempts to make the boy change his attitudes towards his new wife: Clive hints that Roger should call Margaret 'mom' rather than 'Alison's mom' (as Roger always calls her). Roger defends his right to call her whatever he wants to, even if his father is clearly against it. In episode four, Alison's distaste at Clive relaying her mother's instructions is emphasized when she mockingly retorts 'Yes Clive. No Clive. Yes Clive.' The scene ends with Clive telling her what most parents do: it is all for your own good. After being prohibited from talking to Gwyn, Alison tries to obey their parents' rule, but she ends talking to him anyway. Like Nancy with Gwyn, Clive is depicted many times furtively observing his stepdaughter, a surveillance to keep the girl under the parental shadow. *The Owl Service* works on the premise of coming-of-age narratives, where issues of gender and class are disputed only by the teenagers, thus giving hope for a new generation that maybe will not replicate the world (or, at least, contemporary Britain) as it is.

As the series comes nearer to its end, the scratching noises from an abandoned barn accompany the revelation of a locked door. Gwyn later learns Huw is actually the father he has never known and that he has killed Bertram, Nancy's former upper-class lover, thus re-enacting the pagan legend. Hidden in the barn is a stuffed owl in a glass jar, a collection of paper owls made by Nancy and Bertram's motorbike. Gwyn discovers that his mother was once possessed by the same old plates Alison uncovered in the attic. Thus, the past has been repeating itself since the times of Albion, each new generation unable to bring something really new to the future. As such, England is trapped in a present filled with unrealized futures (can Alison and Gwyn break the curse through consummating their relationship?) and a haunting past. The ghostly figures appearing in Roger's photos are those of Bertram or his pagan counterpart, Gronw. But who is, truly, the counterpart of who?

Episode eight reaches the climax with Alison completely possessed and in great danger: her body very weak and her health faltering, she is close to death. At that point Roger asks Gwyn for help, but the housekeeper's son is unable to act. He must kill Roger to fulfill the prophecy. Huw does not tell, and Gwyn remains in a state of shock, with his beloved Alison dying in the bed next to him. It is Roger who calms Alison, forcing the girl to think of flowers rather than owls. In the last scene, Alison looks well and safe. The episode ends there, with a brief coda: three kids (two boys, one girl) walking through the forest find the slab with a hole, hinting to history repeating again.

The end is baffling, as Gwyn, the working-class boy and the 'hero' of the children's story is unable to help the girl he loves while Roger, the series' 'villain', is the one who saves the day. The curse has been, at least, momentarily broken. The legend has failed to win this time and even Huw seems genuinely surprised. Yet, the end of the cycle insinuates that only the upper class has the solution to fix history. Is the series implicitly confirming that young people cannot escape their upbringing?

The end is so complex that Haru Takiuchi dedicates a whole chapter of his *British Working-Class Writing for Children: Scholarship Boys in the Mid-Twentieth Century* to analyse the novel's last part. The question is 'why only Gwyn fails to escape the pattern set by the tale and is incapable of saving Alison' (Takiuchi 2017, 154). There is a happy ending of sorts, with Alison saved but not by her hero. For Takiuchi, Gwyn fails because he has been alienated from a proper role: he is a Welsh boy of working-class status who befriends upper-class teenagers and has been educated as a middle-class lad. 'Gwyn has internalised the dominant culture and thus willingly, not only for his mother's sake, has rejected his Welsh working-class culture' (Takiuchi 2017, 156). We agree with Takiuchi: the three teenagers try to find a foot outside their predetermined roles. Alison falls in love with the poor Welsh boy and Roger befriends him until the curse starts acting on all three teenagers. It is the supernatural legend from the past that places the three kids on a route of prefixed patterns, when all three were, right up to that point, close friends. The three kids represent a future open with possibilities. Gwyn is more than his social and cultural upbringing, while both Alison and Roger can break with social hierarchies that presuppose snobbish attitudes. After Alison is saved, the episode ends abruptly, leaving the future unrealized. What happened with Gwyn? Has the boy found a life as a poor Welsh boy or found a role as a middle-class (why not upper-class?) man? What path do Roger and Alison choose? Will they succumb to their parents' desires and prejudices or build a new non-class future for England?

In this scenario, *The Owl Service* is hauntological in two ways. First, because the story is haunted by a past which tries to asphyxiate the teenagers' lives through cyclical repetition. The future is there as well, as the boys can fall into prefixed patterns and rehearse the tragedy or choose their own destiny. If Takiuchi is right in his argument that Gwyn fails because of his mixed class roles, that is not necessarily a bad thing. After all, the curse has been disrupted. There are unrealized futures lurking on the margins of the series as well, where the past and future intermingle. *The Owl Service* was the first fully scripted colour production by Granada Television and was filmed almost entirely on location in an era when almost all TV drama was made in studio. Technology and modernity (and, by extent, the future) are depicted through 'meta' allusions. The three main actors are dressed in signature colours which at the time were the colours of UK domestic wiring: Alison always wears red, Gwyn black and Roger green, thus pointing not to 'essences' of colours (such as reading red as passion) but to TV itself: red (neutral), green (earth) and black (neutral).

The Owl Service is hauntological in a further way. Seeing it today, the TV series falls into what Bob Fischer calls 'the haunted generation' (2017, 30), meaning, products of popular culture that scared (and scarred) children through the 1960s, 1970s and first years of the 1980s. There is little, for contemporary eyes, that could be read as 'children' in *The Owl Service*. I am not denying here the intelligence of children or the complex ways kids can watch and understand complex stories with shades of horror. Yet, the sombre mood, the talkative nature of most of the episodes and the lack of a proper hero can be baffling for contemporary audiences. *The Owl Service*, arguably, reads more like horror than 'children's fiction'. Still, what prevails through the eight episodes is a coming-of-age narrative that may resonate heavily not only with children and young adults watching the show, but also with adults facing an England who, like Roger, Alison and Gwyn, were trying to figure out their roles in the last days of the 1960s.

I am not arguing here that *The Owl Service* reflects, directly, the economic and social crisis that will shake England through the 1970s. Issues of class and gender, so present in the TV show are, after all, basic tropes of storytelling, in the UK as elsewhere. What makes *The Owl Service* especially relevant in hauntological terms is the time of its production: the series was made through the birth of the British cycle of folk horror. Certainly, *The Owl Service* is an important piece of the cycle. Folk horror is predicated on both the lore of times past and the natural landscapes. The series plays with these two elements. In the weeks the assembled family spends time together, the past returns with a vengeance. In episode two, Huw tells the story of the Mabinogion. He states that the tragedy started when a man took the woman of another man. Clive is framed by a close shot, his discomfort accentuated. Even if he had married a widow, he would have taken the woman of another man. As such, the story is not doomed to be repeated only through the three teenagers, but each generation seems to be a mere reproduction of a past generation. Huw emphasizes this impossibility of flight from the past when he states, 'Yes sir, that is how it is happening [the legend], all times.' This 'all times' refers to a cyclical temporality that dominates not only folk horror but also British history. The country's future was so apocalyptic that a new identity should be found through a return to the past. Only a couple of years later, starting in 1971, BBC would begin anew the Victorian tradition of telling ghost stories for Christmas, another negotiation with the past to find a present.

Garner depicts a Britain where the past, present and future collapse together; as such, roles became ephemeral and alien-like when facing the supernatural. Garner's horror landscapes are subjected to a past brought by cultural memory to replace the lack of contemporary national identity: yet this past comes to haunt with disturbing effects. Identity, national or otherwise, must lie always open to the future, never on the past.

References

Children of the Stones (1977), [TV programme; Director: Peter Graham Scott] HTV West.
Donnelly, K. J. 2007. *British Film Music and Film Musicals*. New York: Routledge.
Fisher, Mark. 2012. 'What Is Hauntology?' *Film Quarterly* 66, no. 1 (Fall 2012): 16–24.

Fischer, Bob. 2017. 'The Haunted Generation', *Fortean Times*, No. 354, June 2017, https://hauntedgeneration.co.uk/2019/04/22/thehauntedgeneration/. Accessed 1 November 2023.

Harrison, Jennifer. 2019. *Posthumanist Readings in Dystopian Young Adult Fiction: Negotiating the Nature/Culture Divide*. Lanham: Lexington.

Heller-Nicholas, Alexandra. 2014. *Found Footage Horror Films: Fear and the Appearance of Reality*. Jefferson: McFarland.

Hogg, Jonathan. 2016. *British Nuclear Culture: Official and Unofficial Narratives in the Long 20th Century*. New York: Bloomsbury.

Julios, Christina. 2008. *Contemporary British Identity: English Language, Migrants and Public Discourse*. Hampshire: Ashgate.

McFarlane, Scott. 2007. *The Hippie Narrative: A Literary Perspective on the Counterculture*. Jefferson: McFarland.

Martín Lopez, Tara (2014). *The Winter of Discontent: Myth, Memory, and History*. Liverpool: Liverpool University Press.

Mitchison, Naomi. 1967. 'Why Not Grown-Ups Too?' *The Glasgow Herald*. 25 November.

Morgan, Kenneth. 2019. 'Britain in the Seventies – Our Unfinest Hour?' *Revue Française de Civilisation Britannique* [Online], XXII – Hors série. URL: http://journals.openedition.org/rfcb/1662. Accessed 13 October 2023.

Pagnoni Berns, Fernando Gabriel, Emiliano Aguilar and Juan Juvé. 2020. 'The Winter of Discontent in Survivors'. In *Apocalypse TV: Essays on Society and Self at the End of the World*, edited by Michael G. Cornelius and Sherry Ginn, 58–70. Jefferson: McFarland.

Rees, Duncan. 2004. 'Resisting the British Bomb: The Early Years'. In *The British Nuclear Weapons Programme, 1952–2002*, edited by Frank Barnaby and Frank Barnaby, 55–62. London: Frank Cass.

Sandbrook, Dominic. 2009. *White Heath*. London: Abacus.

Scovell, Adam. 2017. *Folk Horror: Hours Dreadful and Things Strange*. Leighton Buzzard: Auteur.

Sheeky Bird, Hazel. 2014. *Class, Leisure and National Identity in British Children's Literature, 1918–1950*. New York: Palgrave Macmillan.

Takiuchi, Haru. 2017. *British Working-Class Writing for Children: Scholarship Boys in the Mid-twentieth Century*. New York: Palgrave Macmillan.

'The Owl Service'. 1978. *The Sydney Morning Herald*. 15 October.

The Owl Service. 1969–1070. [TV programme; Director: Peter Plummer] Granada Television.

Threads. 1984. [TV programme; Director: Mick Jackson] BBC TV.

Tribunella, Eric. 2010. *Melancholia and Maturation: The Use of Trauma in American Children's Literature*. Knoxville: The University of Tennessee Press.

Turner, Alwyn. 2008. *Crisis? What Crisis?: Britain in the 1970s*. London: Aurum.

Wale, Kim, Pumla Gobodo-Madikizela and Jeffrey Prager. 2020. 'Introduction'. In *Post-Conflict Hauntings: Transforming Memories of Historical Trauma*, edited by Kim Wale, Pumla Gobodo-Madikizela and Jeffrey Prager, 1–24. New York: Palgrave Macmillan.

Walton, Dale. 2007. *Geopolitics and the Great Powers in the 21st Century: Multipolarity and the Revolution in Strategic Perspective*. New York: Routledge.

Ward, Paul. (2004). *Britishness since 1870*. London: Routledge.
Westfahl, Gary. 2000. *Science Fiction, Children's Literature, and Popular Culture. Coming of Age in Fantasyland*. Westport, CT: Greenwood Press.
White, Donna. 1998. *A Century of Welsh Myth and Children's Literature*. Westport, CT: Greenwood Press.
Wright, Patrick. 2009. *On Living in an Old Country: The National Past in Contemporary Britain*. Oxford: Oxford University Press.
Young. Rob. 2010. 'The Pattern under the Plough: The "Old, Weird Britain" on Film'. *BFI*. https://www2.bfi.org.uk/news-opinion/sight-sound-magazine/archives/old-weird-britain-film-rob-young. Accessed 13 October 2023.

3

'Oh please, let us come undone!' States of independence: Female temporality in the supernatural children's television and literature of the 1970s and 1980s

Fiona Cameron

How do the female protagonists of children's TV and literature of the 1970s and 1980s experience the supernatural? In this chapter, I will explore the idea that individual responses and nuanced expressions of female subjectivity related to the supernatural can frequently be found in some of the innovative and sophisticated writing and TV output of the period. I will argue that these responses can be better understood through examining what French philosopher Julia Kristeva defines as 'women's time', and the mode Mark Fisher defines as 'the eerie'. I will also examine what can be discovered in the mother–daughter relationships implied in these texts. How do these mothers figure in timescapes that actively upend the linear? Mothers are absent from the main action of the texts discussed but are often seen to be 'on their own time' – on different temporal wings or branches. Likewise, all three stories place their teenage protagonists in unfamiliar locations – dislocated from the family home or, in the case of one of the texts discussed, a holiday home, in which a new configuration of family is established and tested.

I will examine the following: Araminta Cane in Helen Creswell's 1987 novel, *Moondial*, and the 1988 BBC TV adaptation; Carrie Willow in Nina

Bawden's 1973 novel, *Carrie's War*, and the 1974 BBC TV adaptation; lastly, I will consider Alison in Alan Garner's 1967 novel, *The Owl Service,* and the Granada Television for ITV adaptation of 1969.

Is it really different for girls?

In her 1979 essay 'Women's Time', Julia Kristeva developed the terms 'cyclical time' and 'monumental time'. These modes speak to the idea that female subjectivity becomes problematic if read through the predominant linear conception of time (Moi 1986, 192). How might Kristeva's assertions help us to locate and define the female supernatural experience as multifaceted and various – these female characters are often enfolded into temporally unstable situations, where it is their ability to embody the asynchronous and see beyond the teleological that helps produce profound meaning and engagement with the phenomena they encounter. How can these definitions help us understand that female characters might engage with the supernatural via temporalities which offer a space for the reciprocal, the transactional and the entangled to flourish?

Kristeva describes linear, teleological and disembodied notions of time as being patriarchal in nature (Söderbäck 2012, 305); time in patriarchal terms is therefore figured as neatly chronological, logical – with a beginning, middle and end. It is understandable as a flat structure in which one can only move forward. She suggests that women therefore face a choice: '*insertion* into history' or the radical *refusal* of the subjective limitations imposed by this [i.e. linear] history's time' (Moi 1986, 195).

So, for female protagonists who encounter supernatural phenomena, we must look beyond the dominant linear mode and ask in what ways they process and understand their times and experiences via non-linear means. How might their perceptions and embodiment of time differ from the dominant patriarchal forms and what do these differences reveal in their own, often temporally untethered experiences? In relation to the supernatural, their 'refusal' of the linear is perhaps less of a genuine refusal, rather it is a state of being that has always been present, but continually effaced by patriarchal time constructs. In the supernatural story, female subjectivity is, to a certain extent, voiced, normalized or given more space. Kristeva (1981) suggests there is need 'to give a language to the intra-subjective and corporeal experiences left mute by culture in the past', meaning that a woman's subjectivity has been undervalued or ignored by patriarchal standards which have come to be accepted as the norm. I would argue that the supernatural is one place we can look in order to see this in action.

Kristeva's definitions of 'cyclical and 'monumental' time offer possible routes into opening out and understanding these experiences. She conceptualized 'female subjectivity as "strung out" between cyclical and monumental time' (Tiwari 2017). Cyclical time deals with the idea of repetitions within natural time and ongoing revolutions (revolutions in the sense of repeating patterns) such as gestation, circadian rhythms, lunar phases and the seasons. Cyclical time might also suggest revenants, a term which is most frequently associated with returns, especially those after death. Monumental time presents the idea of eternity – the vast imaginary space in which the mythical, the all-encompassing and infinite exist, or as Tiwari suggests, 'eternity without cleavage or escape' (Tiwari 2017). Benedict Anderson argues that monumental time is 'a simultaneity of past and future in an instantaneous present.' (Anderson 2016, 265). This definition is particularly useful when we start to consider the individual experiences of our three protagonists – all glimpse the collapse of linear time, be that through encountering revenants or finding themselves enfolded into temporally untethered timescapes. But what is notable in all three cases is the lack of resistance to (or ease of movement into) these states which arise in direct opposition to the constructs of time enforced by patriarchal structures. Therefore, framing their experiences via cyclical and monumental time enables us to address their stories more fully.

An aching fascination

Mark Fisher's 2016 text, *The Weird and the Eerie*, offers a further set of useful ideas which seek to develop modes that push beyond Freud's *unheimlich* and explore a space at the edges of genres such as horror or science fiction which in addition might reveal an extraterritorial space in which the female protagonists' distinct experience of the supernatural can come into sharper focus.

The eerie, in particular, offers some useful routes into exploring the female experience within the supernatural. Fisher suggests that 'it has, rather, to do with a fascination for the outside, for that which lies beyond standard perception, cognition and experience. This fascination usually involves a certain apprehension, perhaps even dread – but it would be wrong to say that the weird and the eerie are necessarily terrifying' (Fisher 2016, 8). For the female protagonists discussed in this chapter, I would argue that there is apprehension and dread but both (as we shall see) are borne from a sense of precognition, an intuition that what they instinctively feel, or sense, is a truth. Can we therefore link their often seamless segues 'through the veil' to Kristeva's assertion that women perceive and embody time in a radically different way? Within this 'fascination' for what lies beyond, is there also the ever-present echo of cyclical and monumental time which enables these characters to adjust to and move through unstable temporalities with ease? Or, as Toril Moi suggests, 'Female subjectivity would seem to provide a specific measure that essentially retains *repetition* and *eternity* from among the multiple modalities of time known through the history of civilisations' (Moi 1986, 156).

Fisher asserts that 'the eerie also entails a disengagement from our current attachments. But, with the eerie, this disengagement does not usually have the quality of shock that is typically a feature of the weird. The serenity of that is often associated with the eerie – think of the phrase *eerie calm* – has to do with detachment from the urgencies of the everyday' (Fisher 2016, 12). This idea has some useful connections with Kristeva's terms if we reflect on some of the unquestioning aspects of behaviour in the female protagonists discussed in this chapter. That is not to say that they lack curiosity or agency, rather that they come to the supernatural with what Fisher describes as 'serenity' – a quiet, deeply embodied acknowledgement that time is (of course) not linear and therefore does not behave as such.

David Annwn, who has also considered the eerie, highlights the risk of what might be termed 'irrational thought' within this area. He suggests, 'Eeriness does of course involve rational *and* non-rational, intuitive thought and feeling; for some writers such approaches to irrationality do, of course risk an inherent danger' (Annwn 2007, 86). Here he is touching on what Kristeva describes as 'subjective limitations' of linear thinking and how voicing a radical female alternative may run the risk of othering and exclusion from dominant narratives. Annwn quotes Alison Croggon, who suggests 'Feminine irrationality courts the seductive danger of appearing to be subversive while in fact satisfying all sorts of time-hallowed prejudices about femaleness, and if valorised within an implicitly male subject, can easily become again a category which leads to the exclusion of dissenting strong female voices' (Annwn 2007, 86). So, it is with interest that I approach the writing of Alan Garner where it could be argued that both male and female characters become vehicles through which a mythic sort of time plays out. I begin to suggest that through his reworking of myth, he enables an articulation of monumental time that is not necessarily figured as an entirely female experience, rather it seems to refer to what Fisher describes as a 'cold fatality' – a cold fatality for all. How, in this case, does the female protagonist, Alison, compare to Minty and Carrie's experiences and where does agency reside, if at all?

Araminta 'Minty' Cane: Moving in time to the moon

Helen Cresswell's spellbinding 1987 novel, *Moondial*, was adapted for BBC Children's TV in a landmark 1988 production directed by the inimitable Colin Cant. Cresswell was commissioned to write the screenplay, and this may, in part, account for why the novel lost none of its beguiling magic in its transference to screen. Cresswell's eerie night-time landscapes are vividly brought to life through an atmospheric theme tune and score by David Ferguson, and the innovative camera work that, even when using day for night filming, still convincingly conjures such an eerie nocturnal landscape, that it's seared into the memory of a generation.

Moondial is the story of the teenage Araminta Cane (Minty) and the sundial (moondial) at Belton House, Lincolnshire, which enables her to move between temporal planes. Minty is sent to the village of Belton to stay with her aged 'aunt' Mary in an old stone cottage next to the house for the summer holidays while her widowed mother continues to work.

Minty's 'time travel' transports her to Belton in the eighteenth century where she befriends the consumptive kitchenhand, Tom. Together they seek to help Sarah, a wealthy child of Belton House, who is ostracized and dubbed 'the devil child' due to her facial difference. Helped by wise old Mr World who lives in the entrance lodge to the house, and hindered by the sinister ghosthunter Miss Raven, the story advances towards the emancipation of Sarah and the inevitable decline of Tom's short and blighted life.

Initially, we encounter Minty (played by Siri Neal in the BBC adaptation) as a sharp, frequently witty teenager. Minty has always known she 'was a witch' and she 'did not talk about these things for the simple reason that they did not strike her as remarkable. Their appearance was as commonplace to her as that of the milkman' (Cresswell 1987, 3). So, we understand that there is a sense of the practical *and* the inevitable in Minty's relationship with the supernatural – it furnishes her every day and is therefore not perceived to be an 'other' or alien state. We also learn that Minty's deceased father's voice has reached her occasionally and that 'at other times she had seen blurred faces hovering over her, and pale hands floating like blossoms in the dark' (Cresswell 1987, 3). Therefore, it is already a given that Minty proceeds through life naturally accepting porous and unstable temporalities. She is, in fact, already operating in both cyclical and monumental time, but it is of note, that she instinctively knows not to voice these experiences, suggesting her awareness of becoming othered within patriarchal narratives about time. She also exemplifies Fisher's eerie calm in the sense that while detachment from her immediate surroundings occurs almost as soon as she arrives at Belton, she doesn't enter this space in shock or with any form of resistance – in fact she almost seamlessly segues from the 1980s to the 1800s and detaches from the 'urgencies of the everyday' (Fisher, 2016, 13). She simply accepts that the moondial will transport her through time.

Arriving at Belton heralds maturation in both Minty's independence, and in understanding her developing relationship with the unseen – which gradually solidifies into a mission to help the children of Belton House in this eerie landscape. Shortly after Minty is deposited at Belton, her family fractures further when her mother is involved in a car crash on the return journey – she now lies in a coma, suspended somewhere between life and death. In thinking about the shift towards adulthood in supernatural children's television, Helen Wheatley suggests 'understanding childhood as an unsettling time of transition, where the family home acts as the key site of this period of uncertainty and when the child must also come to understand their place in wider society' and 'separation anxiety of being removed from one's home and one's family, a fear which, at its root, is a fear of isolation, a growing awareness of a world full of risky strangers – in short, a fear of growing up' (Wheatley 2012, 387). In Minty's case, we see these concerns doubling by the minute. Not only is she transplanted from the family home, there is the threat that she may never find a way back, and now her mother lies close to death on what could be described as another temporal plane. Her past and future lie in the balance. For Minty, it could be argued that her innate alignment with what Cresswell calls her 'sixth sense' or what we might identify as a link to cyclical and monumental time, saves her because it's her one constant – her connection back to the mother, her window beyond overwhelming quotidian and earth-bound realities. Indeed, as the story progresses and Minty and Miss Raven, the ghosthunter, discuss the art of photography, we catch a glimpse of Minty's embodied knowledge of time. Miss Raven declares that a photograph 'has something to do with time for me' (Cresswell 1987, 139). She goes on to qualify this: "'*Capturing* it" said Miss Raven. "Pinning down the passing second"' (Cresswell 1987, 140). Minty doesn't voice her disagreement, but Cresswell's narration shows Minty's interiority at this moment: '"That," thought Minty, "is what you think. Silly bat!" She knew differently. She knew that time is fluid, watery beyond water, even, because you cannot cup it in your hands however fleetingly' (Cresswell 1987, 140).

Later still, old Mr World lends Minty a book about sundials. In it, he reveals, there 'are the queerest things … stuck in my mind all these years' (Cresswell 1987, 164). Mr World goes on to describe how the book shows the difference between clock time, sundial or 'apparent time' (or what we might call linear time) and star time which is the only *real* time. At this, Minty becomes excitable, declaring, '"Star time!" Minty felt a long, delicious shiver. You mean – moontime!"' (Cresswell 1987, 165). For Minty, 'moontime' – or what we might argue is simply another word for the monumental and cyclical – gives name to her intuitive feelings about 'being a witch' or 'seeing things' – these feelings which she keeps to herself. These feelings, which while entirely natural to her, also hold the power to other or isolate her from the dominant narrative around the constructs of time. Internally, she feels a jolt, a physical sort of recognition when Mr World starts to offer the words which can finally explain her feelings. Moontime also allows for the cyclical, the revenant in the form of Tom or Sarah and the illustration of Kristeva's assertion that there must be 'the radical *refusal* of the subjective limitations imposed by this [i.e. linear] history's time' (Mo 1986, 195) if women are to have choice and voice.

Moontime, although Minty does not refer to it as such earlier in the novel, is also a means to understand the nature of a coma. Her mother exists on another temporal plane during her hospitalization and Minty attempts to enter this space through the use of technology – the headphones and portable cassette player on which she plays her unconscious mother a faithful record of her nocturnal adventures at Belton. In the TV adaptation, a set of brand-new headphones are her mother's parting gift before she gets behind the wheel, perhaps visually prefiguring what will be their only line of communication in the coming weeks. This is another example of a temporal breech, this time aided by (what was then) cutting-edge technology. The retelling of Minty's adventures via cassette tape serves as a type of nested narrative within a narrative, which reveals or suggests the bonds and unseen lines between mothers and daughters within the supernatural context. Here we understand that although Minty's mother is unable to communicate in 'clock time', she can still be reached in 'moontime', in the all-encompassing depths of the monumental which they both share.

Carrie Willow: Push and pull

In *Carrie's War*, Nina Bawden's classic tale of growing up in wartime Britain, Carrie Willow and her brother, Nick, are evacuated from London to a small Welsh village where they are billeted with the stern shopkeeper, Mr Evans, and his meek and cowed sister, Auntie Lou. Another evacuee from Carrie and Nick's school (the brilliantly named) Albert Sandwich has found accommodation at Druid's Bottom, a dilapidated manor house situated at the foot of an ancient grove. Here, he settles happily under the care of the housekeeper, Hepzibah Green. Hepzibah cares for not only Albert, but also the owner of the house, the elderly and frail Dilys Gotobed (Mr Evans's estranged sister) and the loveable Mr Johnny who is Dilys's disabled cousin. Initially, Carrie and Nick struggle to adjust to life at the shop, where Mr Evans bullies his sister and dominates their everyday life with a set of strict rules and frothing religious zeal. The siblings find much-needed comfort in the kindness of gentle Auntie Lou, and later at Druid's Bottom, where Hepzibah's cosy kitchen provides succour and relief from their austere existence above the shop. As the novel progresses, the relationships of both adults and children entwine, and the death of ancient Mrs Gotobed sets an unexpected chain of events in motion. This culminates in an explosive denouement which sees Carrie hurl a 'cursed' skull into the depths of a well at Druid's Bottom in order to invoke an ancient curse and stave off what she perceives to be Mr Evans's attempt to sell the manor house from under Hepzibah and Mr Johnny. Carrie and Nick leave the village for good the next morning, and from the train window, as they speed far away, Carrie is horrified to witness a terrible conflagration at Druid's Bottom. For thirty

years, she carries the devastating idea that it was the act of throwing the
skull that caused the fire, which she believes has killed all at Druid's Bottom.

Ostensibly, the least explicitly supernatural of the novels discussed in this
chapter, it could, in fact, be argued that the supernatural in this story is a
near constant presence, but a subtle one – one that seems implied or left to
hum eerily between words and actions. Ultimately, the episode of the cursed
skull brings the supernatural front and centre, however, to focus on this as
the defining supernatural element of the novel would be to overlook the
deep and affective presence of the eerie in this text. I will also argue that
Carrie is an extraordinary example of a female character, who (through
circumstance) becomes disconnected from not only her mother at the advent
of war, but also the channels through which her female subjectivity might
find voice in this charged environment, that is to say, her access to the
cyclical and the monumental.

Fisher's definition of the eerie suggests that 'the sensation of the eerie
clings to certain kinds of physical spaces and landscapes' (Fisher 2016, 61).
And that 'the eerie is constituted by a *failure of absence* or by a *failure of
presence*. The sensation of the eerie occurs either when there is something
present where there should be nothing, or there is nothing present when there
should be something' (Fisher 2016, 61). Applying these ideas, particularly
the 'failure of absence' to the setting of *Carrie's War* is useful as it enables an
articulation of that implied supernatural quality suffused in the text.

Wartime rural Wales as a setting immediately presents a set of landscapes
which by their geography in relation to the rest of the UK and their rugged
topography suggest the distant or lost – a place that time has forgotten.
Wales as a destination for evacuees is understood to be safe and relatively
untouched by the hand of war, however rural Wales is also a repository for
another set of ideas. These are long-held cultural stereotypes which tend
to figure Wales as backward and old-fashioned – essentially untouched
by the modern world. And despite Methodism dominating many rural
communities through the chapel network, Wales also tends to be associated
with the vestiges of a much older religion – the druidic tradition, places of
dark yew groves and an older, deeper magic. These residual energies are rife
throughout *Carrie's War* and are most strongly felt at Druid's Bottom, where
their failure to entirely absent themselves from the landscape is what gives
this location such a vivid charge. Fisher suggests that 'we are compelled to
imagine our world as a set of eerie traces' (Fisher 2016, 63) and on Carrie
and Nick's first dusk visit to Druid's Bottom, Carrie is tuned into these
traces which she finds hard to rationalize. 'She couldn't explain it. It was
such a strange feeling. As if there was something here, *waiting*. Deep in the
trees or deep in the earth. Not a ghost – nothing so simple. Whatever it
was had no name. Something old and huge and nameless' (Bawden 1973,
49). Later, she hears the landscape sigh – 'a slow, dry whisper' (Bawden
1973, 50). Carrie's intuitive feelings also speak strongly to both cyclical and

monumental time – Druid's Bottom seems to exist outside of linear time; beyond the clatter of war, beyond the quotidian life of chapel, school and shop, further away, literally deep down, sunk in a dark grove – a receptacle for the subconscious, where its inhabitants rely only on the progression of the seasons to mark the passing of time. On her return with her own children, Carrie describes it as 'a dark green, silent place, where no birds sang' (Bawden 1973, 13), continuing 'it was certainly a Sacred Grove of some sort. Some old religion. Bad or good – I don't know. But it had a queer *feeling* – you'll see for yourselves when we get there' (Bawden 1973, 12).

While the character of Hepzibah fulfils the role of an intuitive older woman in tune with the old magic abundant at Druid's Bottom (she is rumoured to be a witch and Mr Evans is supposedly frightened of her), she is also intensely practical and no-nonsense. Much like Minty in *Moondial*, she actively dispels the othering or diminishing of the intuitive through her calm manner and her acceptance of her place within the folds of the unseen – she essentially refuses what Annwn and Croggon highlight as the risks of othering the feminine intuitive. In her dealings with Mr Evans, she is placid and accepting – this should not be mistaken for passiveness – there is a strong sense that Hepzibah has the upper hand here. A form of deep intuition which enables her to surpass and rise above the petty family squabbles over money and property – almost as if these issues hold no real value within the vastness of monumental time – the temporal space in which she seems to move.

Carrie, by the opposite token, is young, lost and deeply sensitive. As the older sibling, she immediately assumes a maternal role in caring for Nick once they are separated from their mother. Nick, who has terrible nightmares and 'eats too much' is wholly reliant on Carrie in the earlier chapters of the novel to provide safety and comfort in their new alien setting. As Nick finds his feet and bonds with not only Auntie Lou, but also Johnny and Albert, he leans less on Carrie. However, the damage has been done, for in her attempts to protect Nick from Mr Evans and to 'people please' and smooth the way with every adult she encounters, she has become a pawn in a game of enmity between Mr Evans and his estranged sister, Dilys. Carrie's survival technique and emotional intelligence have rendered her vulnerable at the heart of a tangled web. Mr Evans, in particular, is a focus for Carrie's conflicting sympathies – she intuits his deep sadness and his isolation, which he masks with his gruff exterior, and she finds herself a somewhat unwitting ally. '"He's not so nasty really", she said to Nick. "You shouldn't have pinched his biscuits, you know you shouldn't. … And I know he's nasty to Auntie Lou sometimes but it's her own fault because she lets him be. She's nice Auntie Lou, but she's stupid"' (Bawden 1973, 37). In fact, Carrie's sensitivity ensures that she is gradually detached from her intuitive feelings and, in a sense, 'forced' to relinquish them in order to navigate the complex web of adult emotions around her. This emotional multitasking is yet another rude awakening for Carrie in a world where she has suddenly become adult. The risk here for Carrie is that she is distanced from what Hepzibah, and Druid's Bottom, represent; that is the connection to cyclical and monumental time – the deep intuitive part of her female subjectivity, but also literally the warm hearth and welcome at the bottom of the grove. As the novel progresses, Carrie's suspicions about Mr Evans mount and her sense of disconnection rises. In the scene where Carrie throws the skull into the well, we are witnessing an explosive collision of everyday emotional pressure and the insertion of a more superstitious supernatural and irrational belief system. It should be noted that the curse of the skull is treated (at least by Hepzibah and Albert) as a nonsense, perhaps even a distraction from the deeper magic at play in this space. Carrie's desperate action at this juncture perhaps speaks of what might happen to a young woman when disconnected from deep intuitive cycles.

There is restoration of dreaming, intuition and balance at the end of the novel – the structure of which in itself implies revolutions and recurrences. This is shown when Carrie returns, and cyclically, her young children now stand at the head of the dark grove, ready to make their own descent into Druid's Bottom. In what are particularly moving scenes and passages, we find Carrie, older and now a widow, as deeply sensitive as ever. Her own children intuit her pain 'Now, watching her, … Her smooth, happy look was gone and she was screwing up her eyes and mouth so that her whole face seemed crumpled. … perhaps it was only the hot climb that had tired her but it seemed more than that. As if she were, all at once, afraid of something' (Bawden 1973, 12). The 'curse' is finally broken when Carrie and her children arrive in the grove and find an aged Hepzibah, and Mr Johnny cosily ensconced in the stable block which sits next to the charred remains of the old house – ultimately nothing has changed in their world. Now it would seem that the channels of both cyclical and monumental time are finally able to flow again for Carrie. The important difference between the 'silly' superstition of the curse and the broad string of cyclical and monumental time that underpins the lives of those at Druid's Bottom is writ large in the core of this text.

Alison: Dream girl

Everything about Alan Garner's 1967 Carnegie Medal winning novel, *The Owl Service* and the 1969 Granada Television adaptation of the same name insists upon a refutation of linear time, of neat chronology and of easily located meaning. To accept this and to relinquish control repays the reader or viewer richly through a bewitching entanglement in both cyclical and monumental time. Garner's female protagonist, Alison, of the three discussed in this chapter, appears most passive, but as we shall see, it can be argued that she, along with the other characters, are vessels through which Garner is able to explore the mythic structures which he suggests underpin not only his practice as a writer but also our everyday reality.

However, there is no denying *The Owl Service is* complex – two timescapes play out in constant, often deliberately tangled conversation. And in test screenings of the series, audiences complained of confusion and recaps were therefore introduced ahead of each episode in time for broadcast. But at one level, the story is simply a modern retelling of 'Blodeuwedd', a tale from the ancient Welsh myth cycle, *Y Mabinogi* (*The Mabinogion*). Garner's version centres around three young adults: Alison (Gillian Hills), Roger, her new stepbrother (Francis Wallis) and Gwyn, the housekeeper's son (Michael Holden) who loosely represent and are seen to play out the fates of Blodeuwedd, Lleu Llaw Gyffes and Gronw Pebr from the myth. Like *Carrie's War*, *The Owl Service* presents a remote Welsh valley as both setting and crucible for monumental and cyclical time to play out in, another isolated place where linear considerations of modern time cease to have concrete meaning. In the valley, which seems to act as an amplifier for these cyclical and mythical energies, the three young adults are thrown together by familial circumstance at Alison's family holiday home. Gwyn and his mother present as housekeepers provide stark contrast to the privileged upbringing of Roger and Alison, flanked by Roger's father and Alison's mother, who in the book and series is never seen, although her presence is strongly implied. The presence of the strange groundsman, Huw (later revealed to be Gwyn's father) adds another layer of intrigue to the action. The three teenage characters are wound into a love triangle, which in the original myth, centres on Blodeuwedd's infidelity with Gronw and their hatching of a plot to murder Lleu. Blodeuwedd's subsequent punishment sees her transformed into an owl by the magician, Gwydion. The name, Blodeuwedd, literally translated, means 'flower face', and she is said to have initially been created from the flowers of the oak, the broom and meadowsweet by Gwydion. It is this tension between the owl and flowers as Blodeuwedd's true form which provides the violent denouement of the story. In the novel and television series we are spared the murder and the completion of shapeshifting present in the original, but the threat of this ancient violence and magic is never far from the surface; indeed it seeps into the present-day narrative with terrifying insistence.

Garner's attraction to myth as a rich seam of writerly inspiration is well documented, but it's worth reflecting on what myth cycles might offer in terms of accessing the monumental and cyclical and how mythic or monumental time is essential to understanding not only Garner's practice as a writer, but also his communion with the reader. His writing, which often places heavy demands upon the reader, requires a 'letting go' of what we might consider dominant perceptions of time – he continually invites his reader to unhitch themselves from familiar linear patterns and it is in

The Owl Service, and the later novel, *Red Shift* (1973), that we see this most explicitly through the collapse of neatly chronological plot structure. In *The Owl Service* this instability is shown through the insistent disruption of the present with shimmers and glimpses of another time and another story playing out – these reverberations grow in strength until the two are entwined in a suffocating embrace. The first indication of this intrusion is the scratching Alison hears in the ceiling of her bedroom ' "I heard it the first night I came," said Alison, "and every night since: a few minutes after I'm in bed" ' (Garner 2007, 8). The television series, directed by Peter Plummer, also challenges dominant chronological modes of visual storytelling through the innovative use of jump cuts and subliminal shots. The theme music, a discordant harp playing a traditional folk tune, is interspersed with motorcycle revs, and the sound of water echoing through pipes. This adds much to the viewer's sense of temporal disorientation, as the modern roar of the motor engine fights against the alarmingly off-kilter strains of an instrument we associate with a much older time period.

Fisher describes Garner's distinctive time signatures as 'temporal vortices' (Fisher 2016, 90) and refers to the graffiti which Garner saw in a Cheshire bus shelter that sparked the writing of *Red Shift* – 'not really now not any more'. Fisher asks, 'does this mean that the present has eroded, disappeared – not now any more? Are we in the time of the always-already, where the future has been written; in which case it is not the future, not really?' (Fisher 2016, 91). We already understand that 'women's time' is not linear and we can gain purchase on this idea through the lens of monumental and cyclical time, but is this what Garner is tapping into too? Is the 'cold fatality' (Fisher 2016, 93) of what Fisher describes as 'the mythic time' (Fisher 2016, 90) another way of expressing this? Remember that Anderson, when discussing monumental time, described it as 'a simultaneity of past and future in an instantaneous present'. In the vast eternity of monumental time, the mythical archetypes will play out again and again or as Garner puts it, 'Energy is timeless and inexhaustible. It will never run down' (Garner 1973). Are Alison, Roger and Gwyn therefore only the most recent incarnations in a continuous cycle of repeating patterns? The energy unable to decay and release itself from the echo chamber of the valley – the place alive with the traces of the past?

This cold fatalism not only infects the characters but is perhaps also present in Garner's practice as writer. In a 2017 postscript to the novel, Garner referred to *The Owl Service* as 'a kind of ghost story, in real life as well as on the page. Right from the start things happened that had not happened with earlier books' (Garner 2007, 221). The suggestion here is that the book almost wrote itself and that Garner was subject, or happy to make himself available, to forces of which he was not entirely in control. He had 'the sensation of finding, not inventing, a story … . It was all there, waiting, and I was the archaeologist picking away the earth to reveal the bones' (Garner 2007, 222). This approach to writing seems to suggest a process that's not entirely devoid of agency. Rather, it presents a mode of being in which the author is in fact co-author if he chooses to make himself open to numinous collaboration. Is he acknowledging what Tiwari refers to as 'eternity without cleavage or escape' (Tiwari 2017), simply applying facets of the contemporary in order to acknowledge the insistence and repeating power of these ancient archetypes? There seems no battle to be had here, indeed Garner seems satisfied with the notion that human agency is subject to wider, deeper forces than we would ordinarily feel comfortable acknowledging. The desire to wrest control over a narrative is not the prime consideration here, or as Garner states, 'Myth is not entertainment, but rather the crystallisation of experience, and, far from being escapist, fantasy is an intensification of reality' (Garner 2010, 62).

So, what of the human characters at the centre of this story? Do they also lack agency within monumental or mythic time? And is Alison, in any way, more equipped than her male counterparts to navigate or understand this terrain? All the characters are confused at times and all also show intuitive understanding or a tuning into their situation at other junctures. Alison intuitively understands she must make the paper owls and sometimes poses questions about the stability of time through observations of her surroundings – in the scene where she and Gwyn walk up the ridge, she observes that 'it could be a thousand years ago'. The sheep seen far below them with dyed fleece elicit the reassuring thought 'that's modern' which gives away to sudden temporal vertigo 'Is it? Is it?' (Garner 2007, 125). But she is also capable of cold conformity, as evidenced by her distress at the thought of her mother making her give up choir and tennis lessons if she continues to see Gwyn. This particular episode reveals a shallowness that must wound Gwyn's more romantic sensibilities deeply. However, Gwyn frequently uses scientific reasoning as a defence shield when faced with anomalous phenomena such as the marsh lights. This rationality butts up against the intuitive side of his personality. Roger remains wilfully blind throughout, concerned mainly with his photography and either patronizing or taunting Gwyn. None of the characters could be said to engage with the monumental and cyclical agreeably and certainly none has all the keys to full understanding. But it is Gwyn (against his Grammar school trained rationality), who begins to piece together what is happening, 'not haunted ... more like still happening' (Garner 2007, 69). And, interestingly, it is Roger, prompted by Huw, who finally halts Alison's descent into owl form with the simple words, 'You've got it back to front, you silly gubbins. She's not owls. She's flowers. Flower. Flowers' (Garner 2007, 219). This moment of realization seems to imply that human agency *is* present, but within the bounds of mythic time – Gwyn could stop the transformation too, but he chooses not to, so hurt at this moment that he cannot rouse himself to intercede.

What makes this story so compelling is the central idea that humans are volatile, emotional and vulnerable within these cycles – humans are subject to all of these intensifications of reality, and it is their individual iterations of the myth bound in contemporary concerns such as class which give the story urgency and sting. Gwyn's searing sense of betrayal when it emerges Alison has mentioned his elocution records to Roger is the perfect example of this powerful updating – this is the cyclical and the monumental at work – returning once more with a wicked contemporary swipe designed to hit where it hurts most.

Margaret, Alison's mother, is famously never seen in either the novel, or the television series. We are aware of her presence through references made by the other characters and her shadowy presence, or as Helen Wheatley describes it, she is 'implied in pointedly subjective point-of-view shots which spy on the young lovers' (Wheatley 2012, 388). Margaret is a fascinating character, and unlike the benign and entirely absent mothers in *Moondial* and *Carrie's War*, there is a keen sense of tension and threat implied by her semi-presence. There is also the hint of an old power at work here too; we know that it is Alison's line who are the 'old money' in this new family set-up – Alison will inherit the house from her mother. Roger's father, Clive is referred to as a 'rough diamond' (Garner 2007, 157) by Alison and the suggestion that he's in 'business' of some sort seems to reinforce his *nouveau riche* credentials in this class-ridden familial structure. Clive also seems curiously nervous of Margaret and often uses Alison as a means to gauge her moods 'Er – how's your mother liking it?' (Garner 2007, 151) he asks in reference to the holiday, begging the question – why couldn't he just ask her himself? Most insidiously, we understand that Margaret is opposed to Gwyn, she moves to threaten their relationship by stopping Alison's access to her hobbies. So, what exactly does Margaret represent in this text? Her voyeuristic oversight of the unfolding situation and her deeply rooted power base in terms of house and class would seem to suggest that in the shadows or the unseen aspects of the story resides another sort of power – a female power whose deeper source remains tantalizingly untraceable – an archetypal mother watcher of sorts. Her unknowability hangs over the story like mist, yet there is a sense that somewhere she is pulling all the strings.

At the end of the novel, the cycle is altered, the characters are able to avert the repetition, to change the outcomes and to redirect the energy. But it doesn't dissipate – it just takes another form. The implication is that there is semi-agency for the characters once they have tuned into mythic time – they can make small marks and changes, but the deep, eternal temporality of which they are a part, will continue to cycle on and on. Carrie and Minty are making these marks, becoming entangled and in their own ways locating their place in the vastness with curiosity and acceptance, all the while instinctively aware of the bigger scales at work. Alison, Roger and Gwyn only gain some sort of control once they become aware of their place in the cyclical time of the valley, their place in this eternal story.

Minty and Carrie could be said to represent positive participation with the supernatural which is borne of their open and intuitive personalities – they quietly exemplify what Kristeva recognizes as 'women's time' in action. Alison, Gwyn and Roger could therefore be said to present the human who is constantly pushing back against the unseen, the unexplainable and trying to rationalize the world around them. For them, immersion into the temporally unstable will happen anyway and they must learn to unlearn the chronological, the dominant narrative and start to write their own stories within the vast and circular energies of the universe.

References

Anderson, Benedict. 2016. *Imagined Communities: Reflections on the Origin and Spread of Nationalism*. London: Verso.

Annwn, David. 2007. *The Salt Companion to Geraldine Monk*. Cambridge: Salt Publishing.

Bawden, Nina. 1973. *Carrie's War*. London: Victor Gollancz.

Cresswell, Helen. 1987. *Moondial*. London: Penguin Books.

Fisher, Mark. 2016. *The Weird and the Eerie*. London: Repeater Books.

Garner, Alan. 1973. *Red Shift*. London: Harper Collins Children's Books.

Garner, Alan. 2007. *The Owl Service*. London: Harper Collins Children's Books.

Garner, Alan. 2010. *The Voice That Thunders*. London: Harvill Press.

Kristeva Julia, 1981. 'Women's Time'. Translated by Alice Jardine. *Signs* 7, no. 1 (Autumn): 13–35.

Moi, Toril. 1986. *The Kristeva Reader*. Hoboken: Wiley Blackwell Readers.

Söderbäck, Fanny. 2012. 'Revolutionary Time: Revolt as Temporal Return'. *Signs* 37, no. 2 (January, Unfinished Revolutions. A special issue edited by Phillip Rothwell): 301–24.

Tiwari, Ananya. 2017. 'Women's Time Summary'. Word Press, May 12. https://ananyatiwari.wordpress.com/2017/05/12/julia-kristeva-womens-time-summary-1979/. Accessed 13 October 2023.

Wheatley, Helen. 2012. 'Uncanny Children, Haunted Houses, Hidden Rooms: Children's Gothic Television in the 1970s and '80s'. *Visual Culture in Britain* 31, no. 3 (November): 383–97.

4

'It came from beneath the sink': Children's horror television as an uncanny mirror

Merinda Staubli

Children's horror series regularly mirror the domestic viewing context in their diegeses by revealing the weird among the ordinary in suburbia and the home. These series often combine the normal and the supernatural by drawing on concepts of the uncanny, an experience that Freud ([1919] 2003, 124) labelled *unheimlich*, literally meaning 'unhomely'. The uncanny is pertinent for children's horror television because, as Cynthia Freeland (2000, 235) describes, it is 'something from ordinary life that has a mysterious and familiar feel yet becomes alien and frightening'. Children's horror series can make the familiar unfamiliar or, as Helen Wheatley (2006, 7) describes Gothic television, feature 'the dissolution of boundaries between the familiar and the strange, or the everyday and the disturbing'. Using children's horror television broadcast in Australia during the 1990s and early 2000s as a case study, this chapter draws on textual analysis and audience studies to analyse how these programmes could seem to blur the boundaries between their storyworlds and the viewer's world.

One hundred participants responded to an online survey that asked for their memories of children's horror television they watched growing up in Australia, and three separate focus groups were facilitated with select members from the survey. The participant responses provided direction on the children's horror episodes to focus on for further textual analysis. Participants are hereby referred to by their birth or chosen first names if they opted in to be identified, otherwise they are anonymous. These combined methods analyse seemingly uncanny memories of children's horror television as well as the potential impacts these programmes have had on fans and former viewers.

While there are significant children's horror series that did not reach Australian television, or which aired in other decades, this chapter focuses on a specific national and historical context because, as Andrew Tudor (1997, 456) argues, studies on the horror genre should avoid perpetuating the 'fallacy of generic concreteness'. Genres can have different meanings for different audiences and those meanings can shift over time. According to Tudor (1997, 456), because 'genres are not fixed nor are they only bodies of textual material', there is no universal answer to the meanings or pleasures of horror. He proposes that studies should ask, 'Why do *these* people like *this* horror in *this* place at *this* particular time?', and what are the consequences of this (Tudor 1997, 461, original emphasis)? This chapter therefore explores how the uncanny in children's horror television was experienced and is now remembered by millennial Australian viewers. Filipa Antunes (2020, 17) argues that 'children's horror must be understood as a cultural artifact, fundamentally inseparable from its sociocultural, historical, and industrial contexts'. This research draws on my own national context and has recruited local participants to analyse the 1990s and early 2000s as a rich cultural moment in which horror television made for children was popular and prolific.

The turn of the millennium was an increasingly competitive period in children's television production that facilitated experimentation. In Australia, new commercial channel owners bolstered funding for children's television, allowing Australian children's television producers and other creatives to take more risks with live-action drama series. In the early 2000s, the proliferation of digital transmission and Foxtel, Australia's leading pay television service, further broadened viewing choices for families who could afford a subscription, with speciality children's and animation networks such as Nickelodeon and Cartoon Network. These fledgling cable channels promoted unique brand identities to distinguish themselves from rival networks. Both Nickelodeon and Cartoon Network gave creative freedom to series creators, encouraging them to experiment and produce innovative and boundary-pushing television in order to set the networks apart from their competitors. These series were promoted as being more 'edgy' than children's television by other studios. In this climate, children's television that was neither patronizing nor afraid to frighten young viewers was produced, including various horror television series made for children.

In the 1990s, horror aimed at children was a lucrative industry that millions of young fans consumed every week. As Antunes (2015, 3) observes, 'as a trend, children's horror' in the 1990s 'is best described as a powerful burst, an explosion of horror-themed material that spilled into virtually every sphere of children's culture'. The peak popularity of children's horror is exemplified by the success of RL Stine's *Goosebumps*. The franchise had sold more than 200 million books by the late 1990s (Ciampa 1998) and its live-action television anthology series (1995–98) had become 'one of the highest-rated children's shows in both Canada and the U.S.' (Rancic 2015). Alongside the book and television series, *Goosebumps* produced a plethora of merchandise, from clothing to computer and board games, school supplies and even a Disney World theme park attraction.

Most children's horror series that were broadcast in anglophone nations were from the United States, Canada and the UK, but Australia also produced impactful children's programming at the turn of the millennium that delved into frightening content. Arguably Australia's most renowned children's programme from this period is *Round the Twist*, a live-action series about a family who lives in a haunted lighthouse based in a coastal town, where they regularly encounter supernatural phenomena. With episodes featuring possessed dolls and bedroom-dwelling monsters, the series 'sold to more than a hundred countries' (Edgar 2006, 216) and became 'one of the most successful children's dramas made anywhere in the world' (Potter 2016). The Memory Project, a study led by Dr Anna Potter at the University of the Sunshine Coast 'investigating how adults remember the Australian children's TV they watched when they were young', found that 64 per cent of its 1,000 participants cited *Round the Twist* 'as their favourite TV show growing up' (Potter 2016). While the study was not directly related to children's horror television, many participants also associated the series with horror: 'over a quarter remembered being frightened by some of the show's storylines or characters. Ghosts, skeletons, and a possessed doll were repeatedly mentioned; however most agreed that this was part of the attraction' (Potter 2016). Similarly, in my study, participants describe more episodes of *Round the Twist* than any other children's horror series and it was discussed across all three focus groups as frightening children's horror television. The series juggles horror and humour to different extents in each episode and its horror scenes are a key pleasure and dominant memory for many viewers. Therefore, while Australian children watched a wide variety of overseas children's horror television, local series such as *Round the Twist* are remembered as having an especially high impact which contributed to this period becoming regarded as a significant cultural moment in Australian children's horror television and children's television viewing more generally.

There have long been fears about television's possible harmful effects on children, as evidenced by the enduring popularity of horror films that use television as a portal for the supernatural, especially when children are unsupervised. In *Poltergeist* (1982), cherub Carol Anne is drawn towards the static on the television near her sleeping parents, beckoned by whispers among the white noise. Enchanted, she reaches towards the television screen and her fingers are met by a spectral hand that strikes out from within.

A supernatural force shoots out and becomes embedded in the house. Carol Anne is allowed to play with what she calls 'the TV people', until she is dragged through a portal into an otherworldly dimension. In the final shot of the film, after she has been rescued and the family have escaped to the safety of a hotel, her father is wheeling a television out onto the balcony outside their room, away from his family. In comparison, in *Ringu* (1998), and adapted in its American remake *The Ring* (2002), anyone who watches a cursed videotape is murdered seven days later by malignant spirit Sadako who crawls out of their television. A young boy watches the videotape when left unsupervised by his divorced working mother. Both films articulate anxieties about the ill effects of television on children and caution inattentive parents to monitor their children's viewing. They also depict shared cultural anxieties about the vulnerability of children and their need to be protected from the horror genre. Children's media and television have both historically been viewed as 'space[s] where horror supposedly does not belong' (Hills 2005, 111). This is partly because, as Matt Hills (2005, 119) observes, the genre appears to threaten 'television's deep-rooted discursive links to the safety of hearth and home'. Therefore, in horror cinema, television has been viewed as a potential gateway for evil to enter the home.

While adult guardians may commonly seek to protect children from being afraid of their everyday environments, this blurring of boundaries between the ordinary and the supernatural can be one of the main pleasures of the horror genre for young viewers. Stine (1998, 66) observes that his childhood preferences in the horror genre influenced the *Goosebumps* books:

> Douglas R. Hofstadter, a professor at Indiana University, criticizes my books because the ghosts and other paranormal phenomena are presented as real, as everyday occurrences. He says that such stories blur the line 'between the natural and supernatural'. He praises a ghost story written 30 years ago, in which kids investigate the ghost and discover that he isn't a ghost at all; he's just a strange, lonely boy who lives in a secluded shack. That's certainly a more logical, rational way to end a story. But when I was a kid, my friends and I were always terribly angry and disappointed when the ghost turned out to be a boy. What a cheat! In our horror literature – at no matter what age – we want to escape rationality. We want to face our monsters. We want to confront the supernatural.

Children's horror television dares child viewers to face their fears by making the familiar unfamiliar in thrilling ways.

Everyday settings are a staple of adult and children's horror anthology series and can heighten frightening affect through the diegesis mirroring the viewer's own world. According to Stine (2019), 'a good horror story for kids starts in the backyard. I don't think it starts in a dark castle. It starts in the kitchen or the attic, somewhere close to them, and it threatens reality just enough.' In children's horror television, frightening scenes often occur in domestic or public settings, such as at school. For example, one participant remembers being frightened by 'a bloody skeleton monster' in the *Are You Afraid of the Dark?* (1990–2000) episode 'The Tale of the Dead Man's Float' (1995), in which a malicious ghost haunts a school pool. Another participant recalls, 'familiar settings got to me a lot, that horror is found in the comfortable and the everyday'. As Anna Jackson, Karen Coats and Roderick McGillis (2008, 12) argue, this kind of text warns 'of the dangers mysteriously close to even the most familiar places. It reminds us that the world is not safe. It challenges the pastoral myths of childhood.' The supernatural threatens by violating familiar, everyday spaces rather than being safely physically or temporally distanced in fantastical lands.

These programmes can be frightening because they are viewed on a familiar, domestic medium and reflect the domestic space in which they are consumed. Wheatley (2006, 106) analyses that television is an uncanny object that can function as both a window and a mirror, providing 'a particularly fearful view of another domestic space' while creating an 'uncanny "doubling" of domestic space'. She argues that when an '"unheimlich" presence is felt within the "heimlich" space the horror of the uncanny becomes all the more real' (Wheatley 2002, 159). This can be seen in some episodes of *Goosebumps*, which implicate the child viewer in the diegesis through opening with Stine who directly addresses them as a horror host. John Ellis (2000, 31) observes that since the beginning of television, presenters 'talked directly to their audience to produce the sensation that television was predominantly live' even when programmes are pre-recorded. This creates a sense of co-presence, seeming to diminish the barriers between the viewer's home and the broadcast world. In the *Goosebumps* episode 'Welcome to Dead House' (1997), Stine appears in the attic of the house featured in the episode. The camera ominously moves towards his face and eerie music accompanies his monologue:

> Welcome to Dead House. I think you're going to like your new house. But before you move in, I have a few words of warning for you. Better look under the bed, at night, before you go to sleep. And when you make new friends, always check to see, who's dead and who's alive. Viewers beware, you're in for a scare.

Stine asks child viewers to draw comparisons between the hauntings onscreen and their own home and neighbourhood, warning that they are also at risk.

This segment immediately follows *Goosebumps*' opening title sequence, in which the series' horror physically crosses over thresholds into a representation of the viewer's everyday world, uncovering decay and supernatural threats in suburbia. Stine, signified by his named briefcase, appears like a travelling salesman atop a hill overlooking an unnamed town that may seem to Western child audiences similar to their own. Stine unleashes the horrors of his tales by scattering pages from his books. This is seen through a shadow of the G from the *Goosebumps* logo entering the town and transforming ordinary features so that they become sinister. It floats past a billboard image of a smiling woman whose face becomes sullen and haggard. After passing a golden retriever on a porch, the dog's eyes glow bright yellow. The camera then tracks behind as it travels through a garden and the front door of a house, making *Goosebumps* seem like a malevolent intruder. Once inside, a montage of clips from the series plays, interspersed with imagery of screaming child protagonists, to tease about the horror child viewers are going to experience within their own home. This sequence's mirroring of everyday settings encourages child viewers to question what darkness may lie beneath the surface of their own suburbs.

Round the Twist comparatively subverts Gothic tropes to present an Australian vernacular of children's horror. Jackson, Coats and McGillis (2008, 5–6) analyse that Gothic conventions are fluid and can adapt to different national and historical contexts: 'Gothic conventions and motifs are remarkable for how rapidly and consistently they change, in form and in significance. Its landscapes and conventions change in response to cultural shifts in the fears, values, and technologies that inscribe themselves into our subjectivities. This makes it a genre … particularly responsive to its historical moment and cultural location.' This allows *Round the Twist* to feature 'antipodean reversals of … Gothic conventions' (Jackson, Coats and McGillis 2008, 6). The protagonists live in a haunted lighthouse, a playful reversal of Gothic haunted house tropes, with the lighthouse portrayed as a comforting sanctuary that is a source of light and often depicted in bright daylight. While this setting is likely unfamiliar for most child viewers, the series juxtaposes the weird within the everyday for uncanny affect. For example, some episodes were adapted from Paul Jennings's short-story anthology book *Uncanny!* (1988), such as 'Know All' (1989), in which a scarecrow becomes sentient and terrorizes teenage character Linda. These strange encounters are made more familiar to Australian viewers through Australian actors and characters, accents, colloquialisms, humour and an otherwise suburban, coastal setting.

It is of interest, however, that the only focus group participant who draws associations between children's horror television and their national context is Kit, who grew up in the UK. Kit recalls being frightened by familiar settings in the two-part *Goosebumps* episode 'A Night in Terror Tower' (1996) because they had visited the Tower of London, which is depicted in the programme, and were familiar with the story it is based on. They reflect that the episode 'freaked the hell out of me because it was something that was recognisable and I think that was the most uncanny of his (Stine's) stories for me'. For Kit, this episode was unnerving because it is based on a true story about King

Richard III's two nephews, who mysteriously vanished and were rumoured to have been murdered. Furthermore, being set in a real, familiar location and presenting the seemingly realistic threat of child execution instilled a chilling effect as the horror narrative seemed to reside within their own world. The episode fused historical events with fictional children's horror, fused the past and the present and fused a fantastical Gothic setting with a popular tourist destination. While this memory suggests that Australian locations in children's horror television could be similarly impactful, most participants who grew up in Australia did not have strong memories of local settings in children's horror programmes.

Recognizably Australian locations are generally not mentioned in the questionnaire and most focus group participants deny that children's horror series being Australian impacted their experience or enjoyment, even though *Round the Twist* is the most often recalled series in the study. In fact, focus group members do not remember registering *Round the Twist* as Australian. Harry recalls that 'as a child, I was so indoctrinated by American media as the norm that … the people on *Round the Twist* felt as normal for me as the characters on the American shows … I don't think the Australian aspect of the show connected with me on any deeper level'. Similarly, Katrina posits: 'I think if you were to ask me that question as a kid, I'd actually be surprised that it (*Round the Twist*) was Australian.' It is significant, however, that *Round the Twist* is commonly the first series that participants recall as children's horror television and it was discussed across all three focus groups without any prompting. Jules reflects that children's programmes being Australian likely had an unconscious impact on him as a child because the characters seemed to be 'just silly kids in an environment that looked familiar' whereas American settings could be noticeably foreign. Furthermore, Taylor explains that she enjoyed *Round the Twist* because the series did not obviously signal that it was Australian, whereas other popular Australian series at the time seemed to exaggerate their nationality in off-putting ways:

> I remember thinking that some Australian shows are just too painfully like trying to be Australian. I remember asking 'Why do their voices sound funny? Are they really meant to be us? It doesn't sound like us.' So … *Round the Twist* … I don't even remember that they were Australian, to be honest. But maybe there was that part of me that related to it a bit more.

This made some Australian series at the time seem slightly alien, while *Round the Twist* was unobtrusively familiar.

For children's horror television to be recalled as uncanny, its settings arguably had to be personally relatable to the lived experiences of the child viewer. Participants often recall horror scenes in less distinctly Australian settings such as inside the home or at school because these environments more closely mirrored their own. When discussing their strongest memories of being frightened by children's horror programmes, all the male participants in two of the focus groups describe uncanny objects in children's bedrooms, with *Round the Twist* episodes 'Monster under the Bed' (2001) and 'Toy Love' (2000) independently recalled in both sessions. Catherine Lester (2021a, 126) analyses that the uncanny is seen in children's horror television through 'intellectual uncertainty [as to] whether an inanimate object is alive, as well as the horror of the familiar, as many of these are children's playthings that viewers may have in their own bedrooms'. Focus group member Jake remembers being badly frightened by a sentient porcelain doll in 'Toy Love'. Jake's household had few restrictions on what he was allowed to watch from a young age and he remembers that he was a 'spooky kid' who thought that frightening horror television was 'really cool'. Even though he was accustomed with horror texts made for older viewers, he recalls that the episode 'scared the shit out' of him, and he remains unnerved by porcelain dolls to this day. In comparison, in 'Monster under the Bed', child character Bronson is terrorized by a red-eyed monster formed by masses of lint from his unclean bedroom. Harry remembers the 'lint monster' as 'grotesque' and one of his 'earliest exposures to ... particularly horrific imagery'. This caused some child viewers to fear that the monster may be hiding under their own beds. Survey participant Nick recalls watching this episode when he was eight or nine years old and being afraid to look under his bed 'at night for a year or two'. The fright reactions recalled by participants about these episodes demonstrate how impactful children's horror can be when child viewers' familiar spaces and belongings become uncanny.

While the monster-under-the-bed is a common childhood fear and dolls are prototypical uncanny beings, other more unusual everyday objects can also become uncanny in children's horror television with frightening impact. In the *Goosebumps* episode 'It Came from beneath the Sink' (1996), a household sponge is made sinister. A nuclear family moves to a neighbouring suburb which is very similar to their previous home and yet suddenly unfamiliar. Twelve-year-old Kat enters the house and follows her German shepherd into the kitchen, where the dog begins to paw at the cupboard below the sink. She peers inside and staring back at her from within the darkness is a grotesque monster with red, glowing eyes and needle-like teeth. Once removed from the cupboard, it appears to be a common household sponge. While this concept may seem humorous, for some child viewers such episodes prompted them to imagine the supernatural or the monstrous residing within their everyday world. For example, one participant recalls seeing a *Goosebumps* episode as a child where 'inanimate objects came to life. I went outside to ride my bike because it was too scary and ... I ran over a stick insect and thought that the stick (had come) to life like in the episode. Was pretty terrifying at the time.' Rick Drew, the screenwriter of 'It Came from beneath the Sink', claims: 'to my great surprise ... that's the one that kids (now adults) say scared them the most! Perhaps because it was a household object they could relate to in their real life' (interviewed in Prendes 2020, 337). For child viewers who suspend disbelief, distortions of the ordinary and familiar in children's horror television can seemingly allow the uncanny to infiltrate their everyday realities.

Beyond its viewing context, children's horror television can also reflect its pre-teen viewers, with monsters mirroring the corporeal and psychological transformations of adolescence. As Antunes (2020, 142) describes *Goosebumps*: 'The horror ... always comes, after all, in the form of changes to physical and emotional stability, always to twelve-year-old protagonists, and to both sexes in equal measure'. Such depictions of children undergoing monstrous changes can be seen in *Goosebumps*' premiere episode 'The Haunted Mask' (1995), in which child character Carly Beth's face is replaced by a frightening mask. When trying to remove the mask, she realizes that there is no seam; it has fused with her skin. The mask's mouth moves organically and when looking in a mirror, she exclaims in distress: 'My eyes don't look like that. Those aren't my eyes. Where are my eyes?! Where am I? This isn't me. This isn't me there!' The boundaries of her body and identity are transgressed and she is no longer familiar to herself. While looking in the mirror, she stares into the camera, towards the viewer. The screen is vignetted like eyeholes as if the child viewer is now wearing the mask; the child viewer is encouraged to identify with Carly Beth as if looking at their own reflection and witnessing themselves transformed into a monster. Carly Beth reaches forward and touches the mirror, which also appears like the inside of the television screen, making it both a window and a mirror. 'The Haunted Mask' is one of the episodes mostly commonly recalled as frightening by participants in the survey, and this is arguably influenced by its themes of adolescence and self-identity. Lester (2021b, 46) analyses that 'children are inherently "monstrous" due to their continual growing and changing, both mentally and physically', as seen by 'horrific' child characters in horror films aimed at adults such as *The Exorcist* (1973) and *The Omen* (1976). While child monsters in these films may be threatening to older viewers because they are different from them, these characters in children's horror television may comparatively invite identification for children who have entered puberty and are powerless in relation to their own bodily growths and hormonal changes.

While the programmes discussed thus far are live-action series which use realistic depictions of everyday settings, a sense of uncanny familiarity can also be seen in animation. Drawing on Freud's analysis, Wheatley (2002, 37) argues that 'the uncanny sensation can only be achieved through a disturbance in an essentially realist text, rather than that text which is somehow couched in the realm of the fantastic'. I offer that animated series, even when based in fantastical settings, can have an uncanny affect. For example, *Courage the Cowardly Dog* (1999–2002) uses 'CGI and texture-mapping to create a sort of realism' with a world 'that's full of textured sand and wallpaper and sky' (Dilworth 1999). Series creator John R. Dilworth (1999) reflects: 'I wanted to achieve some sort of believability, so that you wouldn't think you were watching a cartoon and would get into its world.' The series also avoids 'wipes, dissolves and camera pans where possible' to encourage immersion rather than drawing attention to its mechanics (Dilworth 1999). One participant remembers that the series used 'a lot of silence during tense moments' which created a more suspensefully lifelike atmosphere and another participant recalls that it 'seemed realistic'. The uncanny effects of this are described by focus group member Katrina who 'drew parallels' between the series and her grandparents' home where she watched the programme as a child. She reflects that the elderly characters, Eustace and Muriel, reminded her of her grandparents, who had physical similarities and 'lived in the middle of nowhere' just like Eustace and Muriel. She recalls that the series' protagonist, Courage, who is an anthropomorphic purple dog, 'was also a lot like me, neurotic and scared of a lot of things'. Even though the series exists 'in the realm of the fantastic' with Courage's desert suburb visited by new monsters or apparitions in most episodes, Katrina explains that she could 'compare it' with her 'own life and see patterns': 'I could relate to that show quite a lot even if it was set in a completely different universe.' These memories suggest that the series' devices and personally familiar characters presented a warped impression of their domestic viewing context. Through textured and relatable representations, animation can present a funhouse mirror reflection of the home.

Another animated series that participants remember reflecting their own world is *Freaky Stories* (1997–2000), a Canadian anthology programme that adapts urban legends. The series originally presented a few different stories each episode but on Australian television, every episode was a single five-minute urban legend. This short runtime reflects the length of the average urban legend and this can potentially heighten frightening affect. According to popular horror author Stephen King (1981, 304), 'the horror tale works best when it is brief and comes directly to the point'. The series' runtime, bright and non-realistic animation style and omission of blood and gore also could have made it appear innocuous among regular children's programming. As Antunes (2020, 146) argues, children's horror television between the 1990s and early 2000s 'transformed into an inconspicuous part of everyday children's culture'. This arguably allowed it to mediate famous urban legends into children's television without any notable controversy.

Every *Freaky Stories* episode opens with a different offscreen narrator who claims, 'This is a true story, it happened to a friend of a friend of mine.' This device mirrors the sensationalist marketing of horror cinema or the 'based on a true story' convention at the beginning of slasher films which is used to make the narrative more frightening by claiming its authenticity. This might dare the viewer to continue watching, provide hope that the text is as frightening as promised, or become a tired and overused trope. In *Freaky Stories*, the repetition of this line across every episode, as well as the inclusion of 'to a friend of a friend of mine', pokes fun at the apocryphal nature of these stories, which are generally attributed 'to a human source at least three storytellers removed from the first person' (Brunvand 1981, 120). While this opening is tongue-in-cheek, the programme drawing on older urban legends that exist beyond the series invites the possibility that the story might have once been true. Survey participant Jasmine explains that urban legends being 'told for generations outside of the cartoons was scary because they seemed almost plausible' and Angus remembers that 'often urban legends were so famous and well-known that it gave them an additional air of credibility, giving the impression that they could be true ... Even when I knew the programme I was watching was fictional'. David Buckingham (1996, 122, original emphasis) analyses that the power of the horror genre 'is not that it makes you believe in the reality of what is represented, but that it makes you take seriously the *possibility* that similar events might happen in real life'. Similarly, folklorist Jan Harold Brunvand's (1981, 62, original emphasis) research found that young people believe that urban legends '*could* happen, and that makes it seem real'. As one participant recalls: 'I remember the start of *Freaky Stories*, "It happened to a friend of a friend of mine." I didn't necessarily believe it but I assumed its plausibility.' Participants remember it being easy to suspend disbelief because urban legends were recognized as older folklore.

Children's horror anthology series commonly feature twist, unresolved endings, which are another device that can blur the distinctions between the diegesis and the child viewer's world. These endings imply that a threat is undefeated and the characters, as well as the child viewer, may remain in danger. One *Freaky Stories* episode that some participants vividly remember is 'Safe at Home' (1998), which adapts an urban legend often known as 'the licked hand' or 'humans can lick too'. In 'Safe at Home', the child protagonist is home alone at night and hears a strange noise in the house. She gets out of bed to investigate and feels her bare heel being licked, which she assumes is by her dog. She later discovers her dog in the basement before seeing what is referred to as an 'escaped maniac' fleeing from the house, shouting: 'I can lick too!' Of interest is that this is one of the few *Freaky Stories* episodes to feature a reassuring ending, with the child protagonist waking up in bed and realizing that it was a dream. Participants in my study, however, do not remember this ending and instead recall the unsettling twist that is similar to the tale's original oral versions. This could be because this frightening moment is more memorable than the episode's conventional happy ending, or they may prefer the more authentic urban legend ending. As one participant recalls: 'Most kids' shows were really predictable ... *Freaky Stories* ... offered more exciting, more complex stories that had a better payoff for watching. The episode where the main character thinks her dog is under her bed licking her feet but it turns out to be an escaped convict is a great example.' These narratives present the insinuation, chilling and thrilling in equal measure, that the monster has finished with its current victims and is coming for the child viewer next.

Urban legends can perform both conservative and liberating functions. On the one hand, they can be read as cautionary tales with a didactic imperative. Brunvand (1981, 59–60) argues that along with producing 'a good scare', urban legends often 'deliver a warning: Watch out! This could happen to you!' Similarly, one participant remembers enjoying these cautions in children's horror television: '"This could happen to you" was a big thing for me.' These tales warn that the world is full of dangers, especially for young people who venture out on their own. They can also serve as more mundane and everyday cautions, such as the risk of cheap hotels or other 'dirty' establishments. One participant explains that *Freaky Stories* 'always had realistic circumstances that could actually happen. One episode ('Blunder Bed' (1997)) was about a motel with vibrating free beds and they found out it was actually cockroaches under the sheets. I forever questioned the motel beds while growing up.' These warnings can teach children to err on the side of caution and take fewer risks.

Conversely, some children use these tales to enliven their prosaic realities, imagining the monsters of urban legends within their everyday environments. One participant recalls how children's horror episodes about urban legends and ghost stories became a form of social play which travelled across the threshold of the television and into the school playground:

> The urban legends (like in *Freaky Stories*) probably stuck with me more because then I'd go to school and we'd talk about them and make up a lot of crap to scare ourselves. We'd look out the playground fence and see a car parked across the road and it would somehow spiral to being a stalker who was going to kidnap us and someone had seen a headless person in the backseat … When in reality, the car was probably parked there because they lived there or it was a teacher's car! But ghost stories I'd seen on TV would circulate through the playground, making them seem real.

By discussing the urban legends they watched on television, some children attempt to dissolve the boundaries between the ordinary and the supernatural. The familiar settings and twist endings lend to this imaginative play, encouraging the child viewer to feel a sense of dark fantasy within the everyday.

In the 1990s and early 2000s, children's horror programmes challenged child audiences to imaginatively confront their fears by themselves. King (1981, 342–80) argues that horror serves 'as catharsis for more mundane fears' and 'helps us to externalise in symbolic form whatever is really troubling us'. The world can be a frightening place for children and as they grow older, they enter more strange and unfamiliar territory. Facing possessed dolls, haunted masks and the monster-under-the-bed may help some child viewers process more ordinary fears. Some children find comfort in texts that promise that threats are distant and temporary, while others appreciate the thrill and challenge of children's horror programmes that diminish the boundaries between safety and the unknown. Screen critic Aimee Knight offers that *Round the Twist*'s appeal is that 'it trusted young people could process the kind of existentialism and uncertainty from which kids were usually shielded. Hopefully that made some of us feel a bit braver, more capable, less afraid of the unknown and the "other"' (quoted in Bastow 2020). Children's horror television can make the monsters that children are already dealing with tangible. These series invite child viewers to face and perhaps gain a sense of control over these fears within depictions of their world.

References

Antunes, Filipa. 2015. 'Children Beware! Children's Horror, PG-13 and the Emergent Millennial Pre-teen'. PhD diss., University of East Anglia, UK.

Antunes, Filipa. 2020. *Children Beware! Childhood, Horror and the PG-13 Rating*. Jefferson, NC: McFarland.

Are You Afraid of the Dark? 1995. [TV programme; Director: D. J. MacHale] Season 5, episode 1, 'The Tale of the Dead Man's Float'. Aired 7 October.

Bastow, Clem. 2020. '*Round the Twist* Revisited: "It Defined What a Children's Program Should Be"'. *The Guardian*, 25 January. https://www.theguardian.com/tv-and-radio/2020/jan/25/round-the-twist-revisited-it-redefined-what-a-childrens-program-should-be.

Brunvand, Jan Harold. [1981] 2003. *The Vanishing Hitchhiker: American Urban Legends and Their Meanings*. New York: W.W. Norton.

Buckingham, David. 1996. *Moving Images: Understanding Children's Emotional Responses to Television*. Manchester: Manchester University Press.

Ciampa, Linda. 1998. '*Goosebumps* Series a Frightening Success'. *CNN*, 30 October. http://edition.cnn.com/books/news/9810/30/goose.bumps/index.html.

Dilworth, John R. 1999. 'The Triumphant Independent'. Interview by Bob Miller. *Animation World Network*. https://www.awn.com/animationworld/triumphant-independent.

Edgar, Patricia. 2006. *Bloodbath: A Memoir of Australian Television*. Melbourne: Melbourne University Press.

Ellis, John. 2000. *Seeing Things: Television in the Age of Uncertainty*. London: I.B. Taurus.

Exorcist, The. 1973. [TV programme; Director: William Friedkin] Burbank, CA: Warner Bros.

Freaky Stories. 1997. [TV programme; Director: Steve Schnier] Season 1, episode 4, 'Blunder Bed'. Aired 14 November.

Freaky Stories. 1998. [TV programme; Director: Scott Amey] Season 2, episode 2, 'Safe at Home'. Aired 30 January.

Freeland, Cynthia. 2000. *The Naked and the Undead: Evil and the Appeal of Horror*. Boulder, CO: Westview Press.

Freud, Sigmund. [1919] 2003. *The Uncanny*. Translated by David McClintock. London: Penguin.

Goosebumps. 1995. [TV programme; Director: TimothyBond] Season 1, episodes 1 and 2, 'The Haunted Mask'. Aired October 27 and 28.

Goosebumps. 1996. [TV programme; Director: William Fruet] Season 1, episodes 16 and 17, 'A Night in Terror Tower'. Aired 25 February.

Goosebumps. 1996. [TV programme; Director: David Winning] Season 1, episode 14, 'It Came from beneath the Sink'. Aired 2 February.

Goosebumps. 1997. [TV programme; Director: William Fruet] Season 2, episodes 20 and 21, 'Welcome to Dead House'. Aired 29 June.

Hills, Matt. 2005. *The Pleasures of Horror*. London: Continuum.

Jackson, Anna, Karen Coats and Roderick McGillis. 2008. *The Gothic in Children's Literature: Haunting the Borders*. New York: Routledge.

Jennings, Paul. 1988. *Uncanny!* Camberwell: Puffin Group Australia.

King, Stephen. 1981. *Danse Macabre*. New York: Everest House.

Lester, Catherine. 2021a. 'Giving Kids Goosebumps: Uncanny Aesthetics, Cyclic Structures and Anti-didacticism in Children's Horror Anthologies'. In *Global TV Horror*, edited by Stacey Abbott and Lorna Jowett, 121–38. Melksham: University of Wales Press.

Lester, Catherine. 2021b. *Horror Films for Children: Fear and Pleasure in American Cinema*. London: Bloomsbury Publishing.

Omen, The. 1976. [Film; Director: Richard Donner]. Los Angeles: 20th Century Fox.

Poltergeist. 1982. [Film; Director: Tobe Hooper]. Beverly Hills, CA: MGM/UA Entertainment.

Potter, Anna. 2016. 'Lasting Memories of Australian Children's Television'. *Australian Children's Television Foundation*, 26 February. https://blog-actf.com.au/lasting-memories-of-australian-childrens-television.

Prendes, Jose. 2020. *Viewer Beware! The Goosebumps TV Companion*. Orlando, FL: BearManor Media.

Rancic, Michael. 2015. '*Goosebumps, Are You Afraid of the Dark?* and the Canadian Kids' TV Boom'. *New Toronto*, 23 November. https://nowtoronto.com/movies/goosebumps-are-you-afraid-of-the-dark-and-the-childrens-tv.

Ring, The. 2002. [Film; Director: Gore Verbinski]. Universal City, CA: DreamWorks Pictures.

Ringu. 1998. [Film; Director: Hideo Nakata]. Chiyoda, Tokyo: Toho.

Round the Twist. 1990. [TV programme; Director: Esben Storm] Season 1, episode 10, 'Know All'. Aired 15 June.

Round the Twist. 2000. [TV Programme; Director: Esben Storm] Season 3, episode 9, 'Toy Love'. Aired 10 March.

Round the Twist. 2001. [TV Programme; Director: Ray Boseley] Season 4, episode 2, 'Monster under the Bed'. Aired 15 January.

Stine, R. L. 1998. 'Lurking in the Dark'. *Newsweek* 132, no. 18: 66.

Stine, R. L. 2019. '"A Good Horror Story Starts in the Backyard": *Goosebumps* Legend R. L. Stine on Why Fear Is Good for Children'. Interview by Anna McKerrow. Booktrust. https://www.booktrust.org.uk/news-and-features/featu res/2019/february/a-good-horror-story- starts-in-the-backyard-goosebumps- legend-r.l.-stine-on-why-fear-is-good-for-children/.

Tudor, Andrew. 1997. 'Why Horror? The Peculiar Pleasures of a Popular Genre'. *Cultural Studies* 11, no. 3: 443–63. https://doi.org/10.1080/095023897335691.

Wheatley, Helen. 2002. 'Gothic Television'. PhD diss., University of Warwick.

Wheatley, Helen. 2006. *Gothic Television*. Manchester: Manchester University Press.

5

An adult nightmare: Garbage Pail Kids and the fear of the queer child

Max Hart

In May 1986, at a small Catholic elementary school in Ansonia, Connecticut, a strange ritual took place in the school courtyard. Around 200 students ranging from the fourth to the eighth grade gathered around a statue of the Virgin Mary and proceeded to rip up hundreds of trading cards, toss them into trash cans, and promptly light them on fire. The victims? The Garbage Pail Kids. Diane Sacanow, a fourth grader at Assumption Elementary, told a reporter that she thinks the cards are 'ugly' and that 'they make fun of my parents and our country' ('Kids Trash "Garbage Pail Kids" Cards' 1986). The school administration felt similarly. The principal, Susan Kirk, called them 'pretty obnoxious … There's one that says "Sewer Sue". It shows a girl standing in a sewer. Then there's "Sally Slime". I don't ever want to be quoted as to what's coming over her' (Ibid.). Kirk said that until the week before, the cards had been popular with the students and many schools across the country were dealing with a similar problem. However, the children attending Assumption had an apparent change of heart. 'I'm really proud of the kids', said Kirk, 'they willingly wanted to make a statement on it' (Ibid.). The burning (which was voluntary according to the administration) managed to destroy around 500 of the cards and was followed by a 'song for peace' (Ibid.). Kirk said she intended to return the charred remains to Topps, the company responsible for manufacturing the Garbage Pail Kids (it is unknown if this eventually took place). Reflecting on the broader implications of the cards, Kirk said: 'If people look at these long enough, they will be affected by them. They don't belong in a Catholic school. They don't belong in a Catholic home. They don't belong in the world' (Ibid.).

Out of the garbage pail and into the fire

Isolated here in small town Connecticut, it would be easy to dismiss this bizarre ritual burning of children's trading cards as laughably dramatic. But while not everyone went to such lengths as to purify them by fire, the public reaction to the Garbage Pail Kids was certainly on par with this trash can bonfire. Almost immediately after their debut in June 1985, the Garbage Pail Kids were met with public outcries. The cards were lambasted as cruel, perverse and offensive and triggered an explosion of anger and disbelief. Parents, horrified by the grotesque images of mutilated toddlers and oozing infants, tried desperately to purge them from their homes. School administrators, panicked by the vandalizing of classroom desks and bathroom stalls, immediately took action to ban the product from school grounds. Public officials, gravely concerned with their explicit encouragement of antisocial behaviour and disrespect for authority, urged business owners to pull them from their shelves.

But were such extreme reactions really called for? Taken at face value, the cheap bubble gum trading cards appear relatively banal. Sure, they were pretty icky – characters like 'Corroded Carl', 'Junky Jeff' and 'Furry Fran' likely upset some parents' stomachs – and their double function as stickers caused a small vandalism problem. But gross-out humour is nothing new nor unexpected for playground talk, and children will always find ways to deface school property, stickers or no stickers. In short, the humour of the Garbage Pail Kids was puerile, the aesthetic gimmicky and quite clearly meant for nothing more than a cheap laugh. Besides a few crude jokes and some petty vandalism, what truly was the harm?

Despite their trivial nature, it quickly became clear that many did not see the humour in 'Slain Wayne'. In fact, if their critics had been the only people paying them any attention, the Garbage Pail Kids would have been dead on arrival. But there were others who felt differently. While parents, school principals and politicians were revolted by the Garbage Pail Kids, their children couldn't get enough of them. Kindergarteners to high-schoolers saved up their allowance, swarmed convenient stores and lined up in droves to get their hands on the newest pack. Lunch tables across the country were littered with snot covered babies and headless toddlers. Despite all rhetoric to the contrary, what some saw as a disgusting commodity manufactured with cruel intentions became a cultural phenomenon among the very subjects they considered threatened by it.

Faced with such an unprecedented fascination, public discourse exploded into panicked analysis and speculation on what the hell was going on with the nation's youth. But as opinion columns were written and nightly newscasters ran special interest stories, you would have easily gotten the impression that all of America's children were in on some disgusting private joke and that the adults weren't invited to join in on the fun. Thus, the question quickly shifted from 'Who would make such a thing for children?' to 'How could children truly like these?' For aren't the Garbage Pail Kids, with their sick images and cruel intentions, antithetical to all that is healthy for a child to enjoy? Indeed, the Garbage Pail Kids seem to be designed precisely as the opposite of what children are supposed to be; innocence is replaced with perversion, nurture with violence, purity with toxicity.

It is this blasphemy, this unforgivable corruption of children, that this text is concerned with: not to make an ethical argument for or against the Garbage Pail Kids, but to indulge in the horrifying monstrosity they created. As harmless as they may seem today, in a time where the gross-out aesthetic is the norm in commercial children's toys and media, I argue that the Garbage Pail Kids succeeded in tapping into a pervasive social anxiety far exceeding the prudishness of a few uptight parents. This anxiety had, at its root, more to do with the joy that the Garbage Pail Kids gave actual children than the cards themselves. Far more frightening than a cartoon of a child with its head blown off is an actual child who says: 'I like this one. My dolly would look nice with its head blown off too' ('Kids Trash "Garbage Pail Kids" Cards' 1986). Horrifying – and despite desperate attempts to prohibit, or at least understand this cruel fascination, adults remained speechless as more and more children exchanged the grotesque icons, giggling and revelling in the sickness of it all. This laughter, I argue, provoked such fear precisely because it signified an impossible affinity between two culturally opposed figures: the queer and the child.

The framework through which I am making this claim is inherited from Lee Edelman, who argues in his 2004 book *No Future: Queer Theory and the Death Drive* that the ethical discourse surrounding children in Western culture is symptomatic of an oppressive political logic that, far from being concerned with the well-being of actual children, functions to preclude a queer opposition to heteronormativity. The figure of the child, whose supposed innocence solicits our uncompromising defence against any and all who might oppose it, attains its cultural sanctity as the symbol of a future in which the hollowness of identity, the antagonisms of the social and the desire for meaning itself is resolved. This utopian vision of a return to the innocence of childhood is symptomatic of what Edelman calls 'reproductive futurism', a structural predetermination of the boundaries of political discourse that places the figure of the child as its absolute object (Edelman 2007, 2). Thus, to 'fight for the children', an imperative which no legible political platform would dismiss, does not mean to concern oneself with

the well-being of actual children but to insist on the universal mandate of
reproductive futurism for which the child is its most privileged token. But
this, as Edelman insists, is a fantasy, an abstract narrative of meaningful
fulfilment that is based on a misrecognition of the subject as having an
unmediated access to identity. Thus, in order to defer the impossible promises
of reproductive futurism, political discourse must constantly name a social
force that opposes this vision of the future. For Edelman, this antisocial
force is embodied by the figure of the queer. The queer is produced precisely
to figure those divergent subjects who refuse the mandate of reproductive
futurism, those who are coded as immoral, perverse and narcissistic and
whose pleasures oppose the actualization of meaning, the realization of the
social subject and ultimately the future itself.

   In short, it is the child versus the queer; this is the indissoluble antagonism
of *No Future*, on which the central claim of the book turns. Within this
framework, the queer has no option but, as Edelman puts it, to choose
the side '*not* "fighting for the children"', to refuse the oppressive logic of
futurism for which the desire for the child is produced, and to embrace its
structural position as the 'death drive' of the social order (Ibid., 3).

   But while Edelman positions his polemic against representations of
children like those of the film *Annie*, whose titular character's calls for
'Tomorrow! / Tomorrow!' courts the violent mandate of reproductive
futurism, I see another child – one who chooses to play in the garbage rather
than the flowers. The queer child, a signifier structurally paradoxical as it is
ironic, refers neither to an identity nor a speculative project, but to the spectre
of a prohibited encounter – an unholy union between two oppositionally
defined forces that creates a radical perversion. Such a perversion, in turn,
could only provoke fear – the sort of unnamable, abject fear that threatens
to corrupt a foundational logic.

   It is important to stress that these terms employed by Edelman and myself
do not necessarily refer to any actualized subjects with which we might
associate them. While 'child' may indeed refer to humans of a privileged
age, and while 'queer' might denote genders and sexualities outside the
heteronormative imperative, I am speaking of them as they operate
discursively in hegemonic culture as signifiers that, above and beyond any
claims to individual identity, function to reproduce a normative order of
social relations. This does not mean that the task is to 'demystify' the child
or the queer, that is, to cast them aside as arbitrary and historical categories.
On the contrary, it is to insist on an analysis of them as abstract social
figures that have a form and function untethered from the subjects they are
associated with.

   The Garbage Pail Kids phenomenon, while relatively insignificant,
nonetheless presents a unique moment in which the oppressive logic that
Edelman describes was unable to neutralize the threat of a divergent
enjoyment precisely because, as children, the rhetorical framework was

rendered incompatible. Thus, stuck with nothing but the abject image of giggling toddlers excitedly exchanging Garbage Pail Kids cards, the adults could do nothing but look on in horror. This text treats this point of rupture as a catalyst to explore the possibilities of a queer project in which a perversion such as this, that is, *a queering of the child*, might pose a potent avenue for the antisocial queer ethics that Edelman calls for. In other words, to properly choose the side not fighting for the children, the queer may, in fact, have to come full circle – to insist on the radical contamination of the sacred Eden for which they have been produced precisely to look on from the outside, and to release the monster from within.

The cabbage patch

Our story begins with Xavier Roberts, a twenty-one-year-old art student who, through a niche marketing scheme and a few creative thefts, created the most popular children's toy in decades: The Cabbage Patch Kids (Joyce 1983). Instantly recognizable by their cherubic faces and plump features, the Cabbage Patch Kids took the market by storm in the early 1980s. While their mythology was certainly part of their appeal (sex-less children born straight from mother nature's womb), it was the formal gimmicks of the Cabbage Patch Kids – adoption papers, birth certificates and annual birthday cards – that set them apart from their competition. Advertisements for the Cabbage Patch Kids rigorously pushed the perception that these were not dolls but real, living beings, and their ever-increasing price tag seemed to mirror this sentiment. Despite the upcharges, the dolls continued to be a commercial hit, outselling most products around the holidays in the mid-1980s (Ferretti 1984). In their first major year, the popularity of the Cabbage Patch Kids reached such a degree that they began to cause a safety hazard, as holiday shoppers duked it out over the product at strip malls and department stores across the country (Nakahara 1983). News media was there to capture this event, as mothers and grandmothers lined up for hours in order to get their hands on the latest doll. This, it seems, was fuelled only in part by the desires of their children, as many expressed their own inexplicable infatuation with the Cabbage Patch Kids – even when they didn't like them. One elderly woman in Pennsylvania, for instance, said to a reporter: 'I don't like them, I don't like their faces, but I want one' ('Demand for Cabbage Patch Kids Causes Chaos in Stores across America' 1983).

It is this bizarre obsession that the Garbage Pail Kids were created to make fun of. In 1984, Art Spiegelman, Mark Newgarden and a team of artists at the Topps Trading Card company set out to create the Garbage Pail Kids as a parody of what they saw in the Cabbage Patch Kids as a ridiculous commodity craze. Originally conceived as a one-off entry into their already successful line of Wacky Packages trading cards, the Garbage Pail Kids went into development as a stand-alone series and debuted in 1985. The original series featured clear allusions to both the visual aesthetic and brand identity of the Cabbage Patch Kids. However, rather than depict children as innocent babies born of mother nature's womb, the Garbage Pail Kids caricature the cherubic babies in all manner of obscene and unnatural predicaments. 'Adam Bomb', for instance, the lead character of the first series and eventual brand mascot, is a smiling toddler in Sunday school clothes with a mushroom cloud for a head. Other notable entries in the original series include 'Wacky Jackie', a toddler in a straitjacket whose head is popping off like a jack in the box, and 'Drippy Dan', a bottle drinking infant with holes punched out of their body. Besides this trademark bodily humour, other cards like 'Boozin Bruce' and 'Nervous Rex' depict children engaging in adult vices such as alcohol and tobacco. Additionally, the back of the cards features various 'certificates' and 'awards' intended to parody the formal gimmicks of the Cabbage Patch Kids. Unlike the Cabbage Patch Kids however, these are not intended to instruct children on how to care for their adopted child, but to encourage misbehaviour. The 'Pain in the Neck License', for instance, grants the right to 'mind everyone's business, but your own'. Later series would also include 'Wanted' posters for various authority figures, such as a 'Principal', who is charged with crimes like 'Running a school like it was a prison' and 'Impersonating a human' (*30 Years of Garbage: The Garbage Pail Kids Story* 2017).

The first series of forty-one Garbage Pail Kids debuted in June 1985, and the public response was immediate. Concerned parents, media watchdog groups and various Christian associations criticized the Garbage Pail Kids for everything from glorifying violence to making fun of the disabled and encouraging antisocial behaviour. Not surprisingly, the most outspoken opponents of the Garbage Pail Kids were Original Appalachian Artworks, the company responsible for the Cabbage Patch Kids. Original Appalachian sued Topps for copyright infringement, detrimentally affecting the market for the Cabbage Patch Kids and confusing consumers (Frazier 1987a). After a notable effort on the part of Topps to argue for fair use under parody laws, they ultimately settled out of court, agreeing to pay Original Appalachian $30 million in damages and to alter the product's design to no longer resemble the Cabbage Patch Kids (Frazier 1987b). But even before they were tried in court, the Garbage Pail Kids were handed a resounding guilty verdict by public opinion. One of the most publicized criticisms of the Garbage Pail Kids was an editorial written by Bob Greene in the *Chicago Tribune* in November 1985. The story describes a twelve-year-old seventh grader who received an insulting message via a Garbage Pail Kids card. The back of the card featured an award for the 'Most Unpopular Student' on which someone had written the student's name (Greene 1985). The editorial was well circulated, receiving republication in other newspapers and even prompting Topps to make a statement (Ibid.). And although this was the only explicit evidence of any adverse effects, it nonetheless convinced many that their misgivings about the Garbage Pail Kids were correct.

Unsurprisingly, any further development of the product was protested. When CBS announced plans to air a cartoon based on the Garbage Pail Kids in September 1987, there were very public calls for censorship. While CBS asserted that the show would promote the 'fun' aspects of the Garbage Pail Kids rather than their 'creepier' elements, many were not convinced (Haithman 1987). Peggy Charren, president of Action for Children's Television (ACT), a media watchdog group that was instrumental throughout the 1980s in lobbying for federal regulation of children's programming, was quoted as saying: 'I know Judy Price [CBS vice-president of children's programming] says some of the creepier aspects of the cards will not be part of the series ... But to have a show based on the cards is a pitch and an endorsement and a validation of the Garbage Pail Kids cards' (Ibid.). Continuing, Charren said of Price that 'she is promoting a kind of humor that is nasty. ... These cards use stereotypes that are ghastly. It's like allowing a child to call someone a 'retard' in the house – it promotes that kind of thinking. CBS used to be the leading voice in broadcasting, and what are they doing now for children? A series, *The Garbage Pail Kids*!' (Ibid.). It is worth noting that there is no Garbage Pail Kid with the name 'retard', but Charren got her wish. Following the lobbying efforts of the ACT group and other associated organizations like the National Coalition on Television Violence (NCTV) and the Christian Leaders for Responsible Television (a part of the American Family Association), CBS abruptly pulled the show right before it was slated to debut (Haithman 1987b). While it would air partially in other parts of the world, *Garbage Pail Kids* would never air on prime-time television in the United States.

And so, while it was originally intended as nothing more than a crude caricature of a popular children's toy, the rhetoric deployed against the Garbage Pail Kids suggested a much more significant conspiracy. One of the ways this was expressed was in the conviction that its original object of critique, the Cabbage Patch Kids, represented some sort of cultural linchpin that the Garbage Pail Kids had dared to tread on. In this article from *Toronto Star*, for instance: 'Instead of down-home names like Otis Lee or Rebecca Ruby, the Garbage Pail Kids have Bustin' Dustin, a stitched and bruised baby boxer whose bloody nose runs like a faucet; Dinah Saur, a grinning skeleton; Pinned Lynn, a Voodoo doll stuck with nails; and Oliver Twisted' (Nyman 1986). This sort of comparison is intended to stress that, insofar as the Cabbage Patch Kids appeal to all of the 'down-home' qualities expected of a children's toy, the fact that the Garbage Pail Kids are intended to defame them simultaneously implies a direct affront to their associated values. Indeed, many claimed that the Garbage Pail Kids were an offence not only to the Cabbage Patch Kids but were something of a whole-scale assault on US values and norms. The state treasurer of West Virginia for instance,

A. James Manchin, publicly asked retailers to remove the cards from their stores and decried them for the way they 'make fun of everything from the family dentist to Uncle Sam, breed contempt for the American way of life' (Valentine 1986).

The jump to accuse the Garbage Pail Kids of 'breeding contempt for the American way of life' seems to have been made quite easily, despite the fact that there was no evidence to suggest such cultural malfeasance. Even more bewildering is the one who issued the condemnation, as the controversy surrounding a children's trading card wouldn't normally be considered an issue relevant for a state policy maker (a treasurer no less). For Edelman, however, children's lives are not only some of the most politicized, but are in fact positioned – albeit abstractly – at the ethical foundation of Western politics. Within his framework, the figure of the child is emblematic of an oppressive logic of futurism that demarcates the boundaries of the political imaginary (Edelman 2007, 2). Terming this logic 'reproductive futurism', Edelman argues that politics promotes the fantasy of a future in which the structural antagonisms of the social order are resolved, providing the subject with the realization of identity. The universal protagonist of this narrative, whose presence is imagined as an unmediated access to original wholeness, is the figure of the child. Not because actual children are universally desired, but because the sort of meaningful fulfilment promised by politics is synonymous with the fantasy of 'salvation' subtending the figure of the child. Thus, allegorized through heterosexual reproduction as the promise of a better future, the child becomes the 'perpetual horizon of every acknowledged politics' (Ibid., 3). Reproductive futurism is thus a sort of 'secular theology' in which the figure of the child (and the production of it) serves as its emblematic prop, and as such 'shapes at once the meaning of our collective narratives and our collective narratives of meaning' (Ibid., 12).

This fantasy of the child, while perpetually deferred and unattainable, nonetheless ensures that the narrative logic of reproductive futurism is universally reiterated regardless of partisan disagreements. It is thus a particularly powerful, if not the most powerful, rhetorical tool for compelling a political population. Not so coincidentally, we might look to the political climate in which the Garbage Pail Kids emerged, for example. This was the age of 'stranger danger', of 'Have you seen me?' milk cartons. It was a dramatic turning point in US politics where discourse concerning children turned from the language of provision, that is, material threats such as poverty, to protection from moral threats such as a decline in familial values and the threat of urban nihilism (Renfro 2015, 15). This is not to say that these moral threats were not described in material forms – serial child murderers and vindictive drug dealers were supposedly rampant – but that unlike the rising discrepancy in income among working-class Americans (disproportionately people of colour) and the quickly accelerating AIDS epidemic (largely ignored by the federal government) these shadowy immoral villains were not supported by factual data. This was due in large part to a new brand of reactionary conservatism heralded into the mainstream by Ronald Reagan. Early in his presidency, for instance, Reagan catalysed on a couple of regionally specific murder and kidnapping cases to shoehorn the figure of the child to the forefront of his crusade against declining American morale. In a 2015 essay called 'Keeping Children Safe Is Good Business: The Enterprise of Child Safety in the Age of Reagan', Paul Renfro shows how the Reagan Administration utilized the fervour over a couple of kidnappings in the Midwest as a powder keg for many of the social issues the president campaigned on. Dramatically distorting statistics and appealing to the pathos of an increasingly anxious white middle class, Reagan turned 'child safety' into a symbolic and literal enterprise of both private sector morale and conservative institutions. Whether or not the issue of child safety was based on any real surge in violence against children, or the legislation enacted by the government was anything but showboating, did not really matter. What was important was that the president appealed to a growing fear of his constituents that something about their social order was at risk, a fear he tapped into through the image of the vulnerable child he promised to protect.

But perhaps the most obvious example of this came in a televised address from both the president and the first lady, Nancy Reagan, on 14 September 1986. In this now infamous address, the Reagans addressed the nation not from the oval office or the rose garden, but from a couch in the White House residence. Speaking first, the president introduced him and his wife 'not simply as fellow citizens but as fellow parents and grandparents and as concerned neighbours' ('"Just Say No" Address to the Nation' 1986). On their domestic stage, the president and first lady worked hard to impress how familial values were at stake in the supposed drug epidemic, particularly crack, threatening the nation's children. The president, introducing Nancy's efforts to combat the epidemic, stressed that 'while drug and alcohol abuse cuts across all generations, it's especially damaging to the young people on whom our future depends' (Ibid.). The first lady, for her part, hammered it home with this sobering metaphor: 'Every time a drug goes into a child, something else is forced out. Like love and hope, and trust and confidence. Drugs take away the dream from every child's heart and replace it with a nightmare' (Ibid.).

A nightmare indeed – for who would argue with this? When Nancy Reagan speaks directly to the children of America and urges them to 'say yes' to life, who would dissent? (Ibid.). This is reproductive futurism at its finest; like an 'ideological Möbius strip', any attempt to contradict this imperative, to challenge the assertion that our children must be protected, is impermissible (Edelman 2007, 2). This, as Edelman claims, is the 'oppressively political' function of the child, that it is an issue that permits only *one* side (Ibid.). And so, while it may seem misplaced to compare Nancy's drug dealers to the creators of a children's trading card, it remains that whether it is crack cocaine or the Garbage Pail Kids, the rhetoric is the same; a lurking, insidious threat, a scheming other that comes from the outside and is attempting to contaminate the purity within. It doesn't matter that the Garbage Pail Kids were only trading cards, for to suggest that children could enjoy these images, vile caricatures of the syrupy sweet infants they are imagined to be, would be to contradict every ethical imperative necessary for the discourse of reproductive futurism to operate.

But the model of reproductive futurism is only a starting point. For what made the Garbage Pail Kids so especially horrifying was not simply the images themselves, but their circulation. Unlike Nancy and her scheming drug dealers, concerned adults could not cast blame on any shadowy villain for the mass proliferation of the trading cards, for it was children themselves who fuelled their popularity. Despite all expectations, the impossible was happening – against the grain of the child's mythology, the pleasure that the Garbage Pail Kids gave actual children was undeniable. So it was the actualization of this perverse pleasure that was truly at stake with the Garbage Pail Kids phenomenon. The fear – the lurking, unspeakable fear – hiding underneath the panicked attempts to rescue these children from the Garbage Pail Kids were not so much of 'Busted Bob' himself as the giggles he elicited. The possibility that children could be so taken with the image of a dismembered toddler was almost impossible to acknowledge; for to acknowledge this possibility would be to envision an enjoyment so opposed to the child as it is imagined by reproduction futurism that the consequence could only be a horrifying perversion, giving birth to a monstrosity.

An adult nightmare

It is no coincidence that even the small group of adults who publicly supported the Garbage Pail Kids legitimized their counter-argument not in affirmation of the cards, but in such a way that any potential threat was effectively neutralized by rational assimilation into the 'normal' language of child development. This argument, often made during special interest newscasts by a token psychiatrist or behavioural psychologist, suggested (as Irene Goldberg did in one CBS news report) that the Garbage Pail Kids 'give kids a chance to let off steam together, in a not inappropriate way … to be kind of anti-social and anti-conventional in a way that doesn't really hurt too badly' (Drinkwater 2019). This explanation, far more clever and more sinister than to simply condemn the Garbage Pail Kids, is to evacuate them of any subversive potential – that is, of any *real* threat to the narrative of childhood. It is as if to say: Do not worry, your child may be infatuated with 'Nasty Nick' now, but sooner or later they will come crawling back to the cabbage patch from whence they came.

Neither the condemners nor the supporters of the Garbage Pail Kids would dare to suggest that, in fact, they were popular among children *because* of their disturbing qualities – that is, their infatuation with 'Oozy Suzy' was because they enjoyed the image of a dripping, decomposing baby, consciously and selfishly, and that this enjoyment could not be blamed on some nefarious villain or reduced to an Oedipal mythology. For the adult who desires a return to the natural innocence of childhood cannot recognize an enjoyment outside this nostalgia, cannot envision an experience of joy that does not simultaneously insist on the absolute virtues of magical presence which the child is imagined to fulfil. Thus, the adult must find a seamless reiteration of this narrative through the lived experience of actual children, to gaze out at the playground of past innocence as a vanishing point for the object of his desire. This is not to suggest that actual children *do* seamlessly reiterate the narrative of childhood – like any subject of a regulative ideal, actual children only ever diverge from this. But children nonetheless remain the most unquestioned normative identity precisely because any significant divergence is often, and easily, blamed on another, as the narrative of unadulterated innocence precludes the possibility of this coming from the child itself.

Thus, the true threat of the Garbage Pail Kids, that is, of the sort of enjoyment they gave actual children, was the inability for the discourse of reproductive futurism to properly displace this divergent behaviour onto an antagonistic outside. Instead, the threat appears, impossibly, to emerge from within. Take, for instance, in one CBS news segment, when a group of fourth graders were asked to respond to the many critiques levelled at the Garbage Pail Kids by adults. When asked questions like 'Aren't these gross?' 'Isn't that violent?' 'Isn't that mean?' they replied with a level of affirmation, agreeing that there is something unsettling about 'Clogged DUANE'. And yet, even as they performed the interpretive labour that is expected of them, even as they looked into the camera and repeated the adults' words back to them, their faces contorted into smiles and they snickered through their words. There is exhibited in the smirking faces of both the Garbage Pail Kids and the children who adore them a sort of inarticulable pleasure, illegible and unnameable precisely because it is at the expense of themselves. When one fourth grader says 'I think they're disgusting', all the while biting her lower lip and smiling almost maniacally, she does so at the expense of herself and the discourse she takes part in. While their parents gasp, frown and toss heavy rhetoric around, the children exchange heretical iconography and lay out shrines to their toxic taboo. Their parents' concerns are meaningless here; casting aside the ethical disagreements of the adults, they trivialize their school's ban of the Garbage Pail Kids with comments like: 'We can't even play with them at recess time! What are you supposed to do, just sit there? I mean *really*'. In the end, when they are asked if they 'know anybody disgusting like [the Garbage Pail Kids] in real life', their response is only laughter (Ibid.).

What is materializing here, in the form of this perverse, self-effacing pleasure, is what I am calling the queer child. For Edelman, queerness must be understood as 'never a matter of being or becoming', but rather of *jouissance*, of the 'corrosive enjoyment' that occurs at the 'violent passage beyond the bounds of identity, meaning, and the law' (Edelman 2007, 25, 30). Thus, as Edelman so astutely puts it, the fear of an encounter between the queer and the child is to fear a child who 'might find an enjoyment that would nullify the figural value, itself imposed by adult desire, of the Child as unmarked by the adult's adulterating implication in desire itself' (Ibid., 21). Such an enjoyment would, by virtue of its nullifying force, *mark the child as the queer*. What is so unnerving about this laughter, then, is that it occurs *through* actual children *in mockery* of the desire for meaning which the child is imagined to fulfil. This is the true adult nightmare; that of a child who takes pleasure in the perversion of the logic of desire for which it is imagined as its absolute object.

But how could something like the queer child exist? Under the logic of reproductive futurism, the queer and the child can only ever be in absolute opposition. And yet, it is precisely because of the prohibition against such an unholy union that the queer child is made manifest. The queer child is not a being, signifier or figure, but a *spectre*, the kind that the French philosopher Georges Bataille insists 'only truly exists as such from the moment when the milieu that contains it defines itself through its intolerance toward that which appears in it as a crime' (Bataille 1985, 81). The prohibition of queerness that demarcates the boundaries of desire according to reproductive futurism produces as a consequence the very spectral monstrosity that the queer child embodies. It is a horror produced by virtue of its own impossible presence, a haunting perversion that echoes throughout the laughter of children who take unspeakable pleasure in the radical destruction of the normative ideal which they are imagined to embody.

It is in this way that the queer child must be understood as the *abject* of reproductive futurism. Or rather, an encounter with the queer child can only be described as an experience of abjection. I am speaking of abjection here in terms of what the French thinker Julia Kristeva describes as 'the violence of mourning for an "object" that has always already been lost' (Kristeva 1982, 15). According to Kristeva, if the object is that which settles the subject 'within the fragile texture of a desire for meaning', the abject must be understood as that which is 'radically excluded' and draws the subject towards 'the place where meaning collapses' (Ibid., 2). Thus, if we are to treat 'adult' similar to 'child', that is, as a figure meant to affirm a hegemonic order of social relations, then the adult figure is the becoming social subject who imagines the child as the future object whose presence would resolve the social antagonisms of the present. The sort of 'nightmare' appropriate for the adult, then, is one in which the child is radically corrupted – not only at the level of attainability, but at the site of its imaginary production. The adult nightmare is that in which the child is not only lost as an *object* but is in fact *revealed as always already lost* – that is, *that this loss is paradoxically essential to the production of the desire subtending it.*

In contrast, the queer child through which the abject exists is a 'deject', as Kristeva puts it, one who no one can desire, but who nonetheless is never without laughter, as 'laughing is a way of placing or displacing abjection' (Ibid., 8). The Garbage Pail Kids, through their sickness, created for a moment an abject encounter with these perverse, laughing dejects; a nightmare which there can be no waking from.

The queer child

Edelman argues that 'the only oppositional status to which our queerness could ever lead would depend on our taking seriously the place of the death drive we're called on to figure … against the cult of the Child and the political order it reinforces' (Edelman 2007, 30). However, *No Future* did not attempt – nor could it, according to Edelman – to imagine what a radical queer negativity would look like in practice ('Interview with Prof Lee Edelman on State of Queer Theory Today/No Future Project' 2015). And so, faced with the smirking faces of these children and the horror they instilled, I cannot help but ask: is this not precisely the queerness that Edelman calls for? For while Edelman acknowledges that the queer, like the child, is nothing but a figure standing in for the structural antagonism of reproductive futurism, this is not to give queerness an identity, even one characterized by its status as oppositional. To take Edelman's project seriously, to insist 'on queering *ourselves*', is to insist on this negativity not as a position that can be *named,* but as an active, virulent disturbance, one that is unnamable, or that which perverts the oppressive repetition of naming itself (Edelman 2007, 26). With the Garbage Pail Kids phenomenon as an example, I wonder if the application of an antisocial project must not only be to accede to its structural position as the absolute negative, but perhaps take this as an incitement to actively pervert the oppressive narrative of desire produced by the mandate of reproductive futurism. This would mean not only a call to accept the figural status of the queer as the death drive of the social, but also to 'play out' the role of its abject decay.

None of this is to suggest some sort of queer opposition led by misbehaved children (although this intrigues me). Rather, it is to suggest that we might do well not to simply oppose the child and all that it stands for in uncompromising defiance, but to insist, like the Garbage Pail Kids, on its unrelenting perversion – to 'make fun' of it. For in the same way that Edelman tells us to be instructed by the conservative rhetoric that claims (correctly) that the queer is opposed to every country-loving, God-fearing value of the Christian United States, perhaps we should also be instructed by that other familiar accusation; that the queer seeks, above all, to corrupt the minds of our youth, to pervert the innocence of our sacred children. For such an unholy act could only produce monsters – and there is no monster more horrifying than the queer child.

References

Bataille, Georges. 1985. *Visions of Excess: Selected Writings, 1927–1939: Georges Bataille*. Minneapolis: University of Minnesota Press.

'Demand for Cabbage Patch Kids Causes Chaos in Stores across America'. 1983. PIX11 News. New York: WPIX, November. https://pix11.com/2014/08/18/from-1983-demand-forcabbage-patch-kids-causes-chaos-in-stores-across-america/. Accessed 28 February 2019.

Drinkwater, Terry. 1986. CBS News. Los Angeles, CA: KCBS-TV. https://www.youtube.com/watch?v=1qsdYd6A7ZQ&t=7s. Accessed 28 February 2019.

Edelman, Lee. 2007. *No Future Queer Theory and the Death Drive*. Durham: Duke University Press.

Ferretti, Fred. 1984. 'Cabbage Patch Kids: Born for "Adoption" at a Price'. *New York Times*, 16 January. https://www.nytimes.com/1984/01/16/style/cabbage-patch-kids-born-for-adoption-at-a-price.html. Accessed 24 September 2023.

Frazier, Joseph B. 1987a. 'Garbage Pail Kids Trial Centers on What Constitutes Copying'. *The Associated Press*, 28 January: 28.

Frazier, Joseph B.. 1987b. 'Makers of Garbage Pail Kids and Cabbage Patch Kids Settle on Compromise'. *The Associated Press*, 3 February.

Garbage Pail Kids. 2012. New York: Abrams ComicsArts.

Greene, Bob. 1985. 'Topps' Garbage Card Hits Bottom with Boy'. *Chicago Tribune*, 17 November. https://www.chicagotribune.com/news/ct-xpm-1985-11-17-8503190566-story.html. Accessed 24 September 2023.

Haithman, Diane. 1987a. '"Garbage Pail Kids" Plunked on TV'. *The Los Angeles Times*, 8 July. https://www.latimes.com/archives/la-xpm-1987-07-08-ca-2616-story.html. Accessed 24 September 2023.

Haithman, Diane. 1987b. 'The Lid's Not Quite Shut on "Garbage Pail Kids" at CBS'. *The Los Angeles Times*, 10 October. https://www.latimes.com/archives/la-xpm-1987-10-10-ca-8638-story.html. Accessed 24 September 2023.

'Interview with Prof. Lee Edelman on State of Queer Theory Today/No Future Project'. 2015. Interview. YouTube, 21 September, Summer School for Sexualities, Culture and Politics, Belgrade. https://www.youtube.com/watch?v=NjTDLyKP2p0&t=309s. Accessed 21 March 2019.

Joyce, Fay S. 1983. 'Cabbage Patch Kids Spur a Battle over Parentage'. *The New York Times*, 6 December. https://www.nytimes.com/1983/12/06/us/cabbage-patch-kids-spur-a-battle-over-parentage.html. Accessed 24 September 2023.

'"Just Say No" Address to the Nation'. 1986. Transcript. CNN. 14 September. http://www.cnn.com/SPECIALS/2004/reagan/stories/speech.archive/just.say.no.html.

'Kids Trash "Garbage Pail Kids" Cards'. 1986. *The Associated Press*, 30 May: 5.

Kristeva, Julia. 1982. *Powers of Horror: An Essay on Abjection*.
    New York: Columbia University Press.
May, Clifford D. 1986. 'From Acne Amy to Virus Iris, Cards Selling by the
    Gross'. *Chicago Tribune*, 9 February. https://www.chicagotribune.com/news/
    ct-xpm-1986-02-09-8601100753-story.html. Accessed 24 September 2023.
Nakahara, Liz. 1983. 'Chaos in the Cabbage Patch; Buyers Stampede Stores for
    Moon-Faced Dolls'. *The Washington Post*, 28 November.
Nyman, Judy. 1986. 'Garbage Pail Kids a Hot Seller: Children Love Stickers
    Parents Find Disgusting'. *The Toronto Star*, 11 June: 12.
Renfro, Paul Mokrzycki. 2015. 'Keeping Children Safe Is Good Business: The
    Enterprise of Child Safety in the Age of Reagan'. *Enterprise & Society* 17, no.
    01: 151–87.
30 Years of Garbage: The Garbage Pail Kids Story. 2017. [Film; Directors: Jeff
    Zapata and Joe Simko]. United States: Lionsgate. DVD.
Valentine, Valca. 1986. 'Garbage Pail Kids Are the Rage; Cause Some, Too'. *The
    Washington Post*, 26 June.

6

The transgender twist: Mermen and gender nonconformity in *Round the Twist*

Jackson Phoenix Nash

Like Leland G. Spencer (2014), who reads *The Little Mermaid* (both original story and film) as a story 'about a performance of transgender identity' (1), this chapter offers a reading of the episode 'Nails' (1993), from Australian TV show *Round the Twist*, through the lens of a transgender or gender-nonconforming narrative. *Round the Twist* (1990–2001) is an Australian TV show about the Twist family who live in a lighthouse. Dad, Tony, is an artist who lives with his three children – teenage twins Pete and Linda, and their younger brother Bronson, aged eight. The series was based on Paul Jennings's fantastical children's short stories, such as *Unreal!* (1985) and *Uncanny* (1989).

In 'Nails', Linda Twist falls for the new student at school, Andrew, who lives on an island and is surrounded by mystery – particularly concerning why he always wears gloves. An outsider geographically, Andrew is also an outsider in his attitude and gender-nonconforming behaviour. Linda soon discovers that Andrew is growing extra nails on his hands (which turn out to be scales), and the rest of his body, because his mother is a mermaid. Just as Spencer (2014) acknowledges that *The Little Mermaid* is not intentionally a transgender text but that transness is present within it, I also acknowledge that it seems unlikely that the episode 'Nails' is an intentional transgender narrative. At the time of its release in the early 1990s, when I was finishing primary school and heading into secondary, there just weren't out transgender characters in children's television. Where trans characters were present in programmes aimed at adults in the 1990s and 2000s, they were often presented as 'aberrations' or else reinforced stereotypical binary gender roles (Halberstam 2018 in Lamari and Greenhill 2021, 169). Not that I'd have known, on a conscious level, any of this at the time – I was a tomboy who had the sense that I didn't fit in, who perhaps, in hindsight, knew and felt like I wasn't 'one of the girls' but had no way of expressing it fully. I had affinities with gender nonconforming characters, but the reasons why were a murky and painful mystery to be pushed aside and solved later.

In my PhD thesis, I discussed feeling a connection to tomboy George from the TV adaptation of *The Famous Five* (1978–79). But I also loved Buffy in *Buffy the Vampire Slayer* (1997–2003), who seemed to both conform to stereotypical feminine ideals of beauty, and simultaneously break stereotypes by being a strong, kick-ass 'warrior woman' (Early 2001, 12) on TV. It wasn't just the masculine characters I seemed to enjoy, as someone who would later identify as a trans man/trans masculine, but anyone who broke gender norms and stereotypes. Or, in fact, anyone who just stuck two fingers up at the world and refused to change who they were. This chapter explores why I felt such a kinship with Andrew in 'Nails' when I was a young person, before I had the vocabulary and means to fully explore my gender identity.

At about the same time as *Buffy* came into my life, I began painting my nails. Almost exclusively black. Other make-up came and went – I was never good at applying it and it didn't seem right on my face. While foundation, eye shadow and a number of other baffling products soon fell away, eyeliner stuck around until my early twenties. But I never stopped painting my nails. For about twenty-five years it's been a part of my armour, no matter what my gender identity and expression have been. It's still usually black, and I still end up with just as much over the edges as I do on my nails. Wearing my armour is a constant clean-up job.

'Nails' swam back into my consciousness more recently, when Mica, a transgender man in *The L-Word: Generation Q* (2019–present), was painted by his artist boyfriend as a merman. I thought to myself, why is it that trans and gender-diverse people are always connected to merfolk? In 2020, Starbucks in the UK created a mermaid cookie, with 50p from each sale going to the charity mermaids which supports gender-diverse children, young people and their families. In a study in the United States (Galman 2018) in which trans and gender-diverse children were given a scrap-booking task, twenty-five out of thirty-two transgirls aged between three and ten who took part 'drew or otherwise referenced mermaids in their autobiographical material. 12 of these 25 identified the drawings as self-portraits of one kind or another' (166). Children looked to mermaid play and association as a means of reflecting on power, identity, transformation and the movement between the cis and trans worlds (Galman 2018, 175–6).

In *The Little Mermaid*, the mermaid wishes to become human, and goes through a painful process to become so, which some scholars, such as Gerber (2017), have compared to surgery associated with somatic transition. In 'Nails', Andrew at first appears human and his transformation is into a merman, the opposite of *The Little Mermaid*. Despite at first experiencing feelings of being a freak, and being hidden away from society by his father, he eventually seems to find joy when reunited in the sea with his mother, a mermaid. This is an interesting message about happiness among 'your own kind', but at the price of never returning to mainstream society. Shuster and Westbrook (2022) discuss what they call a 'joy deficit' in relation to the sociological narratives told about trans people, noting a lack of focus on what trans people find joyful about their lives as well as what they find difficult (2). Trans people often experience 'rejection, discrimination, violence, uneven access to major institutions such as education and the law, bullying, stigma, and restrictive gender norms' (Schilt and Lagos 2017 in Shuster and Westbrook 2022, 2). Ignoring joy in academic research produces a negative focus which can result in 'unliveable lives' (Shuster and Westbook 2022, 5). The links between the experiences which some people have when they come out, and those of Andrew, are obvious. There can be a simultaneous joy and experience of pain, where something may have to be sacrificed in order to seek out those with tails and fins instead of those who live solely on the land. By identifying with Andrew I not only felt that I understood some of the pain he went through, but was able to cling to the joy he experiences at the end of his narrative journey. I didn't think of it entirely this way as a kid; rather, I was simply captivated as I watched Andrew transform. Very soon, part of me was desperate to find other people who were as 'weird' as me, and dreamed of swimming off happily into a sea of other weirdos, or at least a rippling mosh pit. I had never fit in, I was always 'too' something or 'not enough' something else – too goofy (thankfully braces helped), too studious, too boyish, not girly enough – you get the idea. Gerber (2017) outlines how 'recently the mermaid figure has been used to resist dominant discourses, particularly those surrounding gender' (1). Transgender readings of *The Little Mermaid* have focused on the mermaid's 'desire to transform' (1).

I always felt like the outsider, and Andrew in 'Nails' is no different. From the moment he arrives he is seen as strange, turning up in his old school uniform, complete with a twee straw hat, which the school bullies pick up on right away. Linda Twist is immediately interested in Andrew, and when auditions for a school play are announced, she begins practising with the hope that she'll act alongside Andrew. While she reads lines, her twin brother Pete comments, with a dreamy expression on his face: 'I wonder if that new kid can kiss. I mean act', already setting up a potential queering of Pete/ Andrew, or alternatively a transing of Andrew, if we presume that Pete is straight. It's clear that the audience are supposed to find this moment when Pete forgets himself and says something 'queer' funny. He corrects himself out of embarrassment, rather than let the comment simply speak for itself. Evoking Pullen's theory of the 'hetero media gaze' (2016, 18), potential queerness is treated here as a source of amusement, or even grossness, which becomes apparent again during the auditions. While this is going on, little brother Bronson muses that 'only dorks kiss girls'.

At the audition the children are in pairs to perform a scene where the lead characters kiss, with everyone in a boy/girl pair except two of the male school bullies whose efforts to find a partner are unsuccessful. Linda and Andrew are paired to practise for the auditions. The school bullies notice that Andrew is wearing gloves, which hide the new nails/scales growing beneath, again marking his difference. Two boy/girl pairs go first but fail to kiss; the bullies go next – Linda's brother and the class teacher look somewhat disgusted as the kiss between the two boys nearly happens, but mostly the other children seem amused. However, after the failed kiss between the boys, the teacher exclaims: 'An abomination. An abomination.' While he could be read as critiquing their poor acting, it seems unlikely as he didn't describe any of the boy/girl pairs who failed at the scene as an abomination. Linda, in her nervousness due to her attraction to Andrew, fluffs her line which should be: 'I will never forget the time we kissed on the old pier', and says instead: 'I'll never forget the time we pissed on the cold ear.' Andrew kindly starts the scene again, and with authority silences the other children who are laughing. Here he performs a dual role – stereotypically 'masculine' and dominating the room, but also kind and gentle in a way none of the other boys is, putting him in the stereotypically feminine or queer light that was hinted at when Pete wonders about kissing him. By kissing Linda, Andrew is viewed as a 'dork' if we refer back to little brother Bronson's earlier assessment that 'only dorks kiss girls'. He is masculine, feminine, a dork, different and a success all in one. Andrew and Linda get the scene right, kiss and are given the lead roles in the play. The teacher comments on Andrew's gloves saying they don't do much for him and he should lose them, showing a lack of respect for any possible reasons he could be wearing them and trying to make Andrew look like everyone else.

In my last year of primary school I was cast as Buttons in the school panto, for the reason, according to the teacher, that I 'looked like a boy anyway'. I gave up the part of Buttons in the end out of embarrassment. I was someone who looked both like a boy and a girl (or neither) depending on who was looking, who enjoyed nail varnish, and later *Buffy*, boys tracksuits and occasionally skirts, at the same time as apparently acting and looking like a boy. The me in the present hates how this is all reduced to the gender binary, knowing now that the possibilities for expression and identity beyond male and female, masculine and feminine, are potentially infinite (if you have the space, support and means to do so at least). But in the 1990s, in Essex, during Section 28, I could just about fathom that I didn't necessarily feel wholly one thing or another besides a generalized tendency towards 'the masculine'. In the 1980s, 1990s and right up until I finished my GCSEs in 2000, schools were subject to Section 28, which expressly forbade the 'promotion of homosexuality' (1988) in schools, so good luck ever hearing about trans stuff either. Many schools have yet to engage actively with educating staff and students about trans and gender diverse identities. Consequently, discrimination and bullying are widespread, leading to the isolation and marginality of trans youth (Wyss 2004) as well as higher rates of poor mental health (Becerra-Culqui et al. 2018; D'Augelli and Grossman 2006). There has been a presumption that children have no agency over their understanding of gender, but this is not the case (Riggs 2019, 86). Trans and gender nonconforming youth are subjected to heteronormative models of gender which condone violence against them (McBride and Schubotz 2017). In educational settings which often deny or demonize trans existence, they can experience severe bullying or a lack of acknowledgement that trans people exist (McBride and Schubotz 2017). Galman (2018), citing Schwartz (2012) and Sausa (2005) describes how 'research suggests that all children, but especially those that are transgender, benefit when adults listen to and validate their stories, giving children's expressed identities primacy instead of seeking to reify an adultist gender binary' (164). No one spoke to us about queer identity in the time of Section 28, let alone trans identity, and my efforts to seek advice were usually brushed aside as something that clearly wasn't meant to be spoken about or that would somehow conveniently go away. Making connections with characters on TV, in films and in books was my secret way of finding small slivers of validation – these people were like me, somehow.

As Andrew's transformation progresses, he finds simple tasks increasingly difficult. He struggles with his buttons as he dresses for the journey in his boat to get back to the island one day after school. Linda suggests taking his gloves off. Andrew replies that he can't, because 'er, well … I can't say', shrouding the reason in mystery, and also presenting him as not ready to 'come out' to her yet. Soon after, Linda arrives at school to find that Andrew isn't coming back. She decides to visit him on the island and sails over with her brother Pete. Andrew's reason for leaving school is to help his dad, who is studying the common ghost crab. Interestingly, the common ghost crab, which is the subject of Andrew's dad's research, can change colour, but the process occurs over a long period of time (Green 1964). This compares to Andrew's transformation which seems to be gradual and compares to the process of somatic transition which can take many years, or be a continuing process. 'Why don't you take your gloves off, it won't make any difference to me', says Linda, when Andrew drops a glass as now he cannot even hold things properly due to the scales and gloves. Initially he is angry, saying it's none of her business, but then takes the gloves off after she coaxes him. Andrew has three sets of finger nails and says: 'I'm a freak.' Linda makes a joke of it, offering: 'You could do with a manicure', which softens Andrew.

When Linda gets home she won't reveal to the others why Andrew wears gloves, refusing to out him.

Linda retrieves nail clippers from the bathroom and heads back to the island. When she arrives she overhears Andrew and his dad: 'What's wrong with me dad? Tell me, I've got a right to know. I'm turning into a freak. I wanna see a doctor.' Andrew's dad says that a doctor won't do any good. For someone transgender and under eighteen in the UK, in 1993, this rings true given what I've described with Section 28. Currently there is continual opposition to trans youth having access to support and the means of transition, with groups such as Transgender Trend using scaremongering tactics in their webpage, 'Current Evidence in the Treatment of Gender Dysphoric Children and Young People', calling transition mutilation, and framing transition and transgender identity from a biased perspective as something horrifying which is imposed on young people by adults, rather than something which they have any autonomy and say over themselves. They make vague claims about the number of people who detransition, yet a 2022 study in *The Lancet* showed that 98 per cent of youth who took puberty blockers went on to take gender-affirming hormones in adulthood (van der Loos et al. 2022). Look at the news and it won't be long before you find an article about the oppression of trans people or the 'dangers' of youth transition.

A storm comes, preventing Linda from visiting Andrew for many days as the water is too choppy to sail. Finally, the storm ends and Linda sails out again. However, she finds that Andrew is now in a wheelchair, his legs covered by a blanket, and he reassures Linda that it's alright and he now knows what is happening. Andrew's dad bursts in while they're talking saying: 'She's here! She's here!' referring to Andrew's mermaid mother. In a dramatic scene, Andrew's dad is swept off the rocks as he looks across the water for Andrew's mother. Andrew dives out of his wheelchair and into the water to save him. The scene cuts to underwater and Andrew is swimming, now with a tail instead of legs as the blanket falls away. After saving his dad, they turn and see Andrew's mother on the rocks waving. As Andrew leaves and has fully transformed his dad says: 'it's okay, it's okay'. These are the words gender nonconforming kids long to hear, just that it's okay to be themselves. It is a joyful moment, where we can balance out the 'joy deficit' for a few seconds when reading this as a trans text. They watch Andrew swim away and make a joke about Linda's fluffed line in the audition, and the final shot sees them laughing and happy, while Andrew and his mum swim away, also happy.

It's impossible to say how many times I saw 'Nails' as a kid and teenager. *Round the Twist* was a show I always made time for as it was unusual, funny and offered spooky, gross and weird tales that were unlike anything else on TV for young people at the time. In the hazy glow of my distant memories, it feels as though I watched 'Nails' a hundred times, but perhaps that's more a testament to the trans joy it left me with. Maybe it was a hundred, maybe it was three, who knows. For me, it resurfaced more frequently than any other episode and the image of Andrew would float around in my brain for a while. Andrew seemed to embody different aspects of gender in a more complicated way than George or Buffy. I was bullied at high school for being a 'geezerbird' (I'm from Essex if the language choice didn't give that away. We say it like it is here.). Others saw me as neither wholly a geezer or a bird, and that went for the teachers as well as the kids. Too much and not enough all at the same time. Andrew's transformation was just the briefest window of escape, twenty minutes or so out of a day that had most likely consisted of all the usual stuff kids deal with at school and a big helping of gender-based bullying on top. While I finish writing this, I am of course also painting my nails (black). They're still a mess, but that's okay.

Gerber (2017) highlights the importance of the little mermaid's silence in a transgender reading. In 'Nails' Andrew can speak, but his identity is silenced by teachers, bullies and even his own father when he eventually keeps him away from school on the island. At the time I was watching 'Nails', I was silenced by a lack of vocabulary, a lack of any information at all about who I might be or who I *could* be. When Andrew's extra 'nails' pushed through his skin it not only ignited my enduring love of body horror but, I like to think, also planted a little kernel of hope and joy that one day I might also somehow transform.

References

Anon. 1988. 'Section 28' in Local Government Act.

Becerra-Culqui, Tracy A., Yuan Liu, Rebecca Nash, Lee Cromwell, W. Dana Flanders, Darios Getahun, Shawn V Giammattei, Enid M. Hunkeler, Timothy L. Lash, Andrea Millman, Virginia P. Quinn, Brandi Robinson, Douglas Roblin, David E. Sandberg, Michael J. Silverberg, Vin Tangpricha and Michael Goodman. 2018. 'Mental Health of Transgender and Gender Nonconforming Youth Compared with Their Peers'. *Pediatrics* 141, no. 5. DOI: 10.1542/peds.2017-3845.

Buffy the Vampire Slayer. 1997–2003. [Television series] Mutant Energy Productions.

D'Augelli, Anthony R., and Arnold H. Grossman. 2006. 'Transgender Youth: Invisible and Vulnerable'. *Journal of Homosexuality* 51, no. 1: 111–28.

Early, F. H. 2001. 'Staking Her Claim: Buffy the Vampire Slayer as Transgressive Woman Warrior'. *Journal of Popular Culture*, 35, no. 3:11–27. https://doi.org/10.1111/j.0022-3840.2001.3503_11.x.

Galman, S. Campbell. 2018. 'Enchanted Selves: Transgender Children's Persistent Use of Mermaid Imagery in Self-Portraiture'. *Shima* 12, no. 2: 163–80. https://doi.org/10.21463/shima.12.2.14.

Gerber, Lizette. 2017. 'Transgender Bodies in "The Little Mermaid" and Swim Thru Fire'. *University Of Saskatchewan Undergraduate Research Journal* 4, no. 1: 1–9.

Green, J. P. 1964. 'Morphological Color Change in the Hawaiian Ghost Crab'. *The Biological Bulletin* 126, no. 3.

Halberstam, Jack. 2018. *Trans: A Quick and Quirky Account of Gender Variability*. California: University of California Press.

Jennings, Paul. 1985. *Unreal!* London: Puffin.

Lamari, Lou, and Pauline Greenhill. 2021. 'Double Trouble: Gender Fluid Heroism in American Children's Television'. *Open Cultural Studies* 5, no. 1: 169–80. https://doi.org/10.1515/culture-2020-0127.

van der Loos, Maria Anna Theodora Catharina, Sabine Elisabeth Hannema, Daniel Tatting Klink, Martin den Heijer and Chantal Maria Wiepjes. 2022. 'Continuation of Gender-Affirming Hormones in Transgender People Starting Puberty Suppression in Adolescence: A Cohort Study in the Netherlands'. *Child and Adolescent Health* 6, no. 12: 869–75. https://doi.org/10.1016/S2352-4642(22)00254-1.

McBride, Ruari-Santiago, and Dirk Schubotz. 2017. 'Living a Fairy Tale: The Educational Experiences of Transgender and Gender Non-conforming Youth in Northern Ireland'. *Child Care in Practice* 23, no. 3: 292–304. https://doi.org/10.1080/13575279.2017.1299112.

Putzi, J. 2017. '"None of This 'Trapped-in-a-Man's Body' Bullshit": Transgender Girls and Wrong-Body Discourse in Young Adult Fiction'. *Tulsa Studies in Women's Literature* 36, no. 2: 423–48.

Riggs, Damien W. 2019. *Working with Transgender Young People and Their Families : A Critical Developmental Approach*. Switzerland: Springer International.

Round the Twist. 1993. Episode 'Nails'. Esben Storm Australian Children's Television Foundation.

Sausa, L. A. 2005. 'Translating Research into Practice: Trans Youth Recommendations for Improving School Systems'. *Journal of Gay and Lesbian Issues in Education*, 3, no. 1: 15–28.

Schilt, Kristen, and Danya Lagos. 2017. 'The Development of Transgender Studies in Sociology'. *Annual Review of Sociology* 43: 425–43.

Schwartz, David. 2012. 'Listening to Children Imagining Gender: Observing the Inflation of an Idea'. *Journal of Homosexuality* 59, no. 3: 460–79.

Shuster, Stef M., and Laurel Westbrook. 2022. 'Reducing the Joy Deficit in Sociology: A Study of Transgender Joy'. *Social Problems* (spac034). https://doi.org/10.1093/socpro/spac034. Accessed 13 October 2023.

Spencer, Leland G. 2014. 'Performing Transgender Identity in *The Little Mermaid*: From Andersen to Disney'. *Communication Studies* 65, no.1: 112–27.

The Famous Five. 1978–9. [Television series] Southern Television.

The L-Word: Generation Q. 2019–23. [Television series] Showtime.

Wyss, S. 2004. 'This Was My Hell': The Violence Experienced by Gender Non-conforming Youth in US High Schools'. *International Journal of Qualitative Studies in Education* 17: 709–30.

7

Weird doubling in Wes Craven's *Stranger in Our House* (1978)

Miranda Corcoran

Writing on the phenomenon of Gothic television, Helen Wheatley argues that horror texts, created specifically to be viewed in the home regularly, centre around themes of family and domesticity, self-referentially echoing the site of their consumption. Wheatley outlines how Gothic television repeatedly references 'its domestic reception context, in order to produce its lucid sense of the uncanny' (2007, 7). In this way, a defining feature of TV horror is its discomfiting tendency to remind its audience that the space, in which they are comfortably watching television, could easily become the locus of unimaginable cruelty and violence. Frequently, television horror portrays the disruption of the domestic space, either at the hands of a powerful external force or those of an internal force that had previously been repressed. Paying attention to the deep connection between televisual horror and domestic terror, this chapter explores the presence of weird doubling in Wes Craven's 1978 made-for-TV movie *Stranger in Our House*. Craven's film, which was adapted from the popular YA novel *Summer of Fear* (Duncan 1976), centres on the middle-class Bryant family whose placid existence is disrupted by the arrival of an orphaned teenage cousin, Julia (Lee Purcell). Initially somewhat awkward and reserved, Julia swiftly integrates into both the family and the social circle of their adolescent daughter, Rachel (Linda Blair), through her uncanny capacity to replicate the signifiers of teen culture displayed by Rachel and her friends. As the narrative progresses, we learn that Julia is a witch named Sarah who, rather than being the daughter of Rachel's deceased relatives, was in actuality their housekeeper. Julia utilizes her occult powers to transform herself into an ordinary American teenager and experience the carefree, consumer-driven adolescence denied to her as a result of her family's poverty. Drawing on Mark Fisher's conception of the weird as 'that *which does not belong*', an experience or affect that 'brings to the familiar something which ordinarily lies beyond it' (2016, 10, emphasis in original), this chapter frames Julia as an intrusive force whose essential wrongness destabilizes the conceptual and ideological structures upon which middle-class American domesticity rests.

Stranger in Our House is a film grounded in the uncertainty of adolescent identity. Critic John Kenneth Muir observes that, like its literary source material, Craven's film 'capture[s] the universal fear of being replaced by someone "better"' (2006, 226), an anxiety that is especially potent during the awkward teenage years. After a brief prologue showing the death of Julia's parents, *Stranger in Our House* swiftly moves to establish its protagonist, Rachel, as a child of prosperous middle-class America. She is the responsible young daughter of a comfortable, loving family, helping her parents (Jeremy Slate and Carol Lawrence) and playing with her younger brother (James Jarnigan). Lingering on images of Rachel riding her horse at a nearby ranch and foregrounding the green lawns of her small neighbourhood, carefully watered against the California heat, *Stranger* establishes its setting as a peaceful, all-American suburb. Yet, once her cousin Julia arrives, brought to the West Coast after being orphaned, Rachel's sense of self is displaced. Her cousin begins to assume facets of Rachel's persona – wearing her clothes, styling her hair to mimic Rachel's and eventually stealing her boyfriend (Jeff McCracken) – and as such, Rachel's sense of self begins to falter. She recedes into the background as Julia lays claim to her family, her friends and her essential selfhood.

Julia's power to corrupt the idyllic environs of suburbia is reflective of broader concerns, both cultural and cinematic, as is her capacity to undermine middle-class American values. In her study of the socio-economic factors influencing the evolution of the slasher film during the long 1980s, Kara M. Kvaran observes how a faltering economy and an uncertain future resulted in a glut of low-budget films about suburban landscapes menaced by some anonymous monstrous force. Kvaran points out these films, in which teens are abandoned and betrayed by the adults who are supposed to protect them (parents, teachers, police offices) and left to face an implacable killer alone (2016, 960), embody the anxieties of a generation who knew they would never be as financially successful as their parents (2016, 956). At the same time, the youthful Julia's destructive influence on the family mirrors the fears held by many middle-class adults, who worried that their flight to the placid post-war suburbs would not protect their children from the tumult of the period's counterculture. Wes Craven, who had already directed *The Last House on the Left* (1972) and *The Hills Have Eyes* (1977) and would go on to direct *A Nightmare on Elm Street* (1984) and *Scream* (1996), infuses *Stranger* with a characteristic nihilism, as he utilizes one of his favourite themes, the destruction of the middle-class American family at the hands of a sinister external force. However, where other works in Craven's filmography imagine this destruction in essentially violent terms, *Stranger* is more concerned with the uncanny or weird nature of the invading force. In *Stranger*, Julia unsettles the family dynamic not so much through violence (although, she does commit a number of violent acts), but rather through the incongruity of her presence and her uncanny appropriation of Rachel's identity.

In *The Weird and the Eerie*, Mark Fisher describes the phenomenon of weirdness, as well as the closely related category of the eerie, as grounded in the 'strange – not the horrific' (2016, 8). For Fisher, the weird is not overtly terrifying. Instead, it has a 'fascination, for the outside, for that which lies beyond standard perception, cognition and experience' (8). The weird has much in common with the Freudian conception of the uncanny, the fearful sensation evoked by that which is 'familiar and old-established in the mind and which has become alienated from it only through the process of repression' (Freud 1955, 241). Like the uncanny, the weird is an affect, a mood or sensation, but it is also a mode of perception, a mode of film and fiction, even a mode of being (Fisher 2016, 9). However, where the weird deviates from the uncanny is that while the uncanny 'operates by always processing the outside through the gaps and impasses of the inside', the weird makes a counter movement, allowing us to view the inside from the outside (Fisher 2016, 10). As Fisher further elucidates: 'the weird is that *which does not belong*. The weird brings to the familiar something which ordinarily lies beyond it, and which cannot be reconciled with the "homely" (even as its negation)' (10–11). In *Stranger*, Julia paradigmatically fulfils the function of the weird. Her appearance within the familiar home is strange rather than horrific, as her manipulation of the family is predicated on subtle occult manoeuvrings rather than outright violence. When Rachel's parents bring Julia home, it is immediately apparent that she does not belong, that she represents a discomfiting form of Otherness. She dresses in strange archaic clothing and speaks with an accent characteristic of the remote Ozarks region, despite ostensibly hailing from Massachusetts. Moreover, Julia holds to rural Ozark superstitions, such as a dropped piece of cutlery predicting the ring of a doorbell, and she hides a single tooth in her suitcase. Although the family accepts Julia as their cousin/niece, she does not initially fit in with their bourgeois mannerisms and outlook. Their apparent familial relationship appears puzzling, as Julia seems awkward and uncomfortable in the presence of her supposed relatives.

Julia's appearance within the family home thus evokes a sense of 'wrongness'. She does not belong and so becomes a disturbing, ultimately disruptive, presence within the familiar domestic space. She is, as Fisher claims of the 'weird entity', a being so strange that it makes us feel that it should not exist here. Yet if the entity or object is here, then the categories which we have up until now used to make sense of the world cannot be valid. (15)

Indeed, Julia's presence explicitly troubles the borders that separate self from Other, inside from outside, while also collapsing the social categories that seal off the (sub)urban from the rural, the bourgeoise from the proletariat. As the film progresses, we learn that Julia does not belong in the solidly middle-class milieu of Rachel and her parents. Rather, it is revealed that Julia was never the cousin/niece of the Bryant family, but an employee of their now-deceased relatives, a housekeeper named Sarah. This revelation is hinted at early in the film as we clearly see Julia/Sarah covet the wealth and comfort possessed by the Bryants. As Rachel shows her around their home, Julia/Sarah remarks, 'You sure have a lot of pretty things. Your daddy must make a lot of money.' In the original novel upon which the film is based – Lois Duncan's *Summer of Fear* – Sarah's working-class status is made even more explicit. After being revealed as an imposter, Julia/Sarah explains that she worked as a 'cook and cleaning girl' for Rachel's relatives (Duncan 1976, 198). However, she notes that she was hired because she possessed 'the gift of witchcraft handed down to me from my grandmother', and her employers were interested in learning about this (Duncan 1976, 198). Julia/Sarah goes on to explain that she caused the deaths of her employers and posed as their orphaned daughter because she was envious of their comfortable middle-class existence and felt that this was the only way to escape the generational poverty into which she had been born. When Rachel naively suggests that Julia/Sarah could have just moved to a big city, found a job and lived out the American fantasy of upward mobility, the young witch scoffs:

Without schoolin'? Without trainin'? What would do when I got there – scrub floors? What does a girl like me do, took out of school at the age of ten to help raise the little ones … Sure, I know the art of witchcraft, I learned it from my gram and her from hers, but a lot of good it would do me shut off in the hills. And in the city alone, what good there either? I'd end up as a waitress on some dingy little diner or being somebody's motel maid. (Duncan 1976, 200)

Julia/Sarah's weird intrusion into the Bryant home, the profound sense of wrongness that attends her arrival, suggests that the categories the Bryants had employed to make sense of the world are no longer valid. Class distinctions collapse, and the boundary between the strange and the familiar is effaced. While *Stranger* is less overt in its treatment of class disparity than *Summer of Fear*, Julia's identity, as the housekeeper Sarah, is revealed towards the end of the film. As in the source novel, her socio-economic difference serves as a disruptive force, corrupting the homogenous bourgeois values of the Bryant home and troubling the boundaries that separate the impoverished Other from the stable, middle-class self.

In his massively influential essay, 'An Introduction to the American Horror Film', the critic Robin Wood anticipates Fisher's conception of the weird as that which undermines the categories we use to structure knowledge and experience. Wood argues that in a society demarcated by repression (of sexual, gendered, ethnic and classed Others), the 'true subject of the horror genre is the struggle for recognition of all that our civilization *represses* or *oppresses*' (2020, 113). For Wood, then, the horror movie monster is often emblematic of a marginalized group or identity that (white, bourgeois, heteronormative) American society would prefer not to acknowledge. Among these repressed Others, who invariably return in some monstrous form, we find women, other cultures, various ethnic groups, alternative political systems and those who deviate from sexual norms (Wood 2020, 112–13). Crucially, for any discussion of *Stranger*, we also find the proletariat among Wood's list of Others. Wood observes that the working class often function as an unsettling inversion of accepted bourgeois values, which is simultaneously repulsive and enticing: 'The bourgeois obsession with cleanliness, which psychoanalysis shows to be closely associated, as outward symptom, with sexual repression, and bourgeois sexual repression itself, find their inverse reflections in the myths of working-class squalor and sexuality' (112). In order to maintain the hegemony of bourgeois capitalism, not only must the Other be repressed, but it must also be 'projected outwards in order to be hated and disowned' (111). In *Stranger*, this excision of the working-class Other fails, as Julia/Sarah infiltrates the Bryant home and adopts the superficial signifiers of bourgeois adolescence through her calculated imitation of Rachel. Whatever boundaries might have separated the middle class from the working class are thus seen to waver and become porous.

Concomitantly, Julia/Sarah's corruption of the Bryant home also recalls a series of contemporary anxieties about youth culture, its association with the occult and its inherently transgressive potential. When Duncan's novel was originally published in 1976, American culture was increasingly concerned about its children's engagement with alternative spiritualities and new religious movements. According to Jeffrey S. Victor, the Satanic Panic that gripped the United States and much of the Anglophone world in the 1980s and early 1990s had its origins in the youth culture movement of previous decades (1993, 8). Many young people in the 1960s and 1970s felt alienated by Judaeo-Christian religious traditions and turned to new spiritual alternatives that had their roots in charismatic Protestantism, non-Christian faiths, Asian spiritual systems, the human potential movement and occultism (Victor 1993, 8). While many such groups were comparatively innocuous, a number of high-profile cases like the Tate-LaBianca Murders in 1969 and the mass suicides at the Jonestown compound in 1978 created a widespread perception that new religious movements were dangerous, brainwashing and coercing young people into joining sinister organizations. Victor notes that during the early 1970s, a network of local and nationwide anti-cult organizations was formed to counteract the influence of new religions (8). Often spearheaded by the parents of young people 'lost' to cults, groups like the Cult Awareness Network and the American Family Foundation sought to educate the public on the dangers of cults. Similarly, a variety of fundamentalist Protestant organizations developed effective propaganda for countering the allure of new spiritualities (Victor 1993, 8). Consequently, religious groups such as the Children of God and the International Society for Krishna Consciousness ('Hare Krishna') became the subject of sensational media reporting on the growth of so-called cults (Victor 1993, 9). Young people in particular were thought to be uniquely susceptible to the recruitment tactics of these groups, who were often thought to prey on the vulnerable.

In reality, many ideas and practices associated with the occult and new religious movements – from astrology to psychic powers and astral projection – had entered the mainstream during the 1960s and 1970s. Magazines on astrology and magic as well as courses on channelling and astral projection were available throughout the United States at this time. Indeed, many large cities boasted specialized occult bookstores, while smaller towns may have had to be content with an occult or 'New Age' section springing up in an existing shop. Writing in the early 1970s, sociologist Martin Marty described this mainstreaming of the occult in terms of the development of an 'Occult Establishment'. This process entails the creation of a 'safe and sane "aboveground" expression, whose literature gives every sign of being beamed at what is now usually called "middle America", the "silent majority", or "consensus-USA"' (1970, 216). While this mainstreaming of occultism may have been largely grounded in economic exigencies ('cashing in' on the post-war spiritual awakening), Marty's identification of an occult establishment effectively dismantles the notion that occulture was an entirely underground phenomenon, characterized by antisocial philosophies, sexual deviance and drug use. Nevertheless, the popular perception of new religious movements and alternative spiritualities remained bound up with images of rebellious, disaffected youth whose commitment to abnormal belief systems could result in acts of extreme violence.

One of the most enduring images of this period was the haunting sight of young women, their heads shaved and their eyes blank, sitting on the ground outside the Los Angeles Hall of Justice. Acolytes of cult leader Charles Manson, the women expressed their devotion through the vigil they held outside the building where Manson was being tried for his part in the Tate-LaBianca Murders that occurred during the summer of 1969. When Manson carved an 'X' on his forehead, they did the same. When Manson shaved his head, claiming that 'I am the Devil, and the Devil always has a bald head', the girls followed suit (Bugliosi and Gentry 2015, 571). Although

Manson gathered scores of followers, both male and female, under the banner of his so-called Family, it was the image of devoted young women, in their teens and twenties, professing their willingness to kill and die for Manson that gripped the public imagination. They were collectively known as the 'Manson Girls', and there exists a popular perception that their fanaticism was somehow connected to their youth and femininity. As such, the girls became a byword for the dangers of the counterculture and the propensity for new religious movements to prey on vulnerable, directionless young people. At the same time, early media reports on the slaying of actor Sharon Tate and the other inhabitants of 10050 Cielo Drive suggested that the murders were linked to the occult. Papers mentioned a 'blood orgy', 'ritualistic slayings' and 'overtones of a weird religious rite' (O'Neill and Piepenbring 2020, 22). Though much of this reporting would prove to be inaccurate – a product of the cultural paranoia that was blossoming at the end of the 1960s – the images of young women, little more than girls, who were caught up in the mesmeric thrall of a sinister cult leader, convinced Americans that their children were defenceless against the dangerous new ideas that were circulating in the counterculture.

The Manson Girls embodied a growing fear among middle-class Americans, who worried that their children had become increasingly strange, even threatening. According to Robin Wood, who lists children alongside the proletariat in his enumeration of the forces of Otherness that threaten the bourgeois nuclear family, 'the "otherness" of children … is that which is repressed in us, and what we, in turn, repress in our children, seeking to mold them into replicas of ourselves, perpetuators of a discredited tradition' (2020, 113). Thus, the maintenance of the bourgeois American family, its social and economic primacy, is dependent upon the absorption or destruction of any deviance on the part of its children. Significantly, Wood traces the preoccupation with the child as an unsettling manifestation of Otherness to the late 1960s, as he notes that 'Since *Rosemary's Baby* [1968], children have figured prominently in horror films as the monster or its medium' (2020, 114). From here, Wood goes on to cite examples of monstrous or uncanny children including devil child Damien from *The Omen* (Donner 1976) and child killer Michael Myers who murders his older sister in the opening scene of *Halloween* (Carpenter 1978). He also references Regan MacNeill from *The Exorcist* (Friedkin 1973), the possessed pre-teen played by Linda Blair whose casting in *Stranger* was undoubtedly an attempt to capitalize on her most famous role.[1] For Wood, then, the generational conflict between staid middle-class adults and their wayward children was encapsulated in the image of the monstrous child, a creature often aligned with Satanism, witchcraft or other countercultural practices (2020, 114–15). In horror films

---

[1] Outside of the horror genre, an earlier version of the monstrous child can be found in the 1956 film *The Bad Seed*, which is based on William March's 1954 novel of the same name.

of this period, comfortable, middle-class families are besieged by demonic or uncanny children who imbue their placid lives with chaotic violence. The intergenerational conflict that defines these texts thus seems reflective of a growing rift between parents and children, as well as the fear that rebellious youth might destabilize the order and hierarchy associated with the middle-class patriarchal family unit. In the 1960s and 1970s the bourgeoisie began to worry that the suburban refuges they had constructed for themselves in order to escape the crime, pollution and degradation of the city were vulnerable to the chaotic incursions of the period's sociopolitical upheavals. Indeed, one of the most unsettling pieces of information to emerge about the Manson family was their propensity for 'creepy crawling'. Defining this practice in his study of the social and cultural afterlives of the Manson murders, Jeffrey Melnick writes,

> What the Family meant by creepy crawling was at once simple and profoundly upsetting. Leaving their communal home at Spahn Ranch in the San Fernando Valley, the Family would light out for private homes. Once inside, the Family members would not harm the sleeping family members. Instead, they would rearrange some of the furniture. That's all. Stealing was sometimes part of the agenda, especially toward the end, but it was not the *raison d'être*. (2019, 10)

While creepy crawling did not involve violence, at most entailing some petty theft, it was a deeply unsettling practice, as the family essentially breached the borders of the middle-class home, violating the safety associated with bourgeois domesticity. As Melnick goes on to explain, creepy crawling was a disturbing phenomenon not because it left blood and chaos in its wake, but rather because it simply left behind 'the bare minimum of evidence that the sanctity of the private home had been breached – that the Family had paid a visit to this family' (10).

This conception of the middle-class patriarchal family violated by a threatening manifestation of oppositional youth culture is at the heart of *Stranger in Our House*. Indeed, even the title – changed from *Summer of Fear* for the film adaptation – suggests the incursion of an unsettling external force, an entity that does not belong. Julia/Sarah's presence within the Bryant family home threatens to radically destabilize the strictures upon which the bourgeois nuclear family is founded. In a number of scenes, she is explicitly aligned with the violence thought to be endemic to the counterculture and cultic groups. After all, Julia/Sarah is a witch who uses her abilities to attack the normative bulwark of the American family. Her strangeness is bound up with her occult powers. Throughout the film, Julia/Sarah uses magic to undermine the family unit. She isolates Rachel from her parents and siblings, employing various spells and sundry modes of manipulation to turn the family members against one another. At the same time, she also upends the relational and sexual mores upon which the family rest. Julia/Sarah repeatedly attempts to seduce Rachel's father, her nominal uncle, in order to assume the role of his wife. In one scene, she runs after him as he walks to the car, calling 'Tom, you forgot your suitcase'. Not only does she return the suitcase like a dutiful wife, but she also kisses him before he leaves for work. In another scene, Julia/Sarah, believing she has killed Rachel's mother, dresses in her negligee, symbolically appropriating her role within the household. In this way, *Stranger in Our House* can be situated within a series of broader social transformations that were taking place in the 1960s and 1970s. The film presents the bourgeois family home as a space defined by the fantasy of security and separation, a belief in the domestic sphere as an inviolable structure that screens the family from the chaos of the outside world. However, once Julia/Sarah arrives, she instigates the collapse of the boundaries between inside and outside, private and public. As Vivian Sobchack explains in her study of the home in horror cinema of the 1970s and 1980s, by the second half of the twentieth century, the power of the domestic to repel the tumult of sociopolitical change has been weakened.

> Rather than serving bourgeois patriarchy as a place of refuge from the social upheavals of the last two decades (many of which have been initiated by the young and women), the family has become the site of them – and now serves as a sign of their representation. Not only has the bourgeois distinction between family members and alien Others, between private home and public space, between personal microcosm and socio-political macrocosm been exposed as myth, but also the family itself has been exposed as a cultural construction, as a set of signifying, as well as significant practices. (1987, 178)

Stranger in Our House thus suggests that the American family is a construct rather than an inviolable, a priori institution. As with Fisher's formulation of the weird, *Stranger* brings to the familiar that which exceeds its conventional boundaries, necessitating a collapse of the categories ordinarily employed to make sense of the world. In this case, Julia/Sarah initiates the erosion of the borders that separate strange and familiar, inside from outside, Self from Other.

Although Julia/Sarah's disruption of bourgeois family norms is undoubtedly disconcerting – particularly when her seduction of Rachel's father confuses the categories of lover/patriarch, sexual partner/family member – it is through her unsettling powers of imitation that Julia/Sarah becomes undeniably, irrevocably weird. As noted previously, when Julia/Sarah first arrives at the Bryant's comfortable suburban home, she does not fit in with the rest of the family. Her clothing and appearance are old-fashioned, and her behaviour is awkward. Despite attempting to mask her rural, impoverished origins, her accent repeatedly threatens to give her away. However, not long after her arrival, Rachel brings 'cousin Julia' shopping with her and her friends. Julia slips away and returns, having surreptitiously visited a hairdresser, with a new style similar to Rachel's fashionable cut. When Rachel comments on her new look, Julia responds that she asked the hairdresser to 'make me look half as nice as you'. Later, Julia begins to dress like Rachel, even wearing Rachel's handmade dress to a school dance. Julia/Sarah's usurpation of Rachel's identity is predicated on a form of weird doubling whereby Julia/Sarah brings a sense of strangeness to the familiar, homely space by transforming herself into a replica of her 'cousin', essentially becoming a double of sorts.

In Freud's work on the uncanny, the double is associated with the later stages of the ego's development during which a 'special agency' is formed (234). This agency 'has the function of observing and criticizing the self and of exercising a censorship within the mind' (234). Thus, 'offensive' or incongruous mental material is often projected outwards onto the figure of the double (235). In this way, encountering one's double becomes an uncanny experience because it entails 'coming face to face with long-repressed desires and fears' (Fonseca 2007, 192). Beyond Freud's writings, the double has an even broader cultural resonance. The double, often referred to as the doppelganger, is regularly understood as a 'performer of identity, so that it is not strictly a mirror image, reflecting the subject back exactly as it is, for there must be some subversion and autonomy in its very presence' (Fonseca 2007, 189). Although Julia is not a project of Rachel's mind – she is possessed of a very real and independent veracity – she nevertheless functions as a double. She transforms herself into a distorted reflection of Rachel, adopting the superficial signifiers of middle-class adolescent identity (a fashionable hairstyle and clothing, a peer group, a boyfriend). For Rachel, Julia/Sarah's metamorphic powers are intimately and personally disturbing. As the witch takes on more and more of Rachel's traits, Rachel herself begins to feel that she is losing her identity. This loss of self, its usurpation by the doppelganger is a recurrent motif in Gothic fiction. Herdman notes that while the double often exists in a 'dependent relation to the original', in many texts the 'double comes to dominate, control, and usurp the functions of the subject' (qtd in Fonseca 2007, 189). Yet, as well as portraying the intimate terror of feeling one's identity slip away, *Stranger* also engages with anxieties about the fragility of social categories. In taking on the guise of Rachel's double, Julia/Sarah draws attention to the fluid nature of class boundaries, showing the ease with which socio-economic categories can be traversed. Moreover, Julia/Sarah embodies the conception of the classed Other as a repressed facet of the self that must, according to Wood, be 'projected outwards in order to be hated and disowned' (2020, 111). In this way, Julia/Sarah can be read as a decidedly weird permutation of the double because her presence in the heart of the bourgeois family suggests that the categories of class and identity that we employ to structure the world and make meaningful its experience 'cannot be valid' (Fisher 2016, 15). The suburban home ceases to function as an inviolable bulwark, protecting the family from the world beyond their affluent demographic.

Julia/Sarah's propensity for weird doubling can also be seen in her use of Appalachian folk magic, which she practises throughout the film. In order to remove obstacles and further integrate into the Bryant family, Julia/Sarah employs sympathetic magic. She uses spells to bend people to her will and to harm them when they challenge her. More specifically, the rituals that Julia/Sarah performs can be defined as sympathetic magic. As discussed by the anthropologist and folklorist James Frazer, sympathetic magic is 'based on the principles of similarity and contagion' (qtd in Hong 2021, 255). In his pioneering 1890 study *The Golden Bough*, Frazer writes that

> If we analyse the principles of thought on which magic is based, they will probably be found to resolve themselves into two: first, that like produces like, or that an effect resembles its cause; and, second, that things which have once been in contact with each other continue to act on each other at a distance after the physical contact has been severed. (2009, 36)

According to Frazer's definitions, the two primary forms of sympathetic magic are grounded in notions of doubling and repetition. The first principle of sympathetic magic asserts that 'like produces like', so a magician who performs a specific action in the context of a ritual or spell will cause a similar action to occur in the wider world. For instance, if a magician stabs a doll or poppet through the eyes, then the intended subject of their spell will go blind. The second principle is based on the belief that objects that have been in contact with an individual maintain an enduring connection to that person and can therefore be used to work magic upon that person. It is for this reason that a wide variety of magical rites call for hair, teeth or fingernail clippings taken from the intended subject of the spell. Even though these body parts are no longer in contact with the person from whom they have been taken, their earlier proximity to that individual means that they will nevertheless serve as a powerful magical conduit. In this way, sympathetic magic is all about reflection, replication and doubling.

This mode of uncanny repetition defines Julia/Sarah's magical practice in *Stranger*. When she accelerates her plan to usurp Rachel's social position, Julia/Sarah uses magic to make her 'cousin' sick and prevent her from attending a school dance with her boyfriend. To achieve this, Julia/Sarah steals strands of Rachel's hair from the brush on her dressing table and burns it. Recalling Frazer's second principle of sympathetic magic, Julia/Sarah utilizes biological material that was once in close contact with Rachel to cause a serious physical illness. Moreover, just as Julia/Sarah plucks the hair from Rachel's brush, a symbol of her adolescent vanity, so too does her spell tarnish Rachel's beauty, causing her to break out in a disfiguring, albeit temporary, rash. Later, Julia/Sarah decides to rid the family of Rachel's horse, both as a means of hurting Rachel and in retaliation for the animal's overt dislike of the young witch. In order to achieve this, Julia/Sarah creates a wax figure of the horse, complete with real hair taken from the animal's mane, and destroys it. While this spell does recall the second principle of sympathetic magic – the hair that was once in contact with the horse continues to act upon the animal – it is more closely aligned with the first. The evil enacted on the image of the horse affects the original, so when Julia/Sarah harms the wax totem, the horse itself is also harmed. The forms of magic employed by Julia/Sarah are disturbing not simply because of their results but because of how they are predicated on mirroring, doubling and repetition, creating an uncanny duality that recalls the metamorphic power of the witch herself.

Helen Wheatley argues that 'the uncanny can be found in the very structure of Gothic television' (2007, 7). In television programmes and made-for-TV movies, uncanny motifs manifest both thematically and formally, in repeated refrains, recurring themes and doubled images. As Wheatley explains, Gothic television is marked out by 'a proclivity towards the structures and images of the uncanny (repetitions, returns, déjà vu, premonitions, ghosts, doppelgangers, animated inanimate objects and severed body parts, etc.)' (2007, 3). *Stranger* incorporates and moves beyond these uncanny paradigms, as the figure of Julia/Sarah manifests as something more profoundly disturbing than the traditional uncanny. Where the uncanny, as outlined in Freud's 1919 essay of the same name, articulates the unique sense of unease associated with the *unheimlich* (the unhomely). For Freud, the sensation of uncanniness arises when we encounter an image, idea, object or entity that is not alien or strange, but rather connected to 'something which is familiar and old-established in the mind and which has become alienated from it only through the process of repression' (240). Uncanny sensations thus arise when we are confronted with something 'which ought to have remained hidden but has come to light' (Freud 1955, 240). Although Julia/Sarah can be understood through the lens of the uncanny – she does, after all, embody a form of socio-economic Otherness and youthful rebellion that must be excised to ensure the coherence of the bourgeois family unit – her discomfiting nature extends beyond the boundaries of the unhomely. Her arrival at the Bryant home brings with it an Otherness that cannot be reconciled with the familiarity of home and family, even as its negation or opposite (Fisher 2016, 10). The world Julia/Sarah represents is one in which cultural and class differences coalesce into a preternatural Otherness. While the form of magic practised by Julia/Sarah is a complicated mix of cultural traditions, incorporating elements of European Christianity, pre-Christian practices, Indigenous and African beliefs, and Celtic lore, it is often understood simplistically by both outsiders and scholars studying the phenomenon as a form of irrationality 'whose boundaries in turn constitute "the rational" as the privileged category' (Cunningham 2010, 54). The Appalachian folk magic practised by Julia/ Sarah and passed down from her grandmother is predicated on the belief that Appalachia is itself 'God's promised land' and that those who live there live in the 'time of the original creation' (Humphrey qtd in Cunningham 2010, 57). Using Christian theology as its basis, these belief systems advocate planting crops according to moon signs and 'other traditionary forms of participation in cosmic processes' (Cunningham 2010, 57). Practitioners of this kind of folk magic, despite incorporating Christian ideas into their rituals, are generally condemned by Christian fundamentalists for their eclecticism and engagement with the occult (Cunningham 2010, 57). Julia/ Sarah thus represents a weird intrusion into the Bryants' ordered existence because not only does she embody a disruptive form of class difference, as well as the chaotic potential of oppositional youth culture, but she also signifies an 'irrational', impossible to categorize supernaturalism. Her magic is chaotic, hybrid and unstable. It depends, as noted earlier, on sinister acts of doubling. However, this magic goes beyond being merely uncanny because it brings to the familiar domestic realm something which ordinarily lies beyond it.

The sense that Julia/Sarah functions as a weird intrusion into the ordinarily prosaic space of the middle-class American family can also be seen in the film's use of naturalistic lighting, conventional camera angles and comparatively mundane sets and costuming. Gregory A. Waller observes that made-for-TV movies like *Stranger in Our House* genuinely prioritize narrative over visual creativity or formal experimentation: 'The visual style of the typical telefilm is unobtrusively subordinated to "telling the story"; hence the reliance on close-ups and medium shots, high-key lighting, continuity editing, and function style' (1987, 147). This emphasis on narrative is also characteristic of Craven's style. Aside from *A Nightmare on Elm Street*, which employs surrealistic imagery in order to evoke horrifying dreamscapes, Craven's oeuvre tends to lean more towards realism. His 1970s exploitation films, particularly *Last House on the Left* and *The Hills Have Eyes*, employ naturalistic framing and high-key lighting to create an uncomfortable verisimilitude, while later works like *Scream* (1996) also tend to hew closely towards realist modes of expression, favouring plot and character over formal innovation. *Stranger* is similarly defined by an emphasis on the mundane. The film's colour palette is overwhelmingly beige, reflecting contemporary trends in decor and fashion. Scenes are brightly light, and the camera remains static, capturing performers in medium shots, and only moving in for the occasional dramatic close-up. Editing too emphasizes continuity as opposed to montage or juxtaposition. The atmosphere evoked

is therefore one of staid, suburban normalcy. The only moments in which
the film departs from its realistic aesthetic are when we see Julia/Sarah work
her magic. Especially in the film's climax, she is presented with unnatural
red eyes, wearing a long flowing black dress. In this scene where she utilizes
magic to blow apart doors and chases Rachel with a knife, Julia appears
decidedly wild and witchy. Special effects accentuate her otherworldliness,
positioning her as a preternatural intruder within the mundane environs of
the Bryant family home. However, these moments of explicit supernaturalism
are few and far between, creating a sense that Julia/Sarah exists beyond the
standard experience of middle-class suburban America.

Like the archetypal televisual Gothic described by Wheatley, *Stranger*
foregrounds its 'domestic reception context' (2007, 7). The film, explicitly
referencing the site of its consumption, frames the home as mundane and
secure, a prosaic realm into which something strange and frightening has
penetrated. Julia/Sarah's disruption of the domestic is profoundly disturbing,
bearing traces of the Freudian uncanny. However, *Stranger*'s treatment of
Julia/Sarah, her innate ability to unsettle experiential categories, enables her
to move beyond uncanniness into the realm of the weird. She embodies
an unsettling quality that rather than simply evoking repressed familiarity
extends 'beyond standard perception, cognition and experience' (Fisher
2016, 8). Her disturbing magical abilities, predicated as they are upon acts
of doubling and repetition, efface the boundaries separating the familiar and
the alien, the self and the Other, family and stranger, the bourgeois and the
proletariat. As Waller notes, Julia/Sarah is framed as an evil force, capable
of perverting the family ideal:

> Without the intrusion of external, unambiguously evil, supernatural
> forces, the family would continue its uneventful, unruffled course – with
> no antagonism between affectionate children and their well-educated,
> well-meaning parents, and no rupture between the hardworking, caring
> husband and his supportive, talented, and independent-but-not-too-
> independent wife. However, once evil, clothed in some innocent and
> familiar guise, has been invited in, the average family (which is 'average',
> needless to say, only according to primetime television) proves susceptible
> to temptation and corruption. (1987, 156)

In the final moments of the film, once Julia/Sarah has been expelled from the
Bryant home, the family appears restored, peaceful and loving once again.
Rachel's father even asks her forgiveness for doubting her claims about Julia/
Sarah's sinister intentions. However, the rupture that split the family during
Julia/Sarah's time with them suggests that the family unit is vulnerable to
external corruption and remains so. The weird entity may be expelled, but
her capacity to destabilize familial relationships suggests that the cultural
categories and hierarchies upon which the family depends are fragile.

References

Bugliosi, Vincent, and Curt Gentry. 2015. *Helter Skelter: The True Story of the Manson Murders*. London: Arrow.

Cunningham, Rodger. 2010. 'The Green Side of Life: Appalachian Magic as a Site of Resistance'. *Appalachian Heritage* 38, no. 2: 54–62, 101.

Duncan, Lois. 1976. *Summer of Fear*. Boston: Little Brown.

Exorcist, The. 1973. [Film; Director: William Friedkin]. Warner Brothers.

Fisher, Mark. 2016. *The Weird and the Eerie*. London: Repeater.

Fonseca, Tony. 2007. 'The Doppelganger'. In *Icons of Horror and the Supernatural: An Encyclopedia of Our Worst Nightmares*, vol. 1, edited by S. T. Joshi, 187–214. Westport, CT: Greenwood.

Frazer, James. 2009. *The Golden Bough: A Study of Magic and Religion*. Portland, OR: Floating Press.

Freud, Sigmund. 1955. 'The 'Uncanny'. In *The Standard Edition of the Complete Psychological Works of Sigmund Freud, Volume XVII (1917–1919)*, translated by James Strachey, 217–56. London: Hogarth.

Hong, Ze. 2021. 'A Cognitive Account of Manipulative Sympathetic Magic'. *Religion, Brain and Behaviour* 12, no. 3: 254–70.

Kvaran, Kara M. 2016. '"You're All Doomed!" A Socioeconomic Analysis of Slasher Films'. *Journal of American Studies* 50, no. 4: 953–70.

Marty, Martin. 1970. 'The Occult Establishment'. *Social Research* 37, no. 2: 212–30.

Melnick, Jeffrey. 2019. *Charles Manson's Creepy Crawl: The Many Lives of America's Most Infamous Family*. New York: Arcade.

Muir, John Kenneth. 2006. *Wes Craven: The Art of Horror*. Jefferson, NC: McFarland.

O'Neill, Tom, and Dan Piepenbring. 2020. *Chaos: Charles Manson, the Cia, and the Secret History of the Sixties*. Boston: Back Bay.

Sobchack, Vivian. 1987. 'Bringing It All Back Home: Family Economy and Generic Exchange'. In *American Horrors: Essays on the Modern American Horror Film*, edited by Gregory A. Waller, 175–94. Champaign, IL: University of Illinois Press.

Victor, Jeffrey S. 1993. *Satanic Panic: The Creation of a Contemporary Legend*. Peru, IL: Open Court.

Waller, Gregory, A. 1987. 'Made-for-Television Horror Films'. In *American Horrors: Essays on the Modern American Horror* Film, edited by Gregory A. Waller, 145–61. Champaign, IL: University of Illinois Press.

Wheatley, Helen. 2007. *Gothic Television*. Manchester: Manchester University Press.

Wood, Robin. 2020. 'An Introduction to the American Horror Film'. In *The Monster Theory Reader*, edited by Jeffrey Andrew Weinstock, 108–35. Minneapolis, MN: University of Minnesota Press.

8

Suburban eerie: *The Demon Headmaster* (BBC 1, 1996–98) and *The Demon Headmaster* (CBBC, 2019) as neoliberal folk horror

Adam Whybray

The antagonists of children's horror often appear benign upon the surface. The monsters of adults' horror films – the likes of Jason Voorhees, Freddy Krueger and the Babadook – are generally overtly aggressive and murderous, with more circumspect or surreptitious villains reserved for thrillers and police procedurals. By contrast, the characters that should be feared in texts intended for a child audience, 'often take the shape of the children's parents or other authority figures, including teachers, librarians, sports coaches, and principals. These figures represent forces that often desire to reshape or mold the child into something the society deems acceptable' (McCort 2016, 20). We might think of the alien disguised as a grandma in Nicholas Fisk's *Grinny* (1974), the patrician astronomer Hendrix in *Children of the Stones* (ITV, 1977) or, more recently, the mathematics teacher Baldi Baldimore in the videogame *Baldi's Basics* (2018). The former examples should be familiar to members of 'Generation X', while the latter might be more familiar to 'Zoomers'. However, for British 'Millennials', the character most vividly associated with menacing authority from children's television horror is – likely – the Demon Headmaster.

Brexit folk demons

Since the Brexit referendum in 2016, multiple digital newspapers and magazines – including *Esquire* (Parker 2017), *The London Economic* (as cited in Mellor 2022) and *Vice* (Garland and O'Neill 2019) – have drawn comparisons between the staunch Leave supporter and current Minister for Brexit Opportunities and Government Efficiency of the United Kingdom, Jacob Rees-Mogg, and the antagonist of the 1990s BBC children's television series *The Demon Headmaster* (BBC 1, 1996–8). Superficially the two figures have a similar appearance, with side-parted greying hair, an ovoid face, spectacles and a tendency to wear a formal combination of a shirt, suit jacket and tie. However, the resemblance of the two men is not striking nor immediate enough to explain this comparison being made across different sources and platforms over several years. Rather, I would posit, the comparison being made is – on an implicit level – not just aesthetic, but also ideological.

In the first series of the television programme, the Demon Headmaster (Terrence Hardiman) is the head teacher at a comprehensive school but has the attire – and imposes a system of rules – more typical of a public boarding school, such as Eton College, in the Victorian era. Rees-Mogg was educated at Eton College and his partiality for the Victorian period is such that in 2019 he published *The Victorians – Twelve Titans Who Forged Britain*, which provides biographical accounts of Victorians he believes embodied 'duty', 'honour' and 'work ethic' (Wagner 2019). Hughes (2019) compares Rees-Mogg's project to that of the education secretary under Margaret Thatcher from 1981 to 1986, Keith Joseph, who aimed to provide all state educated schoolchildren with a copy of Samuel Smiles's *Self-Help* (1859) to encourage 'up by the bootstraps' thinking.

Defining neoliberalism: From Thatcherism to the present

Joseph has been referred to by no less than the influential Brexit-supporting right-wing thinktank the Bruges Group – of which Margaret Thatcher was honorary president – as the 'Architect of Thatcherism' (Thoburn 2020). The Bruges Group has ideological affinities with the Centre for Policy Studies, established by Joseph in 1974, which, Thoburn (2020) notes approvingly, 'promoted monetarism' and policies such as 'mass privatisation, deregulation of the markets, unprecedented trade union reform and a huge drive for private home ownership'. Fuchs (2016) has charted the contingencies between Thatcherism in the 1980s and the policies and structuring ideology of the Conservative government in the UK in the 2010s, noting the same individualistic and meritocratic discourse that valorizes work and the traditional family unit at the expense of scapegoated others. In summary, Fuchs (2016, 183) argues that 'like Thatcherism' Cameronism (i.e. Conservativism under David Cameron) 'advances a non-interventionist state in economic politics and a strong state in the realms of law and order, security, and surveillance'.

While some critics (Rieger 2021; Scott-Samuel et al. 2014; Zak 2020) treat Thatcherism as a specific instantiation of neoliberalism, others have offered more discriminating comparisons. Sutcliffe-Braithwaite (2012, 497) argues that Thatcherism's individualism drew its moral impetus from Methodism and its economic principles from Hayek, arriving at an ideology 'not precisely congruent with that of neo-liberal theorists'. Elsewhere, Ledger (2018) has given a whole monograph to precisely delineating the links between what he treats as two separate but intertwined ideologies.

Significantly, for the purposes of this chapter, Gillian Cross's original run of *Demon Headmaster* books – upon which the television series was based – coincided with the premiership of Margaret Thatcher and, latterly, John Major. Indeed, the first two books in the series – *The Demon Headmaster* (1982) and *The Prime Minister's Brain* (1985) – were published when Keith Joseph – the aforementioned 'Architect of Thatcherism' (Thoburn 2020) – was secretary of state for education and science. Notably, after releasing six books from 1982 to 2002, Cross did not write another Demon Headmaster book until 2017, the year in which the Conservative Party under Theresa May defeated the Labour Party under Jeremy Corbyn in a general election. In an interview with the *New Statesman* (2017) Cross is explicit about *Total Control* being written in response to the academization of the UK's schooling system, with interviewer Anoosh Chakelian reflecting that 'the effects of successive Tory government education reforms since the last book in 2002 weigh heavy on the plot and pupils'. The fact that the television adaptation of the first four books was released under Tony Blair's New Labour government does not dampen the series' concern with neoliberalism, reflecting the continuation of the ideology at the level of economic policy across the years of Blair's supposed 'New Way' (Rieger 2021, 113).

Working to the definitions given earlier of neoliberalism in both the original text of *The Demon Headmaster* and *Total Control* as a reboot-cum-sequel, the Demon Headmaster seeks to create a micro neoliberal state in a school that exists within a larger neoliberal state. However alien or demonic the Demon Headmaster may be, he is in perfect alignment with the ideological values of the society he has infiltrated. However, this agenda becomes clearer as the series progresses, with the antagonist's political strategies moving, over the years of broadcast, from hard to soft power.

In the original television series, the headmaster tries to gain domination over Earth through establishing systems of technocratic control that he co-opts from existing institutions. In the first half of Series 1 (1996) he uses the prefect system of a comprehensive school to brainwash children into memorizing facts so that he can win an education-based gameshow because the winning headteacher gets to address the nation via television. Here his system is fascistic and intentionally – on the part of visual cues given by the programme makers – reminiscent of Nazism. In the second half of the series, he assembles a team of child computer programmers to hack into a governmental database with the aim of brainwashing the prime minister. The hypnosis performed by a computer game called 'Octopus Dare' is akin to the propaganda of a Stalinist regime here since it requires not just subservience to militaristic superiors, but also the internalization of ideology at the level of emotional affect.

In Series 2 (1996), the Demon Headmaster has become the head of Biogenetic Research Centre, planning to interfere with evolutionary processes to create a race of purely rational, hyper-intelligent humans. His approach is thus technocratic and Social Darwinist. In Series 3 (1998) he continues a technocratic approach by co-opting a university's artificial intelligence (AI) project to develop a 'Hyperbrain' computer with which he can control all the world's data flows.

Then, in *The Demon Headmaster* (CBBC, 2019), a new antagonist (played by Nicholas Gleaves, later revealed to have been working under the oversight of the original Demon Headmaster) exploits the academization of a comprehensive school to impress his vision of a perfectly orderly, rational society driven by market forces upon the visiting prime minister. The use of drones and digital tablets ensures that not only the students but the parents themselves are also hypnotized in this newer series. While the children in the original series were able to band together in a resistance group called SPLAT (The Society for the Protection of Our Lives Against Them), the children of the newer series are far more alienated and atomized, often turning on each other, unsure of their allegiances.

At this point, the eerie aesthetics of the original show are only recalled in hauntological flashback sequences, with a glossier, digital aesthetic not only characterizing the look of the school environment, but the aesthetic of the programme itself. At this point in the series, the children are, to paraphrase Slavoj Žižek in *The Pervert's Guide to Ideology* (2012), eating from the 'trashcan of ideology' all the time. Žižek, explaining a central metaphor of the film *They Live* (1998), expounds:

> According to our common sense, we think that ideology is something blurring, confusing our straight view. Ideology should be glasses, which distort our view, and the critique of ideology should be the opposite like you take off the glasses so that you can finally see the way things really are … this precisely is the ultimate illusion: ideology is not simply imposed on ourselves. Ideology is our spontaneous relation to our social world, how we perceive each meaning … We, in a way, enjoy our ideology.

Indeed, it is when the Demon Headmaster takes his glasses *off* that he can hypnotize the children and parents of the show, a state of hypnosis that is mirrored in the mise-en-scène of the 2019 school and home environment, the aesthetic embodiment of structured social relations that the characters cannot step out of.

The eeriness of neoliberalism

While neoliberalism is an ideology not an aesthetic, it can be said to have aesthetic *affectivity*. Digimodernism (Kirby 2009) – exemplified by corporate transnational franchises like the Marvel Cinematic Universe – might be regarded as the dominant aesthetic mode of neoliberalism, characterized by digitally disseminated content that exists only to point towards other content across an endless, flat, virtual plane. The emotional or spiritual nourishment promised by such franchises is always eternally deferred, pointing to an *elsewhere* – think, for instance, of the post-credits scenes of Marvel films that hint towards a more revelatory future release, or the increasingly networked storytelling that exists across multiple platforms and formats. This superabundance and superfluity of content becomes such that it is only possible to keep abreast of it via watching YouTube 'Explainer' and 'Reaction' videos, listening to podcasts, and reading articles and opinion pieces – in addition to the social media messages of friends and acquaintances privy to different aspects of the network of content – only adding to the emotional experience of lack.

While this affect is intentionally engineered to encourage further digital consumption, neoliberalism's aesthetic traces often seem aesthetically eerie and emptied-out due to capitalism's tendencies towards resource extraction and displacement. After all, empty and abandoned shopping malls, swimming pools and theme parks do not exist because of the aesthetic, emotional or even spiritual function they serve for posters on subreddits like 'r/LiminalSpace', but as symptoms of the financialization of capital.

Eeriness is both a symptom of neoliberalism's decimation of the commons, as well as a potential site of counter-hegemonic revelation, even escape. Noys (2019/2020, 161) reflects that Mark Fisher 'saw in the weird and eerie, as detailed in the book of that name, experiences of estrangement that not only registered the forms of high capitalism in their psychic dimensions but that also promised us liberation from them'. Noys treats Fisher's *The Weird and the Eerie* (2016) as a companion piece to his earlier *Capitalist Realism* (2009), with weirdness and eeriness as epiphenomena of capitalist realism, micro cultural instantiations of a larger economic and political whole. While Fisher does not offer a precise definition of 'capitalist realism' in that work, in conversation with Jeremy Gilbert, he agrees with Gilbert's description of the term as encapsulating 'both the conviction that there is no alternative to capitalism as a paradigm for social organisation, and the mechanisms which are used to disseminate and reproduce that conviction' (Gilbert and Fisher 2013, 89). As such, capitalist realism might be considered the dominant 'political phenomenology' (Fisher 2009, 64 as cited in Noys 2019/2020, 159) of neoliberalism, in which depoliticized consumer-citizens experience capitalism as an inevitable, implacable force of nature that cannot be challenged or resisted. This experience has the effect of making capital appear to exist independently of capitalists, as though possessed of its own agency. Indeed, Fisher (2016, LOC 770) goes as far as to write that 'capital does not exist in any substantial sense, yet it is capable of producing any kind of effect'. From this description it is difficult to know whether the reader should be picturing 'Eerie Agentic Capital' (*sic.*) (Colquhoun 2018) as one of Timothy Morton's philosophical 'hyperobjects' (2013) or as a Cthulhuesque monstrous entity. Even if we try to avoid both anthropocentricism and animism in our appraisal of capital it nonetheless 'already forms a more-than-human assemblage, one regulated by its own productive and reproductive logics and consuming its various forms of prey – abstract labour, cheap nature – in the process' (Salvage Editorial Collective 2020).

It is unsurprising that, experiencing this lack of positive political agency under a succession of neoliberal governments – the experience Fisher terms 'capitalist realism' – 'parts of the contemporary British left seem to be increasingly enamoured [*sic.*] with the strange, with psychogeography and landscape, with the weird and the eerie and the past; with things that, taken as a whole, look very much like folk horror' (Jones 2020). Taken cynically, this might read as a retreat into magical thinking in the wake of political defeat, akin to individuals turning to astrology in response to the decline of organized religion. However, Jones (2020) reads the tendency more sympathetically, seeing the attraction of folk horror for the left as being rooted in a hope that 'another world, a stranger and more vivid world, might loiter closer to our own than we suspect'.

Arguably the dynamics and contours of folk horror are inherently political. Watson's (2016) potted definition of the genre as 'the projection of the trauma of wide-scale social/religious/political upheaval and conflict – experienced at societal, familial, and personal levels – onto nature and the land itself, manifesting as the supernatural, subverting our perception of the idealised [*sic.*] bucolic setting' captures the political potentialities of folk horror, as well as the genre's potentially reactive qualities. Folk horror challenges the ecofascist romanticization of the countryside, while also insisting upon the primacy of the land – particularly in its relation to the folk – as a site of political and personal struggle. This conflict also involves the (perceived) encroachment upon the land by those deemed by the characters or narrative to be outsiders. Moreover, the mass success of recent folk horror films like Ari Aster's *Midsommar* (2019) suggests that the genre appeals to audiences broader than just a left-wing vanguard, with Calvo (2021) intimating that, while the genre can be theorized via Derrida's concept of 'hauntology' (Shaw 2018 as cited in Calvo 2021, 80), it can also more straightforwardly be seen as yet another example of 'nostalgia and pastiche' as 'the predominant artistic modes under late capitalism' (Calvo 2021, 79). It is not always easy to determine whether a given iteration of folk horror is critiquing political tendencies that the viewer or reader might consider reactionary or, instead, exploiting fears – in the form of scapegoated others, urban or rural – that animate and justify those same conservative ideologies. For instance, the resurgence of interest in folk horror in the wake of the Brexit vote (Newton 2017) could be read as a reflexive interrogation of anti-cosmopolitan isolationism and superstitious prejudice (Scovell 2017a) or, alternatively, a defence of a kind of 'blood and soil' *magick* eco-nationalism characterized by Paul Kingsnorth's controversial 2018 review of Paul Wright's experimental folk documentary *Arcadia* (2017). At the very least, the same can be said of folk horror as has been said of Gothic horror under neoliberalism, that, 'we can see a variety of ideological allegiances of play in gothic texts of the neoliberal age – ranging from the revolutionary to the radical to the downright reactionary' (Blake and Monnet 2017, 1–2).

It would be too reductive to determine whether a given folk horror text is progressive or regressive merely by referring to the stated aims of its creator/s; however, this might be a starting point from which further analysis can proceed. Bearing this in mind, it is worth noting that Cross (2003, 73) has stated that her *Demon Headmaster* books 'stand against systems and in favour of individual thought processes' but has also cautioned that the medium of television risks individualizing the threat of the Demon Headmaster, distracting from the systems' critique of the books (Cross 2003, 74). This is not enough to state that the series is against neoliberalism. Defenders of neoliberalism might claim that the market protects 'individual thought processes' from the state, though one could counter that 'under the ideological veil of non-intervention, neoliberalism involves extensive and invasive interventions in every area of social life' (Jaad-Filho and Johnston 2005, 4).

As such, it must be determined that neoliberalism is the system that can be mapped most effectively onto the allegorical narrative of *The Demon Headmaster*. To do this, it needs to be established how the series does for the suburban environment what folk horror did for the rural. This is because, counter-intuitively, McFadzean (2019) has elucidated how American 'suburban fantastic cinema' of the 1980s upheld the neoliberal values which gave rise to its production. In its original incarnation, *The Demon Headmaster* challenges these values through uncovering and emphasizing the eeriness of suburbia, while in its more recent incarnation it critiques neoliberalism more directly through a combination of satire and hauntological strategies. The original series, discussed first, is a suburban folk horror, while the newest series is more fully a neoliberal horror.

Suburban folk horror

Since the release of Adam Scovell's *Folk Horror: Hours Dreadful and Things Strange* in 2017, several academics (Paciorek 2018; Ingham 2018; Campbell 2017) have identified a number of children's television programmes, such as *The Moon Stallion* (1978), films, such as *Watership Down* (1979), and literature, such as Robert Westell's *The Scarecrows* (1981), as examples of folk horror. Scovell himself (2017b, 68–74) has variably provided examples from children's television with *Children of the Stones* (ITV, 1977), *King of the Castle* (ITV, 1977), *Raven* (ITV, 177) and *Doctor Who* (BBC 1, 1963–89). Scovell (2017b, 14) binds these disparate sources together via the concept of the 'Folk Horror Chain', 'a linking set of narrative traits that have causal and interlinking consequences'. The standard story that emerges following this chain involves an outsider (associated with modernity) coming into conflict against an isolated folk community, staging the incompatibility of the urban and the rural.

While *The Demon Headmaster* takes places within suburban and urban settings, the programme's first series otherwise corresponds to Scovell's Folk Horror Chain. The story's hero, Dinah Glass (Frances Amey), begins the show as an outsider, moving in with her new foster family, the Hunters. Dinah is established as already adept in the sciences and technology, with the second book in the series even opening with a transcript of her coding in BASIC (Cross 1987, 7). As an individual she comes into opposition against the highly conformist community of her new school, who adhere to an older, more traditional form of rote learning than she is used to. When one of the other children, Ingrid, comments that the questions on the 'Great School Quiz' are too difficult for her, Dinah replies that all the children in the school are taught 'parrot-fashion', meaning that they are unable to solve puzzles like those required by the quiz (Cross 1984, 102). This conflict between uncritical groupthink and individual self-determination is the central structuring conflict of all three films of the so-called Unholy Trinity of folk horror, *Witchfinder General* (1968), *Blood on Satan's Claw* (1971) and *The Wicker Man* (1973).

Of course, these three films, as well as the examples of children's folk horror, are all from the 1970s (and a couple of years on either side), the decade that saw the collapse of the British post-war welfare settlement (Rustin 2010; Davidson 2013) and the British folk revival (Young 2011). By the 1990s in British children's television – after a decade of neoliberal politics – the urban had largely subsumed the rural, with eeriness now located within liminal *sub*urban spaces. The character of the Demon Headmaster may harken back to old Edwardian (and Etonian) notions of education and conduct but, as established, he also embodies neoliberal orthodoxies, in favour of technocratic systems, data management, targets, surveillance and manufacturing consent through neuro-linguistic programming, propaganda and behaviour monitoring. Intriguingly, this seemingly counter-intuitive combination of the technological with the outdated and arcane that characterizes the Demon Headmaster and his plans also characterizes many of the hauntological artists like The Advisory Circle, The Focus Group and Pye Corner Audio on the Ghost Box label. Fisher (2014, 134) describes these artists as providing an 'uncanny' 'return to the analogue via the digital', the uncanniness produced by the listener's sense of displaced nostalgia, which evokes the background undercurrents of the 1970s via samples of library music and public information films. Importantly, these samples (and the names of the groups that use them) are signifiers for – and citations of – institutional and governmental authority. The effect is eerie, I would argue, because the analogue traces of the old ideological state apparatus are invoked, experienced by a listener interpolated within the digital smoothness (Kirby's digimodernism) of the modern neoliberal state, where power is ostensibly hidden.

It is notable that when comedian Stewart Lee wrote an article in 2018 about Jacob Rees-Mogg, he used the language of folk horror, proclaiming, 'Jacob Rees-Mogg is upon you, a black darkness over the shire, a shade upon your allotments, a frozen shadow upon all your back garden gazebos'. More straightforwardly, David Mitchell (2021) refers to Rees-Mogg as having an 'eerie aesthetic'. Rees-Mogg's uncanny charge, recognized by Mitchell and Lee, is due to the temporal displacement of his old-fashioned appearance in combination with the anxiety that he holds political views such as the outlawing of all abortion – that we might assume to have been superseded by liberal progressivism and thus question whether they are being held by Rees-Mogg 'authentically'. Toynbee (2017) clarifies this ambivalence when she writes that the politician's 'double-breasted posh-speak, Latin tags and ludicrous names for his six children are all pastiche panache, a country house charade well-crafted to distract from what is genuinely authentic – an extremely reactionary and self-regarding brand of every-man-for-himself Conservatism'. Hyde (2007) captures the aesthetic effect of Rees-Mogg's pastiche – 'He's not just tacking back to things that other people feel should be left behind – he's going past the point from which he even began' – cannily back-projecting his political rise as the fulfilment of a prophecy made by his futurologist father, 'Mystic Mogg', as though Brexit Britain were stuck in a Möbius strip time loop. However, her reflection that 'psychosexual analysis' should be applied to 'Moggmentum', just as it has been applied to 'some Tories' enduring search for a new Iron Lady to fantasise about', misses the fact that Margaret Thatcher herself already used her premiership to construct a proto-Brexit 'return of the repressed', resurrecting a mythic Churchillian spirit that was projected back into the past (Skopic, 2022). This is also Adam Curtis's central thesis in 'The Attic', the third part of *The Living Dead* (BBC, 1995) of which Riley (2013) writes, 'There's a concept of time as malleable here, relics of the past can be called up into the present day, as shiny, brand spanking new, not summoned up as ragged zombies or faded haints. For Curtis, this trend is emblematic of the neoliberal revolution.'

Neoliberalism invokes the past only to reify it, constructing myths that are political commodities, alienated from the commons and thus from any politically progressive or transformative potential. An example of this in *The Prime Minister's Brain* (adapted as the latter three episodes of the first series of *The Demon Headmaster*) is when Dinah is invited to compete in the 'Junior Computer Brain of the Year Competition', taking place at the Saracen Tower, Turk's Island. In their heads, Dinah and her friends imagine 'pictures of grass and water and ducks' (Cross 1987, 37) – perhaps a kind of 'Avalon, Xanadu, Arden' or 'Perfumed Garden' (Young 2011, 5) in the centre of London. When they arrive, however, they are confronted with the fact that Turk's Island is a traffic island, with Saracen Tower represented in the programme by the brutalist Atrium in Uxbridge. The rural imaginings of the children have been concreted over by efficient, technocratic design that evokes a bucolic past only as an empty signifier. Fisher (2009, 4) writes that 'capitalism is what is left when beliefs have collapsed at the level of ritual'. In *The Demon Headmaster*, the countryside rituals of 1970s folk horror no longer exist because folk collectivity has been rendered unfigurable by neoliberalism. The first link of Scovell's Folk Horror Chain – the rural environment – is missing, but we are reminded of it by the missing signified Turk's Island (that would certainly have been a real island in a 1970s children's folk horror).

In this sense, neoliberal late-stage capitalism is always 'eerie' (Fisher, 2016) because it *absences* those aspects of material reality which compromise it. Suburbia – where *The Demon Headmaster*'s family scenes are set – is similarly eerie because its drab conformity (its *realism*) is maintained by urban and rural spaces (and sites of production) which it simultaneously disavows.

In his monograph (2017b, 121–64) Scovell already extends the concept of folk horror to encompass the 'urban wyrd', which he does – like Fisher before him – via the concept of Derrida's hauntology. Elsewhere for the BFI, Scovell (2017b) references Fisher directly, paraphrasing him when he asserts that 'the weird is a sort of "thing-ness", a palpable dread as opposed to the eerie … This contrast is felt most keenly in the city, where the ordinary is a palimpsest under which writhes both human and nonhuman strangeness, sitting in defiant confidence.' Indeed, the 'urban wyrd' case studies Scovell selects – films including *The Lodger* (1944), *Peeping Tom* (1960) and *Death Line* (1972) – largely feature the kind of overtly aggressively and murderous antagonists who often populate adult's horror. The urban degradation which should be repressed underground is, instead, brought to visceral surface of these films.

As children's horror, *The Demon Headmaster* adheres more closely to folk horror's eeriness in its use of locations. The exterior location used to represent the street where the Hunter family live consists of mock-Tudor pebbledash semi-detached houses, which evokes a historic rural style as a stylistic quirk, removed from the original purpose of the post-and-beam half-timbering. Dinah's flattened emotional effect seemed to be mirrored through pathetic fallacy in the grey drabness of these exterior shots, including the concrete uniformity of the school grounds.

In an interview with Fisher (2014, 135), Jim Jupp, co-owner of the Ghost Box label, responds to Fisher's assertion of there being 'a certain grain to 70s British culture that got smoothed away by 80s style culture gloss' by mentioning a friend whose girlfriend dislikes him watching 1970s British sitcoms, referring to them as 'grot TV'. The suburbia of 1990s American children's sitcoms, like that of *Boy Meets World* (ABC, 1993–2000) or *Clarissa Explains It All* (Nickelodeon, 1991–94) was glossy and aspirational, with this gloss even extending into horror-adjacent supernatural children's television from the United States, like *Sabrina the Teenage Witch* (ABC and The WB, 1996–2003), set in a Boston suburb. Since this tendency does not extend to the aesthetic of the more parochial, sparsely populated environments of *Eerie, Indiana* (NBC, 1991–92) or *Gravity Falls* (Disney Channel and Disney XD, 2012–16) – both of which contain elements of folk horror – then this difference might partly be ascribed to the differences between American and English suburbia. American suburbia has infiltrated and replaced the countryside more rapidly, is defined by higher levels of automobile ownership and is, generally, more affluent (Clapson 2003, 14). Moreover, American suburbia is more sparsely populated, with larger spaces between homes.

Theoretically, these larger spaces should make American suburbia *more* eerie than its British counterpart, but the wide-open spaces and vast skies of Amblin Entertainment's suburban fantasy films like *E.T.* (1982), *The Goonies* (1985) and even *Gremlins* (1984) seem to hold the optimistic promise of summer adventure and escapism, compared to the drearier overcast skies of *The Demon Headmaster*, *The Ink Thief* (ITV, 1994), *Johnny and the Dead* (ITV, 1995) or *Knightmare* (ITV, 1987–94). Superficially, *The Demon Headmaster* adheres to the narrative structure McFadzean (2019, 1) identifies in suburban fantastic cinema, by which 'pre-teen and teenage boys living within the suburbs are called upon to confront a disruptive fantastic force'. Importantly, 'the protagonist's melodrama develops in parallel with the crisis of the fantastic, and when the fantastic crisis is resolved, the protagonist's melodrama is also resolved'. Dinah's estrangement from her new foster family is resolved with her defeat of the Demon Headmaster at the end of the programme's first series. While the melodrama is kept low-key, Dinah's emotional life and psychological development are necessarily intertwined with her experiences of the supernatural mind-controlling forces wielded by the Demon Headmaster, which she has to resist and overcome in order to self-actualize.

Dinah, however, is a girl – and Gillian Cross a female author – which marks a significant difference from the case studies that McFadzean profiles. Most of these films are ultimately hegemonic, following a character trajectory in which male protagonists internalize the values of a patriarchal system, ultimately 'co-opted by a society of media manipulation, male domination and the rule of multinational capitalism' (McFadzean 2019, 2). As such, the genre (exemplified by the films of Amblin Entertainment) evokes the values of neoliberal suburbia, while rarely criticizing them. In terms of the impact this has upon an audience, McFadzean postulates that the genre's 'unique combination of terror with wonder is an ambiguous affective mix that approximates the feeling of this new hyper-accelerated turbo-capitalism of the Reagan era, a form of capitalism that has continued to the present day' (2019, 39).

Wonder is characteristic of awe, conjured by a sense of the sublime, metonymically evoked by those impossibly high blue skies of Spielberg's films. Reconceptualized in terms of horror, it is more typical of the impossible presence of the weird than the absence of the eerie (Fisher 2014). The drab monotony of *The Demon Headmaster*'s visuals of pebbledash and concrete exteriors are the eerie residue of 'hyper-accelerated turbo-capitalism' but are unlikely to seduce us in the same way as the extended McDonalds advertisement in *Mac and Me* (1988) (McFadzean 2019, 95) despite the second series' focus on the hypnotic videogame 'Octopus Dare' or the third book's focus upon the television mascot character Hunky Parker and the promotional merchandise of the character. As such, the programme manages to remain critical of such examples of media manipulation, rather than merely replicating them. Moreover, Dinah – though repeatedly defeating the Demon Headmaster, even after he manages to clone her in the second series of the television programme – resists patriarchal authority rather than being co-opted or subsumed by it. In terms of the show's critique of multinational capitalism, a more consistent engagement emerged in the 2019 revival series, *The Demon Headmaster*.

The horror of neoliberalism

The first thing likely to strike a viewer of *The Demon Headmaster* (2019) who grew up with the original series is how glossy it looks. This is faithful to *The Demon Headmaster: Total Control* (2017), which the new series adapts. Writing of the school in that book, Chakelian (2017) reflects,

Fans of the books or the Nineties BBC TV adaptation won't recognise this new school. It has a buzzer, glossy gates, sky-blue memory sticks for parents, an "Information hub" instead of the library, and a member of staff with a badge that reads "Deputy Head, Public Relations". There are livestreams, video conferences, drones and holograms.

The school is the height of digimodernism and – it should be admitted – is superficially highly appealing, composed of gleaming surfaces enlivened by eye-catching graphic design. Speaking of the impact of neoliberalism within higher education in dialogue with Jeremy Gilbert, Fisher (2013, 91) recalled 'an acceptance amongst managers of the inevitability that education would increasingly be modelled on business'. By the near-future setting of *The Demon Headmaster*, this process of privatization has reached the point where students are appealed to as customers and schooled as young entrepreneurs. Angelika Maron (Lori Stott) has established a vegan cupcake and smoothie franchise on the school grounds, taking payments with a card e-reader. Her franchise, 'Angelik Eats'. is reminiscent of Innocent Drinks, the company established by Cambridge University consulting and advertising graduates, majority owned by the Coca-Cola Company. In contrast to this corporate greenwashing, Angelika's mother is revealed to have been arrested due to her involvement with an environmental protest group explicitly modelled upon Extinction Rebellion – their logo being the XR Hourglass with a line through the middle of it. Her memory triggered by the logo, Angelika proclaims, 'To each according to their needs!' and starts giving away the cupcakes in an action reminiscent of Food Not Bombs, before being intercepted by a flying drone declaring 'Warning – unsustainable market model'.

The protest group is reminiscent of the revolutionary actions group SPLAT from the original series, but in the reboot/sequel is shown to be unsustainable in the face of mass digital surveillance. Arguing that revolution is not possible under neoliberalism, Byung-Chul Han (2015) explains that under an earlier model of capitalism, there was a 'concrete' and 'visible' enemy that the masses could fight again. By contrast, neoliberalism 'turns the oppressed worker into a free contractor, an entrepreneur of the self ... Every individual is master and slave in one.' He concludes that 'no revolutionary mass can arise from exhausted, depressive, and isolated individuals'.

This is the situation that the students of the Hazelbrook Academy of the new series are trapped within. A character like Angelika is the very capitalist entrepreneur that she herself works under. In the series, all the show's protagonists are divided against themselves. The main character, Lizzie Warren (Ellie Botterill) spends half her time rebelling against the school and the other half brainwashed into behaving as a militaristic training instructor. Even her rebellious act of vandalizing the school is later shown to have been implanted in her by the Demon Headmaster, this rebelliousness an inauthentically adopted pose. The Headmaster himself often only appears as a hologram, completely insubstantial. In the series' last episode, he is revealed to be something of a pastiche of the original Demon Headmaster – a simulacrum/copy of a demonic, alien entity that was already emotionally and psychologically hollow in the original.

Lizzie's emotional state throughout the series recalls the 'depressive hedonia' Fisher (2009, 21) observed in his students due to their 'ambiguous structural position, stranded between their old role as subjects of disciplinary institutions and their new status as consumers of services' (2009, 22). As with the simultaneous master-and-slave position occupied by Angelika, the entrepreneur, Lizzie – and the other students – are divided against themselves, required to police their own desires as subjects of institutional authority, while simultaneously encouraged to submit to these desires as capitalist consumers. True, lasting solidarity proves impossible between such characters since they are too distracted by battles waged within themselves to effectively turn outwards from their individualism to fight structural, institutional forms of power.

What Fisher identifies as 'Market Stalinism', by which symbols of achievement are valued over actual achievement (2009, 42–3) – think of Innocent's greenwashing by which they claim to champion the environment while selling millions of plastic drink cartons, or the focus on grading over deeper, more embodied forms of learning in the schooling system – has the curious effect of replacing 'narrative memory' with what he calls 'formal memory' (2009, 58). By this, Fisher means 'a memory of – techniques, practices, actions' – that 'privileges only the present and the immediate' (2009, 59).

The learning at Hazelbrook Academy is functionally identical to the uploading of knowledge directly into the brain in *The Matrix* (1999). Rather than cultivate the personal interests the children have developed outside of the school environment, characters are hyper-efficiently trained in skills that seem to reflect stereotypes associated with their demographic categories. So, Ethan Prendergast/Adebayo (Dijarn Campbell) – one of the school's only Black students – is stripped of his interest in computing and, instead, transformed into an athletic football champion. Blake Vinney (Jordan Rankin), who is coded as working class, is forced into a role as a janitor, perhaps reflecting the rise in inequality since Thatcher's government's implementation of neoliberal economic policies (Arestis and Sawyer 2005).

The scenes showing the students' upgraded skills – Ethan's footballing, Lizzie's *Bajiquan* martial arts, and so on – are often edited in short, choppy sequences divorced from the contextualizing contexts of training regimes and practice. As such, they are represented as free-floating signifiers of the academy's institutional achievements, rather than embodied experiences which are meaningful to the children within their wider lives. This is reflective of the commodification of the children at the academy and, more broadly, the neoliberal tendency towards the commodification and standardization of education (Levidow 2004, 157).

Hauntological crazyspace

The reboot/sequel of *The Demon Headmaster* is visually brighter than the original series but a more claustrophobic viewing experience due to the impossibility of true solidarity between the show's characters, foreclosing an imaginary future space of freedom and liberation. This is underscored by the lack of catharsis provided by the ending of the series, which involves the thwarting of two planned explosions – first as tragedy, then as farce. Moreover, the return of the original series' Demon Headmaster is a nostalgic gesture that arrests the future-facing orientation of the show. The fact that the new Demon Headmaster is revealed to be a replicant of sorts suggests an endlessly replaceable series of antagonists who can equally embody the nebulous threat of neoliberalism.

There are few moments in the 2019 series that provide an experience of uncomplicated pleasure. Notably, when the character of Dinah Hunter (now played by Charlotte Beckett) returns, she is brainwashed almost immediately – the hero of the original show now a completely ineffectual agent for MI6 (and thus now part of upholding the neoliberal order herself). One of the few exceptions takes place in the opening scene of Episode 6 'Be Your True Self' in which the child characters come across a website that recalls events from the original series, asking readers, 'Remember the Eddy Hair Show?'

In the first book and series, the Eddy Hair Show is a carnivalesque children's television show with the eccentric and illiterate (or, possibly, pre-literate) presenter Eddy Hair (Daniel John-Jules) existing as an agent of chaos. In the show, he presides over the Great School Quiz like Dave Benson Phillips over a vat of gunge in *Get Your Own Back* (BBC 1, 1991–2004). In the book, he is even stranger – perhaps, magical – described as having a fight with a 'giant plateful of spaghetti' which fights him back (Cross 1984, 125). Dinah characterizes the Eddy Hair Show as 'Mess. Chaos. They fling things all over the place. Flour, soot, chickens … Sometimes they even break windows' (Cross 1984, 100). The Eddy Hair Show is – to use a term Davies (2005) borrows from the books – a form of 'Crazyspace'. Davies (2005, 398) argues that Crazyspace poses a pre-symbolic challenge to the adults' symbolic realm, which explains the importance of Eddy Hair being illiterate. As such, 'Crazyspace is a place where children can safely take political action because, as one of them points out, in Crazyspace, they can be confident that adults will not notice them' (Davies 2005, 392). Unlike the orderly and controlled classroom of The Demon Headmaster, Crazyspace is not a respectable space and is governed more by the ID than the superego. Indeed, 'the thrill of Crazyspace is not simply that it is free from the presence, authority and worries of adults, but that it must constantly and deliberately bring this status into jeopardy in order to reassert it' (Lester 2022, 88). This highlights the precarious liminality of Crazyspace and helps to clarify the threat it poses to the technocratic order.

While it would be facile to argue that ambiguity is anathema to engineers (Pacey 1983, 123) we can avoid individualistic judgements against people within specific professions – such as head teacher, IT director or bio-engineer – by thinking of neoliberalism as *structurally* technocratic. Pacey (1983, 127) posits that the technocractic world view is fundamentally anti-democratic since it involves a 'singleminded' and 'unambiguous' 'view of progress, of problem-solving, and of values', which holds that 'there cannot be any rational alternative technologies because there is only one logical path forward'. A truly threatening children's politics would embrace the messiness of Crazyspace, refusing to adhere to a single logic path in problem-solving. It might even – if we picture Eddy Hair fighting the spaghetti – tend towards animism, anthropomorphization and paganism (Eddy *Hare?*) in its embrace of the irrational. If Gillian Cross comes down in favour of waste and mess in *The Demon Headmaster* – which I believe she does – then it might be worth emphasizing the 'messy complications' to which Pacey (1983, 126) refers:

> Conventional wisdom implicitly encourages the master value such as economic growth; it encourages an unambiguous approach to problem-solving also, frequently favouring a technical fix approach because this may avoid the messy complications of a more human solution, and is often within the capacities of a self-sufficient, specialist profession.

The Eddy Hair Show only exists memorialized upon a website in the 2019 *Demon Headmaster*. The website is a glorious mess of bad graphic design, including a pixelated animated gif of Eddy Hair on a moving green slime background, looping background music and sound effects, and what look like Flash animations. The discontinuation of Flash was announced in July 2017 and it is no longer supported by browsers. It is also now very rare to encounter websites with background music. The website, in short, looks like how a contemporaneous viewer of the 1996 Demon Headmaster might have imagined a cool, futuristic website to look. Since the 2019 show is set in a near or parallel future, the effect of this outdated graphic design is hauntological. It is a vision of a creative and *messy* internet that ultimately did not come to pass due to the rise of social media conglomerates and data harvesting through surveillance capitalism. When Cory Doctorow (2022) speaks about the 'Wondrous World of the Early Internet' it is this 'pluralistic' rather than 'hegemonic' top-down internet that he is picturing – a utopian vision of the technological countercultural that now exists as a melancholy memory.

Beyond neoliberalism?

It is bittersweet that one of the only visions of freedom in *The Demon Headmaster* (2019) comes in the form of a mediated vision only fully explicable to millennial viewers who watched the original series, who can 'Remember Eddy Hair'. The XR-modelled protest group is shown to be quickly defeated by the police state. Vegan smoothies are presented as a greenwashing scan. It is a profoundly pessimistic vision. Glimmers of hope are, however, shown within the classroom in moments in which the children have fun, challenge authority and create mess. Crazyspace is glimpsed in these moments, but never quite emerges. Noys (2019/2020, 193), raising the possibility of creating educational spaces outside of neoliberal capitalism, speculates that, to do this, educators 'would need to articulate the weird "outside" with the eerie spaces of "absence", of the fractures and dialectical tensions of capitalism with its empty appearance'. This is a speculative project and offers little in the way of concrete praxis. However, it is a project that children's horror and fantasy are uniquely suited to attempting, with both series of *The Demon Headmaster* providing bold, counter-hegemonic attempts to do so which are sympathetic to the inner lives of children and their need to play outside of the strictures of capitalist realism.

References

Arestis, Philip, and Malcolm Sawyer. 2005. 'The Neoliberal Experience of the United Kingdom'. In *Neoliberalism: A Critical Reader*, edited by Alfredo Jaad-Filho and Deborah Johnston, 199–207. Fortescue: Pluto Press.

Blake, Linnie, and Agnieszka Soltysik Monnet, eds. 2017. *Neoliberal Gothic: International Gothic in the Neoliberal Age*. Manchester: Manchester University Press.

Calvo, Alberto Andrés. 2021. 'Ghosts of Britain: A Hauntological Approach to the 21st-Century Folk Horror Revival'. *REDEN* 3, no. 1: 79–93. https://doi.org/10.37536/reden.2021.3.1428. Accessed 24 September 2023.

Campbell, Nick. 2017. 'Children's Neo-Romanticism: The Archaeological Imagination in British Post-War Children's Fantasy'. PhD diss., University of Roehampton.

Clapson, Mark. 2003. *Suburban Century: Social Change and Urban Growth in England and the USA*. Oxford: Berg.

Colquhoun, Matt. 2018. 'A Note on Eerie Agentic Capital'. *Xenogothic*, 11 December. https://xenogothic.com/2018/12/11/a-note-on-eerie-agentic-capital. Accessed 24 September 2023.

Cross, Gillian. 1984. *The Demon Headmaster*. London: Puffin Books.

Cross, Gillian. 1987. *The Prime Minister's Brain*. London: Puffin Books.

Cross, Gillian. 1994. *The Revenge of the Demon Headmaster*. London: Puffin Books.

Cross, Gillian. 2003. '"How Do They Do the Eyes?": Televising *The Demon Headmaster*'. In *Children's Literature and Childhood in Performance*, edited by Kimberley Reynolds, 71–8. Lichfield: Pied Piper Publishing.

Cross, Gillian. 2017. *The Demon Headmaster: Total Control*. Oxford: Oxford University Press.

Cross, Gillian, and Anoosh Chakelian. 2017. 'The Academisation of the Demon Headmaster'. *The New Statesman*, 1 August. https://www.newstatesman.com/politics/2017/07/academisation-demon-headmaster. Accessed 24 September 2023.

Davidson, Neil. 2013. 'The Neoliberal Era in Britain Historical Developments and Current Perspectives'. *International Socialism* 2, no. 139: 171–223.

Davies, Messinger. 2005. '"Crazyspace": The Politics of Children's Screen Drama'. *Screen* 46, no. 3: 389–99.

The Demon Headmaster. 1996–8. [TV series; Director: Roger Singleton-Turner] UK: BBC and Simply Media. DVD.

The Demon Headmaster. 2019. 'Control. Command. Conquer!' *BBC iPlayer.* 28:00, 4 November. https://www.bbc.co.uk/iplayer/episode/m000b1mj/the-demon-headmaster-series-1-4-control-command-conquer.

The Demon Headmaster. 2019. 'Be Your True Self'. *BBC iPlayer.* 28:00, 18 November. https://www.bbc.co.uk/iplayer/episode/m000bh4g/the-demon-headmaster-series-1-6-be-your-true-self.

The Demon Headmaster. 2019. Directed by John McKay and Johnathan Fox Bassett, created by Emma Reeves, BBC TV.

Doctorow, Cory, and Nathan J. Robinson. 2022. 'Cory Doctorow on The Wondrous World of the Early Internet & How To Destroy Surveillance Capitalism'. *Current Affairs* (podcast). 31 July. https://play.acast.com/s/current-affairs/1a26cb56-5c8f-4400-aebb-0cb2141a02cb. Accessed 23 August 2022.

Fisher, Mark. 2009. *Capitalist Realism: Is There No Alternative?* Winchester: Zero Books.

Fisher, Mark. 2014. *Ghosts of My Life: Writings on Depression, Hauntology and Lost Futures*. Winchester: Zero Books.

Fisher, Mark. 2016. *The Weird and the Eerie*, 3rd edition. London: Repeater. Kindle.

Fisher, Mark, and Jeremy Gilbert. 2013. 'Capitalist Realism and Neoliberal Hegemony: A Dialogue'. *New Formations* 80/81: 89–101.

Fuchs, Christian. 2016. 'Neoliberalism in Britain: From Thatcherism to Cameronism'. *tripleC* 14, no. 1 (March): 163–88. https://doi.org/10.31269/triplec.v14i1.750.

Garland, Emma, and Lauren O'Neill. 2019. 'No Deal Behaviour: A Guide'. *Vice*, 4 April. https://www.vice.com/en/article/kzdmqy/no-deal-behaviour-a-guide.

Han, Byung-Chul. 2015. 'Why Revolution Is No Longer Possible'. *Open Democracy*, 23 October. https://www.opendemocracy.net/en/transformation/why-revolution-is-no-longer-possible.

Hughes, Kathryn. 2019. '*The Victorians* by Jacob Rees-Mogg Review – History as Manifesto'. *The Guardian*, 15 May. https://www.theguardian.com/books/2019/may/15/the-victorians-jacob-rees-mogg-review. Accessed 24 September 2023.

Hyde, Mariana. 2019. 'Who Could See Jacob Mogg as Authentic?', The Guardian. https://www.theguardian.com/commentisfree/2017/sep/08/jacob-rees-mogg-conservatives-eton-eccentric. Accessed 24 September 2023.

Ingham, Howard David. 2018. 'Happy Day: Folk Horror for Children'. In *We Don't Go Back: A Watcher's Guide to Folk Horror*. Scotts Valley: CreateSpace Independent Publishing Platform.

Jaad-Filho, Alfredo, and Deborah Johnston, eds. 2005. *Neoliberalism: A Critical Reader*. Fortescue: Pluto Press.

Jones, Morgan. 2020. 'Labour Campaign for Folk Horror'. *The Social Review*, 26 April. https://www.thesocialreview.co.uk/2020/04/26/labour-campaign-for-folk-horror. Accessed 24 Spetember 2023.

Kingsnorth, Paul. 2018. 'Elysium Found?' *Paul Kingsnorth*, 20 May.https://web.archive.org/web/20180617035729/http://paulkingsnorth.net/2018/05/20/elysium-found. Accessed 24 September 2023.

Kirby, Alan. 2009. *Digimodernism: How New Technologies Dismantle the Postmodern and Reconfigure Our Culture*. London: Continuum.

Ledger, Robert. 2018. *Neoliberal Thought and Thatcherism: 'A Transition from Here to There?'* Abingdon-on-Thames: Routledge.

Lee, Stewart. 2018. 'Satire only Makes Jacob Rees-Mogg Stronger'. *The Observer*, 11 February. https://www.theguardian.com/commentisfree/2018/feb/11/satire-makes-jacob-rees-mogg-stronger.

Lester, Catherine. 2022. *Horror Films for Children: Fear and Pleasure in American Cinema*. London: Bloomsbury.

Levidow, Les. 2005. 'Neoliberal Agendas for Higher Education'. In *Neoliberalism: A Critical Reader*, edited by Alfredo Jaad-Filho and Deborah Johnston, 156–62. Fortescue: Pluto Press.

McCort, Jessica R. 2016. *Reading in the Dark: Horror in Children's Literature and Culture*. Jackson: University of Mississippi Press.

McFadzean, Angus. 2019. *Suburban Fantastic Cinema: Growing Up in the Late Twentieth Century*. London: Wallflower Press.

Mellor, Joe. 2022. 'Best Comments as New Picture of Jacob Rees-Mogg Drops'. *The London Economic*, 1 August. https://www.thelondoneconomic.com/news/best-comments-as-new-picture-of-jacob-rees-mogg-drops-331189.

Midsommar. 2019. Ari Aster, Square Peg, B-Reel Films, A24.

Mitchell, David. 2021. 'Jacob Rees-Mogg Is Using His Pious Image to Con Us'. *The Observer*, 5 December. https://www.theguardian.com/commentisfree/2021/dec/05/jacob-rees-mogg-is-using-his-pious-image-to-con-us.

Morton, Timothy. 2013. *Hyperobjects: Philosophy and Ecology after the End of the World*. Minneapolis: University of Minnesota Press.

Newton, Michael. 2017. 'Cults, Human Sacrifice and Pagan Sex: How Folk Horror Is Flowering Again in Brexit Britain'. *The Guardian*, 30 April. https://www.theguardian.com/film/2017/apr/30/folk-horror-cults-sacrifice-pagan-sex-kill-list.

Noys, Benjamin. Fall 2019–Spring 2020. 'The Breakdown of Capitalist Realism'. *Mediations* 33, no. 1–2: 159–64.

Pacey, Arnold. 1983. *The Culture of Technology*. Cambridge: MIT Press.

Paciorek, Andy. 2018. 'Albion's Children: The Golden Age of British Supernatural Youth Drama'. In *Folk Horror Revival: Field Studies*, 2nd edition, edited by

Andy Paciorek, Grey Malkin, Richard Hing and Katherine Peach, 328–36. Morrisville: Lulu.com.

Parker, Sam. 2017. 'Jacob Rees-Mogg and the Never Ending Search for an Acceptable Tory'. *Esquire*, 6 September. https://www.esquire.com/uk/culture/news/a17079/jacob-rees-mogg-and-the-never-ending-search-for-an-acceptable-tory.

The Pervert's Guide to Ideology. 2012. [Film; Director: Sophie Fiennes]. New York: Zeitgeist Films.

Rieger, Bernhard. 2021. 'British Varieties of Neoliberalism: Unemployment Policy from Thatcher to Blair'. In *The Neoliberal Age?: Britain since the 1970s*, edited by Aled Davies, Ben Jackson and Florence Sutcliffe-Braithwaite, 112–32. London: UCL Press.

Riley, John A. 2013. 'As If the Nineteenth Century Had Never Happened: Haunting the Documentary Form with Robinson in Ruins and the Attic'. *Desist Film*, 19 July. https://desistfilm.com/as-if-the-nineteenth-century-had-never-happened-haunting-the-documentary-form-with-robinson-in-ruins-and-the-attic.

Rustin Mike. 2010. 'From the Beginning to the End of Neo-liberalism in Britain'. *Open Democracy*, 19 May. https://www.opendemocracy.net/en/opendemocrac yuk/after-neo-liberalism-in-britain.

Salvage Editorial Collective. 2020. 'The Tragedy of the Worker: Towards the Proletarocene'. *Salvage*, 31 January. https://salvage.zone/the-tragedy-of-the-wor ker-towards-the-proletarocene.

Scott-Samuel, Alex, Clare Bambra, Chik Collins, David J. Hunter, Gerry McCartney and Kat Smith. 2014. 'The Impact of Thatcherism on Health and Well-Being in Britain'. *International Journal of Health Services* 44, no. 1: 53–71. http://dx.doi.Org/10.2190/HS.

Scovell, Adam. 2017a. 'Brexit-Is-Iccumen-In: The Wicker Man and Britain Today'. *The Quietus*, 10 March. https://thequietus.com/articles/21954-wicker-man-article.

Scovell, Adam. 2017b. *Folk Horror: Hours Dreadful and Things Strange*. Leighton Buzzard: Auteur Publishing.

Shaw, Katy. 2018. *Hauntology: The Presence of the Past in Twenty-First Century English Literature*. London: Palgrave.

Skopic, Alex. 2022. 'Winston Churchill, Imperial Monstrosity'. *Current Affairs*, 20 April. https://www.currentaffairs.org/2022/04/winston-churchill-imperial-mons trosity.

Sutcliffe-Braithwaite, F. A. 2012. 'Neo-liberalism and Morality in the Making of Thatcherite Social Policy'. *Historical Journal*, June 55, no. 2: 497–520.

Sutcliffe-Braithwaite, F. A., M. Hilton and C. Moores. 2017. 'New Times Revisited: Britain in the 1980s'. *Contemporary British History* 31, no. 2: 145–65.

They Live. 1988. [Film; Director: John Carpenter]. Alive Films.

Thoburn, Ethan. 2020. 'Sir Keith Joseph: The Architect of Thatcherism'. *The Bruges Group*, 1 May. https://www.brugesgroup.com/blog/sir-keith-joseph-the-architect-of-thatcherism.

Toynbee, Polly. 2017. 'Jacob Rees-Mogg's Pose Is Fake. The Contempt Is Real'. *The Guardian*, 14 August. https://www.theguardian.com/commentisfree/2017/aug/14/jacob-rees-mogg-contempt-tory-leadership-pitch.

Wagner, Kim A. 2019. 'Rees-Mogg's Book Is "Sentimental Jingoism and Empire Nostalgia"'. *The Observer*, 19 May. https://www.theguardian.com/books/2019/may/19/jacob-rees-mogg-victorians-sentimental-jingoism-and-empire-nostalgia.

Watson, Paul. 2016. 'England's Dark Dreaming'. *The Lazarus Corporation*, 31 July. https://www.lazaruscorporation.co.uk/blogs/artists-notebook/posts/englands-dark-dreaming.

Young, Paul. 2011. *Electric Eden: Unearthing Britain's Visionary Music*. London: Faber & Faber.

Zak, John M. 2020. 'The Great Wave: Margaret Thatcher, The Neo-liberal Age, and the Transformation of Modern Britain'. *Student Publications* 791 (Spring): 1–30.

9

'My Carnaby cassock': Jimmy Savile, *Jim'll Fix It* and *Top of the Pops*

Benjamin Halligan

Abuse television

Those twin poles of BBC television entertainment for British children – graduating from pre-teen *Jim'll Fix It* to teen *Top of the Pops*, from the after-school, tea-time slot (of around 6 pm) to an early evening slot (around 7.30 pm) respectively – showcased the extraordinary television presence and persona of presenter-anchor Sir Jimmy (James) Savile (1926–2011). *Jim'll Fix It* (hereafter abbreviated to *JFI*, which ran from 1975 to 1994) and *Top of the Pops* (hereafter *TOTP*, which ran 1964–2006) have been described and remembered as spectacularly exuberant and celebratory, and culturally and socially formative, in journalistic and autobiographical writings from those thinking back to childhood television experiences. These two programmes warmed and thrilled countless children, leaving the post-war age of austerity, through the upheavals 1960s and 1970s, and on into the new millennium. Savile, on television, was central to all this.

After Savile's fall from grace – a vertiginous descent on a uniquely unimaginable scale – *JFI* and Savile-fronted *TOTP* were regarded as tainted, triggering, evidence for prosecution and as bitter reminders that justice could not be served posthumously. After this, *JFI* and Savile-fronted *TOTP* episodes seemed odd and unsettling, as one unavoidably pondered the horrors hidden behind each episode – or even caught glimpses of the horrors on the screen. Savile's rapid purging from archival broadcasts (see

Aust and Holdsworth 2017, and Wheatley 2020) must invariably be read as, in part, responding to such concerns through (to extend the metaphor that Aust, Holdsworth and Wheatley all use) exorcising the demon: Savile was removed, with a few hiccups (BBC News 2013), as unambiguously and completely as his gravestone in Woodlands Cemetery in Scarborough (BBC News 2012). Savile went, almost overnight, from omnipresent to never present. *JFI*'s embittered producer, Roger Ordish, accused the BBC of Stalinist behaviour in such 'airbrush[ing]' (2020, 100). Yet the discussion of these programmes in the eventual BBC reports on Savile that followed (Smith 2016) indicated something else too.[1] These programmes were not cultural artefacts that, as per #MeToo readings (Boyle 2019), identify or quarantine various films as arising from moments in which abuse also occurred – so that, for example, one's enjoyment of a certain film is dampened or undone by acknowledging the credit of someone involved who also perpetrated abuse, and even perhaps with their victim in the same film. Rather, *JFI* and *TOTP* were the very enabling processes of abuse itself: programme-making as generating opportunities for sexual assault, the resultant cover for it or cover-up of it and the decades-long continuity of all this. Effectively, these programmes facilitate the creation of ecosystems of abuse: abuse's very strategy and operation, it's very institutionalization and invisibilization. These cultural artefacts are not just redolent of abuse then – they were, as well, abuse television.[2] The *Dame Janet Smith Review Report* concluded that *TOTP* 'effectively provided a "picking up" opportunity' (Smith 2016, 75), not least in that

---

[1]All references to Smith (2016) cite the page numbers of the full report. For commentary on the nature of the evolution of the scandal (as, in part, media-driven and so distorted – as overlapping, then, with historical examples of moral panics), along with a questioning of the base-level assumption of belief in historical allegations of abuse, see Mark Smith and Ros Burnett (2018) and Mark Smith (2017) respectively. Mark Duffett critiques the Smith report, and other Savile-related reports, in respect to a tendency to institutional exoneration (Duffett and Hackett 2021, 187–229) – effectively, then, returning the BBC to their initial stance of denial, as outlined in Greer and McLaughlin (2013).

For this chapter, since I note some actual occurrences of seeming criminal activity against identifiable victims, and victims who may not have engaged in investigations or appeared in the reports on Savile that are cited, and wishing to respect any desire on the part of victims to be forgotten or removed from this discourse, I have not cited precise broadcast dates of some of the programmes discussed. Unless otherwise stated, they are all from the early or first few years of the 1980s.

[2]I have explored this idea elsewhere in respect to analysing 'tainted' popular music: see Halligan (2023a, 97–112).

I will note too that *TOTP*, from its earliest days, may well have enabled or included a side operation of (possibly paedophilic) pornography generation (and consumption, and sex with *TOTP* guests), via the official (and on-screen credited) *TOTP* photographer Harry Goodwin. The BBC were alerted to this in 1969, and the *News of the World* reported allegations in 1971, but the BBC failed to act and Goodwin remained in post until 1973 (Smith 2016, 70, 520–4, 735). Additional allegations from this time include the offer of 'money, gifts and services

the format of *Top of the Pops* created problems. In particular, it introduced into the labyrinthine Television Centre a substantial number of teenage girls. Once there, those girls were unsupervised. Once there, they could make contact with visiting music] groups and their support teams and all sorts of BBC staff. (Smith 2016, 75)

'Teenage' here refers to those over fifteen – but those under fifteen frequently got in, a lack of a ticket notwithstanding. When the entry age was raised to sixteen in 1971, following negative media coverage, the assumption of legal sexual consent could be made, despite the seemingly unenforced ban on sexual intercourse on the premises of the BBC (Smith 2016, 66 and 200). Smith notes that 'it does not appear to have been anybody's responsibility to look after the welfare of the young members of the audience' (2016, 580–1). And, indeed, some of these young girls were already vulnerable – particularly those invited from Duncroft School by Savile, connecting his charitable good works with his stewardship of *TOTP* (Smith 2016, 306–68).[3]

Savile used his association with *Top of the Pops* as bait for young girls … some of these ["frequently invited"] girls became regular attenders; Savile called them his "London Team". They made his dressing room their base. Sometimes he would engage in sexual activity there … he would pick up girls at *Top of the Pops*. (Smith 2016, 77)

Specifically, within the scope of Smith's report, *JFI* and *TOTP* 'were the programmes relating to which victims were most frequently assaulted' (390): nineteen victims in relation to *TOTP*, and seventeen in relation to *JFI*, although such incidents 'took place in virtually every one of the BBC premises at which [Savile] worked' (391–2).[4] One assault was linked to the suicide of a fifteen-year-old girl, Claire McAlpine, in 1971 – a matter which Smith notes as a flunked opportunity for a 'wake-up call' for the BBC (512–19). But, more generally, as other inquiries and reports into abuse have

---

(including sexual services)' for BBC staff with a view to promoting various pop records (Smith 2016, 519); a BBC investigation of this 'payola' scandal eventually led to action taken against some staff.

[3]Duncroft was a residential 'approved school', to which a court might refer troubled teenage girls, rather than a secure hospital unit or prison. Savile was a frequent visitor to Duncroft, and abuse occurred in and around these environs too. The school closed in the early 1980s.

[4]While these figures are significant, they must be viewed in the context of the total number of victims of Savile at the BBC – estimated as *c.* 1,000 (Boffey 2014). And the BBC was only one institution in which Savile operated across a number of decades. Appendix 6 of Smith breaks down these data by programme and year (2016, 771–82). Smith also noted, further to a wider investigation into child sexual abuse (CSA) and murder, Operation Yewtree, that only a small number of victims came into contact with Savile via the BBC, and that Smith's investigation had probably not uncovered or tallied the full extent of Savile's abuse at the BBC (51). On Operation Yewtree and Savile, see Gray and Watt (2013).

shown, the legacy of the experience of abuse (which can include the failure to convince those in authority to believe, and act to intervene), particularly at young ages, can derail or prematurely curtail an entire life (see, for example, IICSA 2019 and Graystone 2021).

Can the dynamics and ecosystem of abuse be detected in the mise-en-scène of *JFI* and *TOTP*, or even be speculatively read as powering or determining the mise-en-scène? This chapter then looks to *JFI* and *TOTP* in this way, through textual readings. (The chapter does not offer a clinical analysis of the scenarios of *JFI* and *TOTP* in relation to CSA). While, as noted earlier, the tally of victims from *JFI* and *TOTP* is relatively small, the Savile revelations were typically read in relation to the ambience of *JFI* and *TOTP*. That is, the revelations ended the assumed joy and innocence of these programmes, as recalled by those old enough to have watched them. But this was more than just a passive matter of 'watched' … I refer to those who affectively experienced the programmes, with these regular broadcasts organizing their childhood and teen days, so that these programmes became embedded in their cultural memory. The extraordinary nature of *JFI*, as television, evidencing Ordish's exceptional abilities as a producer, explains such a collective cultural cache. *JFI* was endlessly varied, arguably deeply inclusive (for a while opening with a 'live' reggae version of the theme tune, from Musical Youth), event-driven and celebrity-studded, delivered to children and about (in the sense of entirely centred on) children (which included members of Musical Youth).[5] *JFI* was a vista of aspiration and opportunity for those who wrote letters – and would have spent long hours thinking about them, composing them, decorating them and comparing them to the letters displayed on the show (some of which did not shy away from attempts at writing by the very young). Savile, as ringmaster, is inextricably stamped on these memories. The revelations then represented a terminal blow to such memory – painting them black, possibly igniting other remembered or forgotten traumas (or revisiting remembering moments that may have been near-assaults), perhaps engendering a frisson of existential crisis for those who encountered Savile in person but were spared his attentions, or know of family members, possibly now deceased, who did. This legacy is the terrible psychic cost or burden of the halo effect, discussed later, lent to Savile by those who saw in him a moral bridgehead in immoral times. But this mistaken reading of Savile as a moral bridgehead, founded on

---

[5] *JFI* attracted 15 million viewers during its first season, in 1975 (Davies 2015, 319). I say 'arguably' as the fixees themselves seem distinctly (but not exclusively) white from the necessarily limited sampling of the programmes that underpins this chapter. Nonetheless, gender balance seems in operation – and some concession to age too, with the occasional fixee of very advanced years (for example, a Vicar undertaking flying lessons, or an elderly couple watching an orchestra performance – conducted by former prime minister Edward Heath – of a song from their own youth).

his young person's television presence, suggests something of the function of Savile across moments of societal and political upheaval. This chapter will conclude accordingly, by moving to a wider context in which to only begin to understand or account for Savile's unchecked life of crime.

The parallel to my methodology, in terms of looking again at *JFI* and *TOTP*, is the 'classic' scenario of suddenly opening a door (to the sacristy, the teacher's office, the scout hut and so on) to behold a scene of abuse about to occur, or that has occurred or is even occurring. One reaction is simply not being able to believe your eyes, and so somehow not to see what is happening – rendering it both clearly seen and yet effectively unseen. And, indeed, this rendering is now apparent: Savile sexually assaulting a *TOTP* audience member on-camera while talking to camera:

> This incident can be seen on video. We can see [witness/victim] B8 jumping about in a most uncomfortable way, although she kept a smile on her face. We can see Savile laughing in what appears to me to be a leery way and hear him saying 'A fella could get used to all this.' Looking at it now, it is apparent that Savile was doing something of a sexual nature [outlined as 'she felt Savile's hand going underneath her bottom. She was shocked and leapt in the air. As she came down, his hand was there underneath her, "fiddling" with her.'] Then the camera moved off Savile. B8 told the [Smith] Review that, when the music started she was able to move away from Savile and she went to speak to a BBC employee (a man with earphones) and told him what had happened. He told her not to worry as it was 'just Jimmy Savile mucking about'. When she remonstrated, he told her to move out of the way as they were trying to move the camera. (Smith 2016, 333)

This moment was broadcast, and so must have been deemed acceptable – presumably just dismissed by producers, editors and director, as with the man with earphones on the studio floor, as just an instance of 'mucking about': something seen, as the footage was viewed, and yet not acknowledged in terms of what is actually seen. Dan Davies's pre-Smith Review biography of Savile is called *In Plain Sight*, and invokes just this problematization of sight and cognition – in this case, as reflecting Davies's incredulous exasperation that the crimes he details, across decades, with seemingly thousands involved, were barely hidden. 'What's staggering', Davies writes, 'is how little Jimmy Savile tried to conceal what he was doing' (2015, 270). And, more generally of children's television, Valerie Walkerdine identifies 'the ubiquitous eroticization of little girls in the popular media and the just as ubiquitous ignorance and denial of this phenomenon' (1998, 254; Boyle contextualizes this denial, in relation to Savile revelations, as gendered, 2018). But many petty criminals understand the seen/unseen dynamic: don't surreptitiously slip shop items into pockets or up sleeves, while trying not to look furtive or shifty … just stroll straight out of the store, with what you want, with the confidence of someone who has paid already and so has nothing to hide. In these respects, *JFI* and *TOTP* offer the opportunity to see again something that had been effectively 'unseen', as it unfolds or happens, and the environment of access to sexual abuse. Indeed, 'as it happens' was one of Savile's catchphrases, meaning 'wouldn't you know – by a happy coincidence'. But this was also a comment with which Savile placed himself at the centre of a narrative of happy happenstance, as the very bringer of opportunities for those in his orbit. Both elements (the in-the-moment present of the broadcast programmes, and the fortunate coincidence of meeting Savile) point to Savile's preternatural control and mastery of his surroundings.

Were it not to potentially diminish the nature of these programmes as crime scenes, this approach to *JFI* and *TOTP* could also be placed in a wider context, of recent years, of a re-evaluation of the strangeness of 1970s British popular culture, and the challenges this raises for contemporary perspectives. In Mark Fisher's terminology, this is the identification of the weird and the eerie, especially in cultural artefacts aimed at children or teenagers, resulting in the 1970s (i.e. the decade itself) effectively being put 'on trial' (Fisher 2014, 88–95, and Fisher 2016; Ambrose 2018). This re-evaluation also includes the emergence of critical writing on folk horror (Bacon 2023; Donnelly and Bayman 2023; Edgar and Johnson 2023; Keetley and Heholt 2023), often understood to fully embrace the weird and the eerie, and transform the once-familiar into the threatening.

'Moral danger'

Smith turns to an arresting term to encapsulate the ways in which the *TOTP* environment was one of a proximity to danger of sexual assault. For audience participants,

> From the description I have given of what it was like in Television Centre on the evenings of a *Top of the Pops* recording, with the benefit of hindsight, it is obvious that some of the young girls in the participating audience were at risk of moral danger … [c]learly, looking back, the same risk applied to young boys. (Smith 2016, 508)

Smith notes the 'old-fashioned ring' to 'moral danger' – a description used repeatedly across the Report – but finds this formulation accurate, and useful, in respect to the:

> risk to which young people (mainly young girls) might be exposed as the result of finding themselves in the company of older men and liable to be

involved in sexual conduct which might be unlawful on account of their youth or might be inappropriate and emotionally damaging to them on account of their lack of maturity. (Smith 2016, 68)

The question of morality and danger – particularly with respect to popular culture and its environs, and media culture for impressionable young people – was a major concern of that group of opinion-formers and activists that I have identified elsewhere as the 'Anti-Permissives' of the 1970s (Halligan 2022a). Shared concerns and high-profile interventions – most notably the pro-censorship Festival of Light gatherings, for example, or the commentary emanating from Mary Whitehouse's National Viewers and Listeners Association (NVALA) – often centred on media for children and the permissible limits of expression for media for adults, so that the BBC and the British Board of Film Censors were typical targets. And Savile was among the Anti-Permissives – lending support to ideas of remoralizing a faltering British society, and intervening accordingly, as well as appearing with Whitehouse (in, for example, NVALA's newsletter (see Anon 1978, 1)). Davies also notes Whitehouse with respect to Savile's moves to establish a powerbase via acquaintances, 2015, 276–7). Savile was an (unproductive) member of Lord Longford's investigative team looking into the apparent explosion of pornography (Davies 2015, 280) as emblematic of the moral degradation engendered by the permissive society, further to a verbose House of Lords debate (HL Deb 1971) and with a wildly anecdotal report eventually produced as a paperback (Longford Committee 1972). As a gatekeeper or interlocuter of popular culture, Savile, on the one hand, was the exemplar of 'wholesome' family entertainment, for 'Auntie' (the affectionate familial name for the BBC) – despite his unusual appearances. Episodes of *JFI* are peppered with Savile's discrete 'God bless you's, kindly experts giving up their time to entertain and educate children, excursions into institutions of care (particularly hospitals, particularly for the young), encounters with senior establishment figures (Margaret Thatcher appeared twice, in 1977 and 1983, the latter as prime minister), and (sometimes grumpy) pop stars corralled into engaging in good deeds (Culture Club and Boy George, for example, enlivening a school morning assembly, or Kajagoogoo allowing one of Savile's fixees to be a co-vocalist).[6] On the other hand, Savile could

---

[6]Transcriptions/records of Thatcher's appearances are available at https://www.margarett hatcher.org/document/103173 and https://www.margaretthatcher.org/document/105269 respectively.

Commentators often talk about Savile's startling sartorial appearance, matched with his unique yodelling exclamations, but his appearance was ever-changing, from the wildly outlandish (jangling, blingy accessorizations, shiny tracksuits, sometimes an exposed and taunt torso beneath, long and unruly dyed hair, which became increasingly straggly as he aged, sunglasses and substantial cigars) to entirely business-like (sober tailored suits). One is tempted

orchestrate condemnations of 'serious' entertainment on the grounds that it
energized dormant delinquency, in respect to a discussion of *A Clockwork
Orange* (Stanley Kubrick, 1971) with the source novel's author Anthony
Burgess (Burgess 1990, 256–7). Savile's public profile presented Whitehouse
with a dilemma: *TOTP* was an NVALA target – taken as a showcase for
violence and anarchy (Whitehouse 1978, 43; see also the Whitehouse-esque
educationalist Elizabeth Manners 1971, 111, 179). For Whitehouse, the
programme stimulated group masturbation among 'small boys' (Thompson
2013, 101–2). And Savile, famous for his lifelong bachelor status, had gone
on record about his enthusiasm for sexual pursuits, in the press and in his
own writing (Smith 2016, 403–34). But, on the other hand, as evidenced in
JFI, Savile was seemingly a force for a renewal of national moral propriety.
Whitehouse turns, with determination, a blind eye to the former flaws.
Further to watching (and seemingly being involved with) *JFI*, she writes:

> Jimmy spoke very kindly about our [NVALA] work and he was
> very touched by the 'We've fixed it for Jim' medallion which we had
> specially made for him. The team responsible for the show is quite
> obviously committed to something way beyond just the production of a
> programme. Some of the stories they told about the way in which they
> get involved with the children were very moving, like the one about the
> little girl Jimmy said he was going to marry and they got engaged with a
> huge cuddly toy just a few days before she died. … [Savile] added 'While
> Mrs Whitehouse possibly wouldn't agree with my personal lifestyle, it is
> through organizations like hers that there is some semblance of decency.'
> Well, I don't know anything about Jimmy's lifestyle and, in any case, it's
> no business of mine. (Whitehouse 1994, 88–9)

The halo lent to Savile then shone for decades, despite gossip and innuendo
as common currency in media circles and beyond, and seemingly further
formal notifications and allegations of inappropriate conduct (Smith 2016,
435–50 and 451–89 respectively). The halo dazzled even the most cynical.
Journalist Lynn Barber, for a 1990 *Independent on Sunday* profile, daringly
aired rumoured allegations of pederasty ('into little girls') but later agreed
with Savile that his recently awarded knighthood represents a state-level
verification of his good character ('the fact that the tabloids have never
come up with a scintilla of evidence against Jimmy Savile is as near proof
as you can ever get', 1991, 249). Fellow light entertainer David Mitchell
could still advance the same assurance or exoneration decades later, on the

---

to find the kind of wrong-footing strategy of some (British) managers in this spectrum: to
jarringly or counter-intuitively recast interactions as friendly and informal, or professional and
formal, so disorientating those under their management. But the tracksuit seems to have had
a utilitarian function too: ease of removal, to enable rapid sexual assault (Smith 2016, 447).

very cusp of the revelations ('child molestation – it rings true without being true', 2012, 117). Investigative documentary-maker Louis Theroux would be wholly outmanoeuvred and ethically compromised by Savile, even as he edged towards asking about pederasty and violence, and thereafter treated Savile and himself as comedy promotional figures for his BBC documentary, *When Louis Met … Jimmy* (Will Yapp, 2000). Theroux and Yapp, in their limitations, but undoubtedly without intention, illustrate Duffett's thesis of institutional exoneration – a process which would finally break surface in the scandal following a cancelled BBC *Newsnight* profile of Savile (see Greer and McLaughlin 2013).

It is Whitehouse's 'the stories … were very moving' element that may be a key to the abrogation and emotional trajectories of each fix-it segment that seemed to have been made for the oddness of *JFI*. There is a tendency to put pre-pubescent children and young teenagers in positions of measured mild distress – for example: riding a ghost train, asking for a repair of a much-loved teddy bear or publicly overcoming some sort of emotive impediment, such as an inability to eat with chopsticks. But there is a tendency too to put nervous rather than extrovert children in the spotlight. Sometimes this involves dressing the fixees up for an adult-like performance, as with the children's pop show *Minipops*.[7] So, for example, a boy is directed and coaxed through the filming of the James Bond opening sequence, with himself as 007, and a girl (of maybe thirteen–fifteen) whose mother despairs at her inability to tidy her bedroom, is transformed into the character Wonder Woman, in a midriff-exposing outfit, and is seen to tidy her room with superhuman speed. But there is intimacy to much of this, centred on the singled-out and now isolated child: a prolonged sequence with a softly spoken make-up artist transforming a young boy into a werewolf (make-up, hair gel, fangs), or a young girl reading Savile a bedtime story as he pretends to sleep under a blanket, with the studio lights dimmed. Another fix, involving a trip to the Bahamas for fishing, includes shots of the sleeping boy selected, presented as seemingly parent- or guardian-less. (There is no indication that any of these specific abovementioned fixes involved children who were Savile's victims).

This tendency to single out individual children from the crowd – finding something special about them or particular in them, and taking them to one side for further attention (both on-screen but then, as per the reports cited here, off-screen, typically to Savile's dressing room, and often via Savile's non-BBC assistants) – is familiar from the ambience of artefacts claimed by paedophilic cultures, particularly Luchino Visconti's 1971 film adaptation of Thomas Mann's *Death in Venice* (see Halligan 2022a, 257, 264 n. 10).[8]

---

[7]*Minipops* was broadcast on Channel 4 in 1983; a number of tie-in albums were also released.
[8]Generally, Savile seems not to have fraternized with BBC colleagues, or been part of the BBC's social culture, Smith (2016, 48–9).

And Savile's 'special' chair, with semi-hidden compartments containing prizes and surprises for children, offers further draws and fascination for individuals who draw close to Savile. The *JFI* studio beanbags were used too, to immobilize guests. Once the children were sat, this allowed Savile to select potential victims, and join them, in a squash, on their beanbags (Smith 2016, 344, 357, 616). This was in the 'privileged subgroup of the audience' picked out (in Smith's description; 2016, 592) to surround Savile for the opening of each episode of *JFI* – vibrant, jostling, huddled, welcoming, fun-filled shots familiar from *TOTP* too. Each fix culminates with the child back in the studio with Savile, and ceremoniously given the chunky 'Jim Fixed It for Me' gold medal – a moment akin to a royal award, with the child bowing their head before Savile (or proxy star guest) and a branding of 'Jim' on the recipient.

But the journey may have continued beyond the dressing room. *JFI*, with shots of request letters for fixes (themselves a form of intimacy: children writing directly to Savile, sending letters which are often confessional, and sometimes sharing a secret), effectively enabling access to the children. Addresses are shown, at length – even telephone numbers (and this in the early years of video recorder use too) – and then with the names of the children repeated in the end credits, prefaced with 'Jimmy Savile OBE KCSG Fixed It for'.[9]

In reality, Savile did little in terms of preparation for *JFI*, despite the suggestion that he himself sifted through these letters and personally arranged the fixes (Smith 2016, 50, 255–6), and despite the nature of the marketing of the programme in the *Jim'll Fix It Annual* tie-ins (Ordish 1980 and 1981). Roger Ordish, who produced *JFI* for two decades, was clear as to Savile's minimal involvement after the series. This 'front man' had 'virtually nothing to do with the programme that bore his name. When he arrived in the studio on recording days, he would ask me, "What have I fixed today?"' (2020, 101, 100).[10] And this lackadaisical approach is also apparent in some of his presenting – Savile fluffed autocue readings, or distractedly looked at

[9]The giving of addresses of correspondents was seemingly not unique to *JFI*; the BBC's *Multi Coloured Swap Shop*, broadcast between 1976 and 1982 also did this.

OBE: the Queen-bestowed Order of the British Empire, awarded in 1972, and Savile was Knighted in 1990; KCSG: a Vatican-bestowed Knighthood, of the Pontifical Equestrian Order of St Gregory the Great, awarded in 1990. Savile, a practising Roman Catholic (although seemingly with some formal warden-like positions in the Church of England too), could not be stripped of the latter after this death, despite the request from the Archbishop of Westminster (RTE 2012).

[10]This observation is found too in Ordish (1992). Ordish had undergone the 'profoundly distressing for him' experience of the Smith inquiry (Smith 2016, 82), effectively into the majority of his life's work, and was found to have no case to answer. But his unhinged, self-published autobiography, railing against the bad faith of lawyers and victims in various Savile inquiries (2022, 95–9) and the perceived absurdities and affront of political correctness and ideas of privilege (170–3) could reasonably suggest that the revelations after Savile's death may

or adjusted his clothes, and he constantly seemed to be in a rush. But the implication of Savile's authorial control also arises from Savile's centrality to *JFI*, which results in his on-camera direction. He handles and adjusts the children as he presents them to others, and arranges them for the camera, often holding them from behind, and with difficult-to-track, sleight-of-hand hand movements, and sometimes seemingly (as if accidentally, in the crush) brushing his hands over backsides. Savile assembled and operated within crowds, as if to dissipate responsibility for stray hands, and maximize a sense of witnesses and so safety for those around him. *JFI* opened with Savile in the middle of the above-mentioned crowd of children, as if the epicentre of a party already in full swing (and from audio from moments before the broadcast, he can be heard authoritatively shifting and arranging the children next to him). This is in stark contrast to the standard shot of the lone presenter or presenters, of *Blue Peter*, of news programmes or the weather, of chat shows, of *Jackanory* – but more generally before technology allowed a wider democratization of television broadcasts, with the ease of an ability to move outside studios, and a sense that the everyman should have their say too.[11] For *TOTP*, at times, but particularly during the 1980s, Savile sometimes seems to emerge, for his introduction to each group, from within the crowd crush (on the studio floor, on the balcony, etc.), as if momentarily squeezed out from an entanglement of bodies and limbs, only to be sucked back in again once the camera has panned away. Savile proactively arranged this tableau vivant – instructing guests to move forward, to move closer in to him (Smith 2016, 286). All other *TOTP* presenters, perhaps mindful of preserving their star status in the fray of guests, seem to maintain some distance, and appear as placed or arranged in the shot – the others with them now downgraded to extras, and not fully integrated as 'straight-men' for Savile's jokes and performances, or foci for his attentions. These audience members would be selected by the floor manager or Savile himself (Smith 2016, 67). Smith records one assault facilitated this way, on a sixteen-year-old in 1969: an audience member was invited up to the podium by 'a man with a clipboard', whereupon Savile undid her hotpants from behind and pushed his hand 'underneath her bottom'. She complained to the man with the clipboard, who told her she must be mistaken, summoned security and 'she was taken outside and left on the street' (Smith 2016, 5). Nearly one quarter of a century later, and 'I must admit, ladies and gentlemen', Savile

---

have taken their toll. The latter element of his book, in the context of this chapter, can be read as an enraged rejoinder to the Fisher-identified 'Jimmy Savile and "the 70s on trial"' (Fisher 2014, 88–95) and the unfairness of imposing today's standards on yesterday. As Smith notes, 'I have lost count of the number of witnesses to the Savile investigation who have told me that "things were different in those days"' (2016, 46).
[11]*Blue Peter* was first broadcast on the BBC in 1958 and continues at the time of writing. *Jackanory* was broadcast on the BBC from 1965 to 1996.

exclaims, with disconcertingly Christian (specifically Roman Catholic) terminology, and while looking directly at (even angling his head into) the chests of the women either side of him, 'that being surrounded by so much beauty has got grave problems if you aren't stern of will'. Another near quarter of a century later, with Savile at almost eighty, a further *TOTP* assault is recorded (Smith 2016, 363–4).

Savile's differences from other presenters finds an arresting reflection in an official history of *TOTP*, *The Story of Top of the Pops* (Blacknell 1985; with the inevitable 'Foreword by Jimmy Savile OBE, KCSG'). On shifting Savile from *Juke Boy Jury* to the new programme, *TOTP*, in 1964, a producer for the former, Tom Sloan, is quoted as advising 'I don't want that man on the television' (20). And, upon Savile's instalment – this 'non-regulation', 'bizarre', 'buoyant', 'not the typical … hardly typical at all', 'a bit strange alright', 'outlandish', 'very much a law unto himself' presence – producer Alastair 'Johnnie' Stewart 'would always give Savile a free reign' in sartorial matters. These wary quoted observations, incredibly, come in the first few pages of Blacknell's book. Stewart himself was interviewed by Savile on the occasion of the 500th edition of *TOTP* (transmitted 4 October 1973), with Savile's arm around him, and seemed cowed and scared, taking refuge in laughing, during a sequence that also included Cliff Richard sporting a large cross (familiar garb from his Festival of Light appearances) and joking about marijuana, and Kenny Everett's seemingly mid-LSD hallucination (on Everett, see Leith 1993). Bill Cotton, who became Head of Light Entertainment upon Sloan's death in 1970, was also part of the interview. He 'believed too much in Jimmy Savile' for Ordish, who failed in his attempts to secure a different presenter at the outset of *JFI*.

Stewart's obituary posits that *TOTP* itself was a concept he had translated from Savile's Radio Luxembourg show, *Tween and Twenty Disc Club* (Sweeting 2005). If so, then it seems to have taken until the early 1980s for *TOTP* to be further Savile-ized: in the step away from watching performing groups (or cutting to performances filmed elsewhere) and towards a further and fuller integration of the studio audience. That is, *TOTP* went from an arrangement of looking on at the group performing (sometimes with the audience as little more than shadowy movement, denoting the supposedly live nature of the event) to the kind of crowded, supposedly semi-controlled chaotic arrangements that opened the boisterous *JFI*. *TOTP* in the early 1980s resembled a wilder office party in fancy dress, or themed night in a package holiday resort disco. Groups were now sometimes placed in the middle of the audience, with the crowd as the backdrop – wittingly (in the case of the dancing troupe Zoo) or even unwittingly (in the case of standard audience members) becoming backing dancers. The aesthetic was neon (orange and purples predominated), the jingles peppy, the chart update given with an urgent air against a propulsive soundbed. More studio space seems to have been opened up and fully lit – with the clothes of guests bright, the hair big, the dancing demonstrative, the flow nonstop and the presenters barely punctuating the ongoing music and festivities. One episode (transmitted 2 September 1982) installed a circus merry-go-round in the studio. This kind of performative silliness, along with novelty songs, had been a strain of the now-forgotten 1970s pop music (Hodgkinson 2022), and had always been present in *TOTP*, notably with producer-singer Jonathan King: singalongs, dance-alongs, clap-alongs and with clothing to mimic – as with the multicoloured, outsized wigs of 'One for You, One for Me' of 1978 (which now, with its celebratory flag-waving, appears to be deliberately countering the Sex Pistols' 'God Save the Queen' of 1977). King had used the Surrey teen disco, the Walton Hop, as a testing ground for his songs and routines, and a catalyst for their promotion, as well as a way of keeping in touch with, and drawing inspiration from, the changing tastes of the young – a disco that, it emerged during King's later trial, was also a stalking ground for paedophilic predators (Ronson 2001).[12] And, in December 1973, Savile dressed as a womble, Orinoco, so that he could flirt anonymously with guests (two of whom – both children – became his victims (Smith 2016, 317).[13] One assumes Orinoco was the chosen suit by Savile since his long red scarf could potentially obscure hand movements, or lasso victims. To be precise about the gravity of these crimes, Smith includes recollections of Savile, in and partial or fully out of a Womble costume, raping a ten-year-old boy, and seriously sexually assaulting a twelve-year-old girl, together, in his dressing room (2016, 320; Smith notes the credibility of these accounts: 325), on 18 December 1973.

---

[12]Selecting popular music for such purposes seems not to have been unusual. Petronius's guide to 'underground' Swinging London advances the suggestion of establishing a pop star fan club in order to access young fans: a 'happy hunting ground ... you may even deflect [fan club members'] passion from their idol to yourself, and at least give them more than an autograph ... there are the schools – comprehensive or not. Here you are on your own. And watch out – or you may end up doing a stretch' (Petronius 1969, 3, 98–9).

King, who was the US correspondent for *TOTP* in the early 1980s, was accused of enacting a more localized version of Petronius's advice, in Surrey, whereas Savile saw *TOTP* 'as bait for young girls' (Smith 2016, 76). Ronson offers a summary from Wham!'s manager Simon Napier-Bell (who had been subjected to Tam Paton's attempt to pick him up when younger; Paton managed the Bay City Rollers): 'the great difference between the British and the American pop industries is this: the American impresarios are traditionally driven by money, while their British counterparts were historically driven by gay sex, usually with younger boys – and that British pop was conceived as a canvas upon which older gay svengalis could paint their sexual fantasies, knowing their tastes would be shared by the teenage girls who bought the records' (Ronson 2001).

[13]Blacknell notes that others also wore Womble costumes. The Wombles were popular *TOTP* performers in the early 1970s (1985, 97): stop motion anthropomorphic upright creatures for a BBC children's show (which first ran 1973–5), given over to litter collection, and based on Elisabeth Beresford's books. On the Wombles see Johnston (2010), and on children's pop music, including the Wombles and other novelty acts, see Maloy (2022).

This shift to greater audience participation in *TOTP* mirrored (and boosted) shifts to New Romanticism, late disco, watered down rap (as with Wham!) and Hi-NRG genres, eradicating punk and post-punk (and, to invoke a cliché, their miserabilism and anger) and Prog Rock (and its studiousness) – as if relics of the 1970s, along with the Labour Party and the mythology of social strife of the 'Winter of Discontent' years of 1978/9. In dance music's ascendency, groups that seemed to want to engulf the crowd in the performance, decentring the group itself as the sole point of focus, began to characterize *TOTP*. The music now lent itself to the party and to fun times: a depoliticization of music for the coming neoliberal times, drawing on the legacies of Glam Rock showmanship and (via King at least) the Walton Hop teen cultures. Savile, who rarely passed judgement on music, was in sympathy: disliking 'message' music, and positioning himself as an 'atmospheresmith' (as opposed to the Beatles, and Bob Dylan, and their wordsmithery, Mardles 2007). At this point, Savile seems to step down from the podiums and ceiling walkways from which he often presented in the 1970s, and into the midst of the party.[14] This reworking of the *TOTP* format anticipates the managed pandemonium of live performances for *The Word* (see Halligan 2023b) and the relocation to actual nightclubs for *The Hitman and Her*, by the end of the decade.[15]

As it happens

What was actually occurring in Savile's inter-song introductions? Many Savile episodes of *TOTP* pass by with nothing alarming, and Savile is often entirely perfunctory – just one quick quip and funny face per introduction. Other episodes move from one inter-song introduction to another, with each containing elements that are difficult to process. This is true of their cryptic, seemingly coded, utterances and often (Spike Milligan-like, or *Goons*-like) surrealism: one inter-song moment begins with Savile proclaiming 'good morning to you!' And this difficulty to process is true too of a series of on-camera gropings that can be taken to be assaults. I turn to emblematic examples of these elements of the cryptic and the criminal.

---

[14]These observations draw on sample viewings of available material; a fuller survey of the hundreds of hours of still-existing programming (much now beyond reach, but also much wiped rather than archived over the decades) would need to occur to empirically verify these observations as typical.

[15]*The Word* was broadcast on Channel 4, 1990–5. *The Hitman and Her* was broadcast on ITV, 1988–92. Jeremy Deller, in his documentary/lecture *Everybody in the Place: An Incomplete History of Britain 1984–1992* (2019) posits rave as ending this kind of silly, celebratory music event by the late 1980s, and badly wrong-footing *The Hitman and Her* in the process.

A 10 September 1981 episode featured a performance by *TOTP* regulars, the Black British trio Imagination, of their single 'In and Out of Love', from the album *Body Talk*. As these titles suggest, Imagination sang of eroticism – but often romantically, and aligned to a post-disco, semi-easy listening drift to muted soul and very smooth funk. The single's cover showed the trio, naked from the waist up, with an intimation (via a leather belt or strap across a torso) of bondage of a sexual or – as prompted by this performance, and recollections of Isaac Hayes's appearance in gold chains in the 1970s – of a slavery kind.[16] The actual *TOTP* performance features the trio dancing, stripper-like, as if hired for a hen party, in front of three seated white women (backs to the audience). Imagination thrust at and gyrate before them, with one woman simulating groping Leee John's chest. This racialized fantasy could be read as performing to a white/Western sexualized fear or fascination with the 'unleashed' Black man or, Hayes-like, a post-colonial subversion of ideas of oppression and othering, transforming objectification into empowerment. What this clearly is not is an integration of Black and white, in terms of personnel and music or, ultimately, a shared class perspective of oppression – as exemplified by the Specials and particularly *A Message to You Rudy* of 1979. The Imagination class perspective is apparent in the official music video for the single: cocktails sporting chunky slices of orange at (studio-recreated) beach bars, dancing around swimming pools, fake 'tropical' greenery and jewellery-accessorized bikinis, as per a package holiday (for example, Club 18–30), and an array of mostly non-Black women enticed by the singers (offering definition to the 'in and out of love' – the singers seem to fall for a succession of women, seen here lined up in swimming pools, harem-like and so on). In these respects, 'In and Out of Love' seems perfectly in tune with *TOTP* of the 1980s, musically, aspirationally and (a)politically. Savile then perhaps alludes to the video's setting, or the ethnicity of the singers, when he quips (with a cut back to him, at the song's end): 'Hey – I'll tell you something: this is much better than being on a desert island!' The 'better' then would be his own supposed harem of lined-up available women (Savile was then in his mid-fifties, in distinct contrast to the youth of the programme); the 'this' is presumably the *TOTP* studio and environs; the 'you' casts the viewer, again, as privy to direct confession. The shared joke is that one does not need a desert island or generally freer holiday environment to gain or amass sexual advantage. Savile's pragmatic opportunism is presented as trumping Imagination's Orientalism. Time and again, Savile talks explicitly of what will or can happen off-camera – for example: 'should I tell you the secrets of these

---

[16]On Hayes, and the political contexts of his performance and presence, see Fairclough, Halligan, Persley and Rambarran (2023, 2, 6). But the subversion/eroticization of chains became true of other Black groups too – for example *Ecstasy* by the Ohio Players (1973).

ladies [around me], ladies and gentlemen? Or should I introduce you to Dexy's Midnight Runners? Or ha, oh-ha, ah-ha!'

After the performance from Dexy's, Savile is seen with Coleen Nolan on a podium, introducing a performance by the Nolan Sisters: 'Ladies and gentlemen, there are more Nolans than meet the eye. This is a Nolan here. She is not old enough to join in but the rest of them [the Nolans] are, down there – my goodness gracious yes!' As he talks, he places an arm around her, way above her waist, and so pushing her chest up, and bouncing her body: in short, sexualized groping, presumably with Coleen immobilized and muted by being on camera. This same move is seen with a number of other women placed next to him for such inter-song introductions – possibly part of a Savile modus operandi that seemed to involve a haptic 'sounding-out' of potential victims: a stress-test to find those who do not object, sometimes done with kissing up the arm (see, for example, Guardian/Press Association, 2014), or even licking (Smith 2016, 263, 349, 366 *et passim*). Nolan, then fourteen, does not outwardly register objection – and later went on record concerning Savile's attempts to have sex with her (Bullock 2021).

'My Carnaby cassock'

In a documentary profile of Savile broadcast for 'Schools and Colleges' (i.e. educational television for children), *Scene: Personal View: Jimmy Savile* (first transmitted in the early afternoon on BBC 1, 27 November 1969, and produced by Julian Aston), Savile is seen delivering a talk or sermon in a church in Ilford, Essex. This is presented as one facet of Savile's diverse portfolio of interests and activities in the profile: hospital porter work (at which he appears – on camera – exceptionally good), undergoing Marine training, entertaining disabled young people, and DJ'ing. But Savile appears in a bizarre fashion in the church: hooded vestments of baroque, psychedelic design, first glimpsed in the procession of clerics down the aisle of the church and towards the altar, with Savile with them, moving in step with the cleric's halting, respectful pace. This is not a free-for-all hippy service of the type, of this moment, described in an imaginary documentary in David Lodge's 1980 novel about contemporary Catholicism, *How Far Can You Go?* Rather, Savile appears as an emissary of the contemporary world and social mores, then in enormous flux, or even a returning missionary, back in the midst of the establishment, as per the psychedelicized clerical clothing. He comments on this in the documentary: 'My Carnaby [Street] cassock is the envy of all Vicars and prelates that see it.' In this respect, verified in the documentary by the young people in the church, listening to Savile, he is both emissary of the outside world and the revitalizer or renewer of this older, staid (church) world. He seems to exist as a bridge between the two social spheres: the baffling flux of the new, the staid of the old. But, more than this, Savile seems able to safely channel the priorities of this new world into the older, staid world: a gatekeeper of the new, even a spy in this world, and a figure able to orchestrate and defuse the new, to counter the counterculture at a moment of societal and civil crisis (around 1968) – meaning renewal or revitalization as reformist rather than revolutionary propositions. Savile functions as the anti-Daniel Cohn-Bendit, or anti-Che Guevara or anti-Tariq Ali: an iconographic figure in the slipstream of revolution – understood to be channelling and directing enormously potent waves of youthful energy. This function, in the context of the discussion of this chapter, begins to explain the paradox of Savile's endless confessions and comedy enactments of his own criminal behaviour. The effective anti-revolutionary fully engages with the revolutionary world, rather than setting themselves against it. Savile then presents himself as immersed in the fleshpots, and as familiar with the Permissive Age as any jaded exponent of free love. As he ogles, gropes, licks and leers, this much is understood to be apparent. The missionary has returned home – but brings with him some of the wildness of the heathen lands. And yet that ogling, groping, licking and leering is a grotesque caricature: Savile critiques permissiveness with this performance – free love as base and immoral opportunism rather than a considered position against Victorian strictures of sexual propriety. And intent, in Savile's performances, is misread as comic irony by those with editorial control. What he actually says to the congregation can be read as meshing Good Samaritan-ism with self-aggrandisement: he has done well for himself but, rather than privately enjoy that wealth, he has allowed it to free him up to help others.[17]

A certain worldly saintliness redeems Savile's performance of sinfulness: Savile's Catholicism, his 'God bless' refrains, his presence in *Scene* as a cleric, his work for and with the sick, his writing about religion (Savile 1979; on this book, and its shared authorship, see Smith 2016, 13–14, 101–2, 408–9), and even an appearance on the BBC's *Songs of Praise* the month after the televised profile (28 December 1969; Savile seemingly in the same cassock as *Scene*). *Scene* in this respect might be considered in relation to another documentary of the moment – the one that established the figure of Mother Theresa, thanks to Malcolm Muggeridge (one of Longford's pornography investigators/co-authors, closely associated with, and indeed the namer of, the Festival of Light, and sexual assaulter too; Halligan 2022a, 97–8, Levy 2015). This was the BBC's *Something Beautiful for God* (Peter Chafer, 1969). Both *Scene* and *Something Beautiful* single

---

[17]This reading anticipates Thatcher's own biblical parable, of a *Weekend World* interview (6 January 1980): 'No-one would remember the good Samaritan if he'd only had good intentions; he had money as well' (Transcript via https://www.margaretthatcher.org/document/104210).

out godly individuals, whose mission is not derailed by the contemporary world – negotiating poverty in the Global South (in St Theresa of Calcutta's case) and post-austerity age hedonism in the West (in Savile's case). (And Mother Theresa would also come in for criticism – partly on the Savile-esque grounds that her saintly status precluded any criticism or investigation of her work, alleged to have been far from the best interests of the sick – most notably by Christopher Hitchens (1995).)

The same 'two worlds' dynamic makes sense of Savile's presence in young people's television, and the licences and invisibility that he seems to have been afforded in this – in the exalted context of Savile as 'really seriously important' to the BBC and, as per a 'witness … well placed to speak on this', that Savile at the point of *JFI* was the BBC's 'biggest asset' (Smith 2016, 50 and 260 respectively). In this mediated respect, and in tandem with Savile's insider connections to politicians and Royals over decades (Booth 2012), his positions in various hospitals and on executive boards (around, for example, attempting a crude diffusing of industrial action – enacted via political backing; Davies and Mason 2014), his status as the great orchestrator of charity solutions over state interventions, his inside track friendliness with the police and his ennoblements, Savile can only really be taken as a semi-renegade operative of the coming neoliberal state. But Savile appears as a state operative *within* the crowd – as identified in *JFI* and *TOTP* here and, beyond these, in packed charity marathons, on the ward with hospital workers and the unwell, and so on – rather than isolated from the crowd. I have explored elsewhere, in respect to television coverage of history-freighted events such as Royal funerals, the tendency towards isolation of the presenters, and the silencing of the massed crowds (Halligan 2022b). In this, presenters are understood to speak both of and for the multitudes, in shoring up myths undergirding the attempted renewal of senses of national identity, and with this assumed mandate becoming increasingly threadbare and untenable. Savile, deep in the crowd, can be read as the reverse: multitude-mandated and hands-on.

Moving beyond 1968, and thinking about this role or function during the next youth culture crisis (punk), Savile's positioning is clear: a 17 April 1980, 7.25 pm BBC 1 episode of *TOTP*, with a suited Savile, contains performances from groups that parents might associate with danger for their children or teenagers (charting punk groups Sham 69 and The Ruts, and hard rock group Girl, with 'Hollywood Tease'), offset by groups self-presenting as harmless fun (The Nolans, some disco and Barbara Dixon's 'January February'). Savile – still the kindly Jim who fixed it for so many children – represents assurance for parents, mitigating any frisson of danger of exposure to the former, rebarbative strain (punk and sexualized rock), and negating it with the latter, easy listening strain. Savile becomes the vector through which popular youth culture, then in revolt once again, passes as it is mass disseminated, so making it palatable to concerned parents: Savile as state safeguarder, proxy babysitter, cuddly womble, cassocked cleric, remoralizer, restorer of control, curator-defanger of culture.

References

Ambrose, Darren, ed. 2018. *K-Punk: The Collected and Unpublished Writings of Mark Fisher (2004–2016)*. London: Repeater Books.
Anon. 1978. 'Jimmy's Special Award'. *The Viewer and Listener* January: 1.
Aust, Rowan, and Amy Holdsworth. 2017. 'The BBC Archive Post-Jimmy Savile: Irreparable Damage or Recoverable Ground?' In *The Past in Visual Culture: Essays on Memory, Nostalgia and the Media*, edited by Jilly Boyce Kay, Cat Mahoney and Caitlin Shaw, 170–84. Jefferson: McFarland.
Bacon, Richard. 2023. *Future Folk Horror: Contemporary Anxieties and Possible Futures*. Maryland: Lexington Books.
Barber, Lynn. 1991. *Mostly Men*. London: Viking.
BBC News. 2012. 'Jimmy Savile's Headstone Removed from Scarborough Cemetery'. *BBC News*. 10 October. https://www.bbc.co.uk/news/uk-engl and-york-north-yorkshire-19893373.
BBC News. 2013. 'BBC Receives 216 Complaints for Tweenies Jimmy Savile Spoof'. *BBC News*. 21 January. https://www.bbc.co.uk/news/entertainm ent-arts-21108337. Accessed 24 September 2023.
Blacknell, Steve. 1985. *The Story of Top of the Pops*. Northants: Patrick Stephens.
Boffey, Daniel. 2014. 'Revealed: How Jimmy Savile Abused up to 1,000 Victims on BBC Premises'. *The Guardian*. 18 January. https://www.theguardian. com/media/2014/jan/18/jimmy-savile-abused-1000-victims-bbc. Accessed 24 September 2023.
Booth, Robert. 2012. 'Jimmy Savile Caused Concern with Behaviour during Visits to Prince Charles'. *The Guardian*. 29 October. https://www .theguardian. com/media/2012/oct/29/jimmy-savile-behaviour-prince-charles. Accessed 24 September 2023.
Boyle, Karen. 2018. 'Hiding in Plain Sight: Gender, Sexism and Press Coverage of the Jimmy Savile Case'. *Journalism Studies* 19, no. 11: 1562–78.
Boyle, Karen. 2019. *#MeToo, Weinstein and Feminism*. London: Palgrave Macmillan.
Bullock, Andrew. 2021. '"He Said He'd Look After Me": Coleen Nolan Reveals Paedophile Jimmy Savile Invited Her Up To His Hotel Suite When She Was Just 14'. *Daily Mail*. 18 March. https://www.dailymail.co.uk/tvshow biz/article-9375681/Coleen-Nolan-reveals-paedophile-Jimmy-Savile-invi ted-hotel-suite-just-14.html.
Burgess, Anthony. 1990. *You've Had Your Time: Being the Second Part of the Confessions of Anthony Burgess*. London: Heinemann.
Davies, Caroline, and Rowena Mason. 2014. 'Jimmy Savile: Detailed Investigation Reveals Reign of Abuse across NHS'. *The Guardian*. 27 June. https://www.theg uardian.com/uk-news/2014/jun/26/edwina-currie-shocked-jimmy-savile-role.
Davies, Dan. 2015. *In Plain Sight: The Life and Lies of Jimmy Savile*. London: Quercus Editions.

Donnelly, Kevin J., and Louis Bayman, eds. 2023. *Folk Horror on Film: Return of the British Repressed*. Manchester: Manchester University Press.

Duffett, Mark, and Jon Hackett. 2021. *Scary Monsters: Monstrosity, Masculinity and Popular Music*. London: Bloomsbury Academic.

Edgar, Robert, and Wayne Johnson, eds. 2023. *The Routledge Companion to Folk Horror*. London: Routledge.

Fairclough, Kirsty, Benjamin Halligan, Nicole Hodges Persley and Shara Rambarran. 2023. 'Y'all! The Diva and Us'. In *Diva: Feminism and Fierceness from Pop to Hip-Hop*, edited by Kirsty Fairclough, Benjamin Halligan, Nicole Hodges Persley and Shara Rambarran, 1–21. New York: Bloomsbury Academic.

Fisher, Mark. 2014. *Ghosts of My Life: Writings on Depression, Hauntology and Lost Futures*. London: Zero Books.

Fisher, Mark. 2016. *The Weird and the Eerie*. London: Repeater Books.

Gray, David, and Peter Watt. 2013. '"Giving Victims a Voice": A Joint MPS and NSPCC Report into Allegations of Sexual Abuse Made against Jimmy Savile under Operation Yewtree'. Metropolitan Police and National Society for the Prevention of Cruelty to Children. https://library.nspcc.org.uk/HeritageScripts/Hapi.dll/filetransfer/2013GivingVictimsAVoiceSexualAllegationsMadeAgainstJimmySavile.pdf?filename=CC18C70DB7C8C3D49403BB94EB176F95207E5F66235DCA89651F5ED2BA5DA9311A3547010EB1745F9098C8189E66B54F16BBCA4419250DDAE584462476E362622BD259A20D1597309210AC995C99F449C7702D4CF7627CBCEC72291068BFEAFDDC8C9625B71658F22EAD1E815FED12FF6D0DEB5CDBB40AEA4EF5D058E57168353BEB2DA3730B57DF729865CC3271FEE73BB1D434AB645BB5&DataSetName=LIVEDATA. Accessed 20 September 2023.

Graystone, Andrew. 2021. *Bleeding for Jesus: John Smyth and the Cult of Iwerne Camps*. London: Darton, Longman and Todd.

Greer, Chris, and Eugene McLaughlin, E. 2013. 'The Sir Jimmy Savile Scandal: Child Sexual Abuse and Institutional Denial at the BBC'. *Crime Media Culture: An International Journal* 9, no. 3: 243–63.

Guardian, The/Press Association. 2014. 'Jimmy Savile's Hospital Abuse: The Full Dossier'. *The Guardian*. 26 June. https://www.theguardian.com/media/2014/jun/26/jimmy-savile-hospital-abuse-full-dossier. Accessed 20 September 2023.

Halligan, Benjamin. 2022a. *Hotbeds of Licentiousness: The British Glamour Film and the Permissive Society*. New York: Berghahn Books.

Halligan, Benjamin. 2022b. 'Multitude Void: The Regal Mode of Imperial Legitimation'. In *Politics of the Many: Contemporary Radical Thought and the Crisis of Agency*, edited by Rebecca Carson, Benjamin Halligan, Alexei Penzin and Stefano Pippa, 115–31. London: Bloomsbury.

Halligan, Benjamin. 2023a. 'Aaliyah's Voice and After'. In *Diva: Feminism and Fierceness from Pop to Hip-Hop*, edited by Kirsty Fairclough, Benjamin Halligan, Nicole Hodges Persley and Shara Rambarran, 97–112. New York: Bloomsbury Academic.

Halligan, Benjamin. 2023b. ''90s "It Girls": Britpop at the Postfeminist Intermezzo'. *Journal of Feminist Scholarship* 22, Spring. https://digitalcommons.uri.edu/jfs/vol22/iss22/3/. Accessed 22 September 2023.

Hitchens, Christopher. 1995. *The Missionary Position: Mother Theresa in Theory and Practice*. London: Verso.

HL Deb (House of Lords debate). 1971. 'Pornography in Britain.' 317, cc. 639–754, 21 April. https://api.parliament.uk/historic-hansard/ lords/1971/apr/21/ pornography-in-britain. Accessed 22 September 2023.

Hodgkinson, Will. 2022. *In Perfect Harmony: Singalong Pop in '70s Britain*. London: Nine Eight Books.

IICSA (Independent Inquiry into Child Sexual Abuse). 2019. 'Anglican Church Case Studies: Chichester/Peter Ball Investigation Report'. https://www.iicsa. org.uk/reports-recommendations/publications/investigation/anglican-chiches ter-peter-ball.html. Accessed 24 September 2023.

Johnston, Keith. 2010. 'Underground, Overground: Remembering the Wombles'. In *Culture and Society in 1970s Britain: The Lost Decade*, edited by Laurel Forster and Sue Harper, 154–63. Cambridge: Cambridge Scholars Publishing.

Keetley, Dawn, and Ruth Heholt, eds. 2023. *Folk Horror: New Global Pathways*. Cardiff: University of Wales Press.

Leith, William. 1993. 'Kenny and Holly Find Positive Ways to Face Up to a New Kind of Fame'. *The Independent*. 10 April. https://www.independent.co.uk/ news/uk/kenny-and-holly-find-positive-ways-to-face-up-to-a-new-kind-of-fame-celebrities-may-own-up-to-hiv-freely-or-under-pressure-but-the-result-is-usua lly-the-same-writes-william-leith-1454707.html. Accessed 24 September 2023.

Levy, Geoffrey. 2015. 'The BBC "Saint" Who Pounced on Any Woman in Reach'. *The Daily Mail*. 27 February. https://www.dailymail.co.uk/ news/ article-2972833/The-BBC-saint-pounced-woman-reach-New-book-exposesunholy-truth-moralist-Malcolm-Muggeridge.html. Accessed 24 September 2023.

Lodge, David. 1980. *How Far Can You Go?* London: Secker & Warburg.

Longford Committee. 1972. *Pornography: The Longford Report*. London: Coronet Books.

Maloy, Liam. 2022. *Spinning the Child: Musical Constructions of Childhood through Records, Radio and Television*. London: Routledge.

Manners, Elizabeth. 1971. *The Vulnerable Generation*. London: Cassell.

Mardles, Paul. 2007. 'Sir Jimmy Savile.' *The Guardian*. 22 April. https://www. theguardian.com/music/2007/apr/22/features.musicmonthly11. Accessed 24 September 2023.

Mitchell, David. 2012. *Back Story*. London: HarperCollins.

Ordish, Roger. 1980. *Jim'll Fix It Album*. Maidenhead: Purnell Books.

Ordish, Roger. 1992. *The Jim'll Fix It Story*. London: Hodder & Stoughton.

Ordish, Roger. 2020. *If I Remember Rightly …* . Oxford and Shrewsbury: YouCaxton Publications.

Petronius. 1969. *London Unexpurgated*. London: New English Library.

Ronson, Jon. 2001. 'The Fall of a Pop Impresario'. *The Guardian*. 1 December. https://www.theguardian.com/lifeandstyle/2001/dec/01/weekend.jonronson. Accessed 24 September 2023.

RTE. 2012. 'Savile's Papal Knighthood Died with Him – Vatican'. *RTE*. 27 October. https://www.rte.ie/news/2012/1027/343363-jimmy-savile/. Accessed 24 September 2023.

Savile, Jimmy. 1979. *God'll Fix It*. London: Mowbrays.

Smith, Janet. 2016. *The Dame Janet Smith Review Report: The Jimmy Savile Investigation Report*. (Second volume of the report). https://www.bbc.co.uk/bbctrust/dame_janet_smith.html. Accessed 24 September 2023.

Smith, Mark. 2017. 'A Cautionary Tale Regarding "Believing" Allegations of Historical Child Abuse'. *Ethics and Social Welfare* 11, no. 1: 62–76.

Smith, Mark, and Ros Burnett. 2018. 'The Origins of the Jimmy Savile Scandal'. *International Journal of Sociology and Social Policy* 38, no. 1/2: 26–40.

Sweeting, Adam. 2005. 'Obituary: Johnnie Stewart'. *The Guardian*. 6 May. https://www.theguardian.com/media/2005/may/06/guardianobituaries.broadcasting. Accessed 24 September 2023.

Thompson, Ben. 2013. *Ban This Filth! Mary Whitehouse and the Battle to Keep Britain Innocent*. London: Faber and Faber.

Walkerdine, Valerie. 1998. 'Popular Culture and the Eroticisation of Young Girls'. In *The Children's Culture Reader*, edited by Henry Jenkins, 254–64. New York: New York University Press.

Wheatley, Helen. 2020. 'Haunted Television: Trauma and the Specter in the Archive'. *Journal of Cinema and Media Studies* 59, no. 3: 669–89.

Whitehouse, Mary. 1978. *Whatever Happened to Sex?* London: Hodder & Stoughton.

Whitehouse, Mary. 1994. *Quite Contrary: An Autobiography*. Auckland: Pan Books.

PART TWO

Memory, Process and Practice

10

The technological uncanny: The role of memory prosthetics in hauntological practice

Michael Schofield

Much of what we might consider to be hauntological today has less to do with supernatural spirits and literal ghouls, as it appertains to childhood memory and its mediations by technology. 'Hauntology isn't about hoky atmospherics or "spookiness" but a technological uncanny' (Fisher 2006). 'Hauntology is exercised by the problem of memory and its imperfect recovery' (Fisher 2013, 45). An ongoing cultural fascination with the strange and unsettling media of the 1970s and 1980s is largely filtered through hazy recollections of that time, revisited and reimagined by those who grew up during this specific period. The media artefacts that have endured also behave akin to ghosts, grainy and timeworn, yet digitally reanimated on new platforms, and denying their own mortality by continuing to haunt our screens, seemingly indefinitely. As we look back through this heavily mediated time, organic and technological memory can seem to conflate or disrupt one another – and this often provides the impetus for new hauntological works and explorations. Years on from the original 'spectral turn' in critical cultural theory (Weinstock 2013), hauntology still shows no signs of dying, periodically resurrecting itself in different cultural areas, and evolving as it inspires new generations of academics, critics and artists, to look back and embrace the ghostly. As it does so, it is necessary to take stock and reflect on what we actually mean by hauntology in these shifting contexts and to try and bring into focus its formative yet indefinite relationship with both memory and technology.

For many years, my own experimental practice as an artist has attempted to probe similar concerns and questions, exploring the hidden and haunted qualities of different media technologies, from archaic glass plate photography to modern webcams. *Zoetrope.space* (Coldwell 2019) was an audiovisual archive based on a personal media archaeology, unearthing television shows and video tapes that I half-remembered from my own childhood, and repurposing them as short looping projections. The clips I selected for the work all possessed a certain eerie quality for myself, but I couldn't always fully deduce why that was. They were often seemingly quite innocuous, and not the usual folk horror tropes, or the deliberately scary public information films that routinely traumatized children in the late twentieth century, and that we often see recurring in contemporary British hauntological work. The haunted quality I was tapping into didn't appear to originate solely in the strange content of the media sampled, rather it seemed to have something to do with the treatment of memory itself (Figure 10.1).

Paramnesia, confabulation and misremembering all became key concerns in the creative work as it developed. Looping and re-scoring the archived clips seemed to render them more unsettling, emphasizing the gaps, disruptions and recontextualizations that eventually transform and erase all memory.

FIGURE 10.1 Zoetrope.space *by Conflux Coldwell (2019). Reproduced with permission.*

A fear of amnesia, or of me losing my grip on what was real, seemed to be the primary source of the most haunting phenomenon I encountered in the project. This should not have come as a surprise, as some of the earliest hauntological works and theories primarily concerned disturbances of memory and memory loss. The Caretaker began similar experiments in electronic music in 1999, with his album *Selected Memories from the Haunted Ballroom* (Caretaker 1999); a long-term investigation of amnesia and technology ensued, that finally culminated in a multi-part portrayal of the progression of Alzheimer's disease, entitled *Everywhere at the End of Time* (Caretaker 2016). The late Mark Fisher – a highly influential music critic and cultural theorist, who arguably did more than anyone else to popularize hauntology and explain its cultural significance – used The Caretaker's work in his theory on the subject, to expound the differences between hauntology and nostalgia in the normal mode, and the key role played by disruptions to memory. Writing in 2008 on his K-Punk blog, Fisher suggested,

> it is the very foregrounding of temporality that makes hauntology differ from the typical products of the nostalgia mode ... The great sonic-theoretical contribution of The Caretaker to the discourse of hauntology was his understanding that the nostalgia mode has to do not with memories but with a memory disorder. (Fisher 2018, 716)

In both *Zoetrope.space* (Coldwell 2019) and the work of The Caretaker, this 'foregrounding of temporality' was done through the manipulation of the recording technologies' innate properties – the foregrounding of their own noisy materiality and physical presence – which worked to emphasize certain innate spectral qualities of the media they carried, and the loss and absence those veiled features seemed to convey. For Fisher, the ominous crackle of the sampled vinyl used by The Caretaker made 'the dimension of time audible' (Mark Fisher 2018), something he went on to explore much further in *The Metaphysics of Crackle* (Mark Fisher 2013), charting similar patterns of foregrounded decay in the work of William Basinski, Philip Jeck, Burial and the Ghost Box record label. If we're to explore what hauntology means today, and its as-yet fully articulated relationship to memory, this seems as good a place to start as any.

Returning to the originating theory, Fisher's conceptualizations of hauntology can be traced back to Jacques Derrida, who coined the term in *Specters of Marx* (Derrida 1994). This influential book revisited and deconstructed Karl Marx's infamous 'spectre of communism', shortly after the fall of the Soviet Union, and addressed how this phantom continued to exert a powerful effect on Europe, while no longer being present as such. A homophone of ontology in French – and something of a joke by Derrida – hauntology was characteristic of a larger project by the philosopher, undermining simplistic metaphysical conceptions of presence, through the invocation of traces, ghosts and haunting. Long before *Spectres of Marx* (1994), Derrida was interested in the spectrality of media too – and his sporadic writing on this topic is probably more useful to a Fisherian view of hauntology, than the book in which the neologism originated. As far back as the early 1980s, Derrida was musing on the importance of ghosts in the modern world, and the increasing role of media technologies in their perpetuation. He appeared in Ken McMullen's film *Ghost Dance* (1983), stating in the interview that 'cinema is the art of ghosts, a battle of phantoms' and that the technologies of communication enhance 'the power of ghosts and their ability to haunt us'. For Derrida, all media was spectral.

> Spectrality is at work everywhere, and more than ever, in an original way, in the reproducible virtuality of photography or cinema. (Derrida 2005, 108)
>
> Spectrality … far from being reduced by the rationality of modern technology, found itself, on the contrary, amplified … Every culture has its phantoms and the spectrality that is conditioned by its technology. (Derrida et al. 2010, 39)

It doesn't seem like a coincidence then, that cultural hauntology is 'amplified' at roughly the same time as the 'digital turn' (Westera 2012), with new media technologies and practices of communication keeping our ghosts alive in new ways. This is also acknowledged within memory studies, to an extent, with media seen as playing an increasingly important role in deciding 'what we remember and how we remember it' (Daković 2021, 3). I began to explore this and Derrida's notion of media spectrality in my creative practice research, wondering why, if these technologies are *all* intrinsically spectral, as Derrida suggested, only certain examples have the power to genuinely haunt us? This spectrality seemed to be on a spectrum of some kind, usually hidden from view, but nevertheless a latent potential within recorded media that could be brought to the fore in certain contexts. What was it then that made these ghosts appear, and why were they hidden the rest of the time? 'Technicity is hauntology, in that technical artifacts haunt their users with the possibility and actuality of absence' (Gere 2016, 105).

Charlie Gere's research into the hauntology of the digital image offered something of a clue – it was the 'possibility' of 'absence' that could lead to media haunting, and this potential could sometimes be rendered visible or audible through the foregrounding of the technology's own material *presence* – as we saw in Fisher's meditations on 'crackle'. In most cases, media technologies offer a very immersive and normalized illusion of presence, and it is only when this deception is disturbed that we can be made aware of a recording's inborn spectrality, and even its own mortality. In *Aura and Trace* (Schofield 2018), I postulated that this was because recorded media isn't just one type of thing (a ghost), but more like two (a spirit and a medium).

'A material ghost must have a dual nature: the present object, the support or "medium" (which can often be invisible to us), and the spectral trace of the past that it channels' (Schofield 2018, 24). When the physical object that we are actually co-present with (the media technology) becomes more perceptible in some way – often through decay or damage to the recording – we have the 'possibility' of seeing the present trace of the 'absent' for what it is: a ghost.

A couple of years after *Zoetrope.space* (2019) I moved on to another creative research project that, while utilizing similar methods – and addressing more or less the same theory on spectrality – didn't start from my own childhood recollections of specific media, but instead from a box of unlabelled VHS tapes that I found at my parents' house. Most of the video recordings were very badly damaged. Some of them I remembered immediately, a couple of tapes even including examples of my own early work. Others were forgotten, totally unknown and seemingly random. Scraps of old science documentaries from my mother's Open University course in the late 1980s. A programme about natural disasters and extreme weather taped off the television. A film about the history of the London Underground. Several old b-movies and war films. And *lots* of noise.

Looking through the corrupted tapes made me realize the ultimate fragility of all our recordings and the memories they can potentially hold for us. These analogue cassettes only have an estimated lifespan of twenty-five years, and this artificial afterlife is only granted to the videos we actually decide to keep. The vast majority went to landfill when the world went digital – I began to wonder what might have been lost in this waste. The assumption that *everything* has now been digitally preserved and made available online forever is surely mistaken. There are gaps and absences. Media can still die. I decided to try and recover what I could from this little archive and make something new out of the various remnants. An overarching theme emerged from what I created: entropy and legacy. This marked a shift from personal to cultural memory in my artistic preoccupations. What will survive of this time for future generations? What will be destroyed? What if this random selection of decaying tapes was the last evidence of life on Earth? *Memorex Mori* (Coldwell 2023) was the audiovisual work resulting from these questions and my various VHS experiments, and it functioned like a piece of technological vanitas. Once again, the background noise of the media technology itself was a vital ingredient – this time I made it the primary focus. The work presented the flickering media ghosts as unidentifiable, as fatally fading, as nearly absent, as the not-quite-alive and as the soon-to-disappear-completely (Figure 10.2).

Interference and defects: A particularly hauntological medium is an obsolete, archaic medium (such as audio or videotape), because it imparts a new spirit to dead matter (Drenda 2013).

FIGURE 10.2 Memorex Mori *by Conflux Coldwell (2023). Reproduced with permission.*

Mark Fisher wasn't the only writer on hauntology to notice the noisiness of the ghostly media emerging from late postmodern culture. Olga Drenda, Elodie Roy (2015) and Katharina Niemeyer (2014) have all made note of the use of anachronistic technologies and the foregrounding of their characteristic noise in hauntological practice – with Niemeyer asserting that this was 'a strategy of re-enchanting an object through aesthetic defamiliarization, as it is characterised by deliberate imperfection' (Niemeyer 2014, 34). For the most hauntological, this wasn't just an exercise in nostalgic fondness for primitive technologies. The tendency towards foregrounding 'the noise, not the signal' (Niemeyer 2014, 34) is redolent of ghost hunters endlessly searching for voices in meaningless static. The desire to commune with the lost is the same, as is the hallucinatory quality of what is ultimately found. What is often missed is that the presence of noise is an acknowledgement of a failure of presence of something else – a physical rendering of that loss, a reminder of the passage of time and of death itself. It is this that can have the most haunting effect in hauntology. Roland Barthes noticed a similar phenomenon in photography, in his meditations on what he termed 'punctum' (Barthes 1993). This visceral emotional reaction to an image can be triggered by some unexpected detail, but more often than not, it embodies a form of haunting, as Barthes details in his writing on 'time as punctum' (Barthes 1993, 96) – he recognized that all photographs have the potential to haunt us as memento mori, and that this is the medium's greatest power. In this form, the punctum is an example of the technological uncanny. In certain images we can feel haunted as we are made aware of the presence of what should be dead and buried, reappearing but now disembodied, many years later, by some technical trick of the light. While Barthes was speaking only of photography, similar affects can be found in other media, including film, television and recorded sound.

> Hauntology functions as a kind of deconstruction; to acknowledge that cinema is a haunted medium is to submit to its capacity to perpetuate ghost stories, but also to the technological uncanniness of the very concept of cinema. (Clanton 2012, 69)

We only perceive these different technological reproductions as uncanny if they do decompose somehow, and we are suddenly surprised by their essential unrealness – the temporal disjuncture and absence/death of the traces reproduced before us. So accustomed are we to engaging with life through media that we don't often see this: we look through the reproductive technology as if it was Barthes's 'transparent envelope' (Barthes 1993, 5), as if we were looking upon life itself through a window, rather than an unnatural copy of life that ultimately disrupts time and space. Hauntological practice often seeks to break this illusory envelope and renders the familiar copies of media strange. We can experience our own memories as uncanny once this happens. Noisy media is just one tool in that hauntological armoury.

Media technologies can become uncanny in this way because they have become a key part of the modern self, but a part we don't yet fully understand or often acknowledge. Ciano Aydin explores this psychoanalytical aspect in relation to robotics and the uncanny valley, but the concepts explored in the writing are potentially translatable to memory technology and to hauntological media:

> The technology within is not completely strange or foreign, since it is a constitutive part of our subjectivity and selfhood ... Technology is strange and familiar, at the same time. [This] explains why it can be experienced as uncanny. (Aydin 2022, 312)

Prosthetics are a key consideration on Mori's original graph of the uncanny valley –'when a prosthetic hand that is near the bottom of the uncanny valley starts to move, our sensation of eeriness intensifies' (Mori 1970). Mori is referring to physical artificial limbs in this famous investigation, but in recent years the concept of prosthetics has expanded to include the technologies of memory (Landsberg 2004, Lury 2013). David Bate and Celia Lury have also written extensively on photography as a memory prosthetic, but this can be expanded to include all the other forms of recording and producing media texts – all the technologies that we routinely use to remember for us – and those that become an integral part of our own organic memories of childhood.

If, like Freud, we count photography as one device among the long history of different techniques of "artificial" or "prosthetic" devices for the support of human memory, then the question it raises is what specific impact photography has had on human memory and the cultures that use it. (Bate 2010)

Hauntology includes an indirect examination of these kinds of questions – of media technology's increasing role in human memory and the cultures that use it – the uncanny glitches in time, the false memories and confabulation that can occur once a generation grows up using such prosthetics from a very young age – consuming the majority of culture through various technologies of reproduction. Hazy yet formative memories are just as likely to be the television programmes we watched as children as they are family holidays, Christmas presents or learning to ride a bike. As technologies that form a 'constitutive part of our subjectivity and selfhood' (Aydin 2022, 312), memory prosthetics should be some of the most influential of all.

The uncanny valley graphs familiarity against human likeness – but this doesn't fully acknowledge the contradiction that we experience the uncanny when something is both familiar and strange at the same time – or once something very familiar (usually something about ourselves) is rendered or revealed to be somehow disturbing. It is depicted as a valley because we can climb the other side towards things that are so similar to human beings, that we feel they are safe and familiar again, despite being artificial. Modern media creates such a powerful illusion of presence (and we are so accustomed to it), that as a form of prosthetic, it may be functioning firmly on the other side of this allegorical gorge. Older media is certainly less perfect an illusion in many ways – with all its aforementioned noisy imperfections – and the memories it preserves are further removed from our current lives, reducing their familiarity through time. What has the potential to render memory uncanny here is media's ability to create disjunctures in time, to make us doubt the veracity of our own organic memory in the process, sometimes unsure of which memory we should trust, or just unsettled by blurred 'boundaries between real and simulated' (Landsberg 1995, 189) memory. This fallibility can be an instinctive source of great unease, as memories are revealed to be as slippery and illusory as ghosts – but ghosts that are as devastatingly subject to transience and decay as our own bodies.

It must be acknowledged that thinking about technological memory as a form of prosthesis is merely a metaphor (Hutton 2022), and any similarity between Mori's uncanny valley and the technological uncanny of memory is therefore just a thought-provoking correlation. Memories are not bodies, after all, and technology seems to disembody memory yet further. However, using this comparison as an analogical model to further unpick hauntology, we can see that something must take us out of our usual memory 'comfort zone', before media begins to have its implicit haunting and eerie affects – something

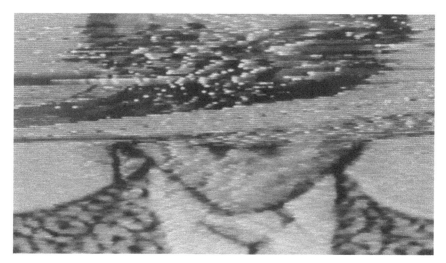

FIGURE 10.3 Memorex Mori *by Conflux Coldwell (2023). Reproduced with permission.*

must remind us of its unfamiliar and hidden deadness – and much like the uncanny valley, this spectrality probably falls on a spectrum, as mentioned earlier. When mediated memory glitches, when the prosthetics we rely on fail or the illusion is otherwise broken, that is when we are most haunted by it, as we tumble into the 'uncanny valley' of malfunctioning memory (Figure 10.3).

In *Memorex Mori* (Coldwell 2023) the aging technology used readily created ghosts. It was important to the project that this wasn't a fabrication on the part of the artist, but always a highlighted feature of the decaying media itself. Bad tracking and playback errors lead to normal dialogue sounding like demonic voices from a bad horror movie. Glitches and noise obscure faces making them appear unrecognizable or even dehumanized in some way. In the section entitled 'Moulding', figures and faces are paused on the video, but they continue to flicker and move by virtue of the looping analogue substrate. The uncanniness of the images and sounds presented here seems to stem from the same dichotomy highlighted by Freud himself (via Jentsch), 'whether an apparently animate being is really alive; or conversely, whether a lifeless object might not be in fact animate' (Freud 1919, 226).

Seemingly familiar scenes are made strange in this way by the broken technology, presenting people in some ambiguous state between animate and inanimate, between alive and dead. This uncanny atmosphere seems to permeate the whole work, spilling over into its depictions of places and objects, as well as those unsettling human representations. Towards the end, in a section called 'After Math', the signal seems to disintegrate completely for several minutes, before slowed-down figures begin to emerge from the walls of noise, ostensibly coming back from the dead.

For us to find something familiar in the first place is to invoke memory to some extent. Even the video materials I didn't recognize from my own past could therefore trigger memories – my familiarity with the particular characteristics of the video medium itself was enough to transport me to an earlier time. Certainly, the tapes I used in the work that had more of a personal connection would induce a deeper emotional response, but if I remembered them too well, I was unlikely to experience them as uncanny, even as the technology distorted them into eerie forms. It was always with the half-remembered that the ghosts seem to materialize most, and perhaps this is where the depths of this specific uncanny valley lie. It is here that we feel uncertainty about memory prosthesis, and where we ultimately confront the potential for paramnesia within ourselves.

> Any kind of distinction between "real" memories and prosthetic memories – memories which might be technologically disseminated by the mass media and worn by its customers – might ultimately be unintelligible. (Landsberg 1995, 183)

It isn't when we notice a prosthetic as artificial that we experience the uncanny, it is when that prosthetic makes us realize we have forgotten what is real – when we become cognizant that those boundaries have become blurred internally. In *Zoetrope.space* (Coldwell 2019) there was a sense that the looping and re-scoring of the video clips was an act of defamiliarizing my own childhood memories. The technological uncanny came into play because these simple technical manipulations jarred with my own mnemic sense of self. To break time yet further, some of the clips were re-scored with looped recordings of my own children watching these television shows and playing along on xylophones and old keyboards. These sounds, in turn, were defamiliarized by the technology. Working with loops and echoes is to work with the fabric of time and push it closer to the disjointed form of memory, which works through repetition and is non-linear in nature. My own children watching these shows with me was itself a form of technologically aided time-loop and the creation of new memories of media that cannibalized old ones. In this project the distinction between real and prosthetic memory certainly became unintelligible in the way Landsberg suggested, but the processes and technologies used in the creative practice mirrored those that we use in everyday life. Recording, returning and repetition are routinely aided and encouraged by modern media technologies. We can show our children pieces of our own childhood. We can revisit lost fragments of our past at the click of a button, completely out of context of time and our real memories of it.

To fully explore the role of memory prosthetics in hauntology we need to extend these ideas beyond personal memory and look for similar effects in the wider sharing of cultural memory, but any clear boundary between personal and cultural memory also becomes blurred with time.

Much of popular hauntology has a yearning quality, and I wondered whether the movement was, at least partially, an attempt to rationalise (and fill in the blanks of) a collective childhood that has become a delicious, jumbled mish-mash of fleeting memories. (Fischer 2019)

Within hauntological-related work there is also often a deliberate mis-remembering of the past, filtering it through your own personal vision, reimagining it in your own form. (Prince 2018, 123)

However deliberate the reimagining of these fleeting memories is in hauntological culture, it nevertheless mirrors the real problems of fading and distorted memory already discussed – and in turn, this memory 'remix' becomes part of cultural memory itself, distorting it further. The 'yearning' Bob Fischer alludes to is no doubt symptomatic of a memory loss that has already happened, and this then becomes hard-coded when it is embodied in new cultural texts that reference the past. What separates the hauntological from mere nostalgia, as Mark Fisher explored (Fisher 2018, 716), is that rather than just 'filling in the blanks' with pure phantasy, it highlights those gaps and temporal disjunctures – foregrounding their uncanny nature – and revealing all memory as potentially phantasmatic in the process. It is the uncanny nature of memory prosthetics that separates hauntological practice from the merely retro, and hauntological affects from those of nostalgia. Without this acknowledgement, hauntology is in danger of moving ever closer to the usual retromania and postmodern pastiche, with memories of past forms recreated lovingly within present ones, yet the malfunctioning role of memory in haunting is forgotten. For Mark Fisher there was a philosophical and political dimension to this too. To forget these haunting absences is to somehow uphold ideological phantasies that habitually paper over the many mnemic cracks; 'whereas postmodernism glosses over the temporal disjunctures, the hauntological artists foreground them' (Fisher 2013, 46).

For Fisher, postmodernity finally succumbed to a static 'spectral time' and the 'technologies that made us all ghosts' (2013, 48), but simultaneously it screened out any detectable spectrality of those recording devices, hiding it from view, and naturalizing its uncanniness. Hauntology exists to upset this prosthetic illusion of presence and reveal postmodernism's permanent revivalism as fundamentally artificial. For Fisher, it is the future that has been stolen from us, and we can only see that by looking back in time and finding the gaps – 'we must listen for the relics of the future in the unactivated potentials of the past' (53).

In Mark Fisher's early writing on hauntology, the outputs of the Ghost Box record label seemed to embody this tendency as much as any other hauntological practice. The Ghost Box was television, or more correctly, 'a television that has disappeared, itself become a ghost' (Fisher 2005). The recreated memories of this lost media were knowingly artificial. They were warm, hazy and nostalgic but also strangely unsettling. Fisher saw this as a direct contrast to the irritating 'citation-blitz' of postmodernism, and also a key exploration of the lost futures of 1960s and 1970s modernist ideals. Quaint retro science fiction references rubbed shoulders with folk horror and the unique quirkiness of public service broadcasting of the time, but this wasn't just a trip down memory lane for its own sake – the technological uncanny was there in the background, disrupting linear temporality and the assumption of progress. 'Ghost Box is implicated in a web of pulp esoteria: Children of the Stones, New English Library paperbacks, Hammer films, Lovecraft, Lewis, The Tomorrow People, Blackwood, Timeslip' (Fisher 2005).

In *Ghosts of My Life* (2014) Fisher acknowledges that Ghost Box have been 'accused of nostalgia' (136), but that their work presented something more paradoxical than that – it was a nostalgia for the future, or at least a future we thought was coming when we were children. For Fisher, Ghost Box were at their strongest when they 'foregrounded dyschronia, broken time' (137), and once again, this was often achieved through rendering the technology of reproduction perceptible – 'the joins are too audible, the samples too jagged, for their tracks to sound like refurbished artefacts' (137). In recent years it could be argued that Ghost Box has lost some of this lo-fi dyschronic aesthetic. If you compare early releases by Belbury Poly and The Focus Group with Plone's *Puzzlewood* (2020) or Belbury Poly's own *The Gone Away* (2020), the latter seem much more like straight pastiches of an outmoded sound. The uncanny disjunctures now seem to be missing, or at least buried deeply in the retro aesthetics.

A similar, but less pronounced, trajectory can be noticed in the work of Richard Littler, working under the name Scarfolk. Initially published as an obscure blog of fake artefacts from the archive of a fictional town council, Scarfolk has grown into a successful series of publications with a mainstream media attention. Dark and uncanny esoterica gave way to narrative material with a much more overtly satirical intent, although the humour was often still pitch-black. While the joins and disjunctures were arguably more visible in his earlier outputs, the dystopian nature of the satire somehow maintained the hauntological ethos. It did so via what Adam Harper calls the 'hauntological layer' – with the layer, in this case, being the humour itself. 'The second, "hauntological" layer problematises, compromises and obfuscates the first layer, undermining or damaging it in some way' (Harper 2009).

Harper noticed that in hauntological practice an ideal view of the past is often presented alongside something which disturbs it and our memory of it. Whether this layer is an innate feature of the technology such as noise, or some key element added afterwards – memory damage is still key to hauntology. This second layer defamiliarizes cultural memory, raising questions about what might be missing or deliberately omitted. For Fisher, cultural hauntology always had this imperative to 'unsettle the pastiche-time of postmodernity' (Mark Fisher 2013, 47) – it had to be a haunting with a purpose.

With *Zoetrope.space* (2019) and *Memorex Mori* (2023), I hoped to avoid such pastiche time by sampling the old media directly and then decontextualizing it, using innate features of the technology. It wasn't a recreation of a past fondly misremembered, it was the technological ghosts of our past re-emerging and misremembering themselves. With *Memorex Mori* the hauntology became increasingly purposive as the project progressed, although this was still very much subtextual. An unforeseen apocalyptic tone began to permeate the work. The subtext in question concerned environmental destruction and climate change. An idealized view of the past was presented in some of the gathered materials, such as vintage science documentary footage of nature. Juxtaposed with fragmentary scenes of destruction and the palpable erosion of the media itself, the 'hauntological layer' seemed to be indicating a lost future without the impending threat of a mass extinction event on the horizon – a past future where we saw what was happening and acted soon enough. We have known about 'global warming' since the 1980s when there was still optimism that we would be able to avert it – a naïve hopefulness we seem to have forgotten. These memories slip between the cracks, barely visible but still haunting the noisy video as it disintegrates and finally disappears. Neither nostalgia nor pastiche are words I would use to describe the haunting feeling this leaves me with.

While not always this overt, the technology of memory is key to all hauntology. Even when the spectrality of media isn't foregrounded in the ways we have discussed, its supporting technology is the key medium that makes these hauntings possible. The ghosts we can be sure of existing are uncanny features of memory – both personal and cultural – that are 'amplified' by memory prosthetics, most notably when they fail. Placing technology at the centre of this argument certainly opens it up to accusations of technological determinism – which has been rightly criticized as ahistorical and reductionist (De la Cruz Paragas and Lin 2016). However, while I would agree that all media is socially constructed and socially employed, one of the key aspects missing from a 'hard' socially deterministic view is the role played by accidents, by certain unforeseen and unplanned features and properties of technology. Glitches, errors and noise are accidental characteristics that most media technologists would strive to remove or 'gloss over' – as Mark Fisher might have said – but it is when these technologies go wrong that certain truths about them (and us) can be revealed.

> The accident (and thus the glitch) shows a system in a state of entropy and so aids towards an understanding of the ultimate functioning of a system. This opens up space for research and practice, and the arts are a special domain for this. (Menkman 2011, 32)

Paul Virilio saw the importance of such accidents for art, and explored 'technology's many unintended social consequences' (Dawes 2019, 118) in his work. For Virilio, such errors in the systems we rely on have the ability to reveal things we would not 'otherwise know how to perceive' (Lotringer and Virilio 2005). Hauntological glitches in time and memory were not an intended function of media technologies, but they *can* fulfil various social purposes. How we choose to use these ghosts is still up to us.

If hauntology is to remain critically imperative, it should continue to explore the relationship between memory and technology, using this as prime territory for fresh ghost hunting. Re-establishing this as a core tenet of any hauntological 'movement' (Mark Fisher 2006) is important to prevent its cultural outputs from sliding into the nostalgic revivalism it emerged to disrupt – which is rarely all that haunting anyway. Contemporary hauntology's strong links to childhood memories from the mid-to-late twentieth century are clear to see, but these cultural references will change again, and more important to the general concept of hauntology are the accidental ways in which that memory has been mediated, altered and even erased by prosthetics. While these technologies continue to mediate memory for us and produce their own ghosts, the hauntological will stay relevant to culture in some form. Paradoxically, in our late postmodern epoch, dominated as it is by such technology, and in which much more of our past is recorded and accessible to us than ever before, it seems to be our fear of forgetting that has the potential to haunt us the most.

References

Aydin, Ciano. 2022. 'The Technological Uncanny as a Permanent Dimension of Selfhood'. In *The Oxford Handbook of Philosophy of Technology*, edited by Shannon Vallor. Oxford: Oxford University Press.

Barthes, Roland. 1993. *Camera Lucida: Reflections on Photography*. London: Vintage.

Bate, David. 2010. 'The Memory of Photography'. *Photographies* 3, no. 2: 243–57.

Belbury Poly. 2020. *The Gone Away*. Ghost Box.

Caretaker, The. 1999. *Selected Memories from the Haunted Ballroom*. V/Vm Test Records.

Caretaker, The. 2016. *Everywhere at the End of Time. History Always Favours the Winners*.

Clanton, Carrie. 2012. 'Hauntology beyond the Cinema: The Technological Uncanny'. *ManyCinemas* 3: 66–76. https://www.carrieclanton.com/journal-article-hauntology-beyond-t. Accessed 24 September 2023.

Coldwell, Michael C. 2019. *Zoetrope.space*. Crooked Acres. https://www.michaelcoldwell.co.uk/archived/zoetrope/. Accessed 24 September 2023.

Coldwell, Michael C. 2023. *Memorex Mori*. Subexotic. https://www.michaelcoldwell.co.uk/work/seafaring-hmek5. Accessed 24 September 2023.

Daković, Nevena. 2021. 'Digital Turn – Memory Studies.' *The IPSI Transactions on Internet Research* 17, no. 2: 2–7.

Dawes, Simon. 2019. 'Paul Virilio and Media Theory: An Introduction.' *Media Theory* 3, no. 2: 117–20.

De la Cruz Paragas, F., and T. T. Lin. 2016. 'Organizing and Reframing Technological Determinism'. *New Media and Society* 18, no. 8: 1528–46.

Derrida, Jacques. 1994. *Specters of Marx: The State of the Debt, the Work of Mourning, and the New International*. New York: Routledge.

Derrida, Jacques. 2005. *Paper Machine*. Stanford, CA: Stanford University Press.

Derrida, Jacques, Hubertus von Amelunxen, Michael Wetzel, Gerhard Richter and Jeff Fort. 2010. *Copy, Archive, Signature: A Conversation on Photography*. Stanford, CA: Stanford University Press.

Drenda, Olga. 2013. 'The Alphabet of Hauntology'. *Czas Kultury [Time of Culture]* 2. http://czaskultury.pl/en/the-alphabet-of-hauntology/. Accessed 24 September 2023.

Fischer, Bob. 2019. 'The Haunted Generation'. https://hauntedgeneration.co.uk. Accessed 24 September 2023.

Fisher, Mark. 2005. 'Unhomesickness'. K-Punk. http://k-punk.abstractdynamics.org/archives/006414.html. Accessed 25 September 2023.

Fisher, Mark. 2006. 'Phonograph Blues'. K-Punk. http://k-punk.abstractdynamics.org/archives/008535.html. Accessed 25 September 2023.

Fisher, Mark. 2013. 'The Metaphysics of Crackle: Afrofuturism and Hauntology'. *Dancecult: Journal of Electronic Dance Music Culture* 5, no. 2: 42–55.

Fisher, Mark. 2014. *Ghosts of My Life: Writings on Depression, Hauntology and Lost Futures*. Winchester: Zero Books.

Fisher, Mark. 2018. 'No Future 2012'. In *K-Punk: The Collected and Unpublished Writings of Mark Fisher*, edited by Mark Fisher and Darren Ambrose, 713–18. London: Repeater.

Fisher, M., and J. Barton. 2019. 'On Vanishing Land'. In *On Vanishing Land: Flatlines*. https://hyperdub.bandcamp.com/album/on-vanishing-land. Accessed 24 September 2023.

Freud, Sigmund. 1919. 'The 'Uncanny'. In *The Standard Edition of the Complete Psychological Works of Sigmund Freud, Volume XVII (1917–1919): An Infantile Neurosis and Other Works*, edited by James Strachey, 217–56. London: W. W. Norton.

Gere, Charlie. 2016. 'The Hauntology of the Digital Image'. In *A Companion to Digital Art*, edited by Christiane Paul, 203–25. New Jersey: Blackwell.

Ghost Dance. 1983. [Film; Director: Ken McMullen]. UK: Channel 4 Films.

Harper, Adam. 2009. 'Hauntology: The Past Inside the Present'. *Rouge's Foam: Excessive Aesthetics* (blog). http://rougesfoam.blogspot.co.uk/2009/10/hauntology-past-inside-present.html. Accessed 24 September 2023.

Hutton, Margaret-Anne. 2022. 'Putting Metaphor Centre-Stage: A Case Study of Alison Landsberg's "Prosthetic Memory"'. *Memory Studies* 15, no. 1: 230–42.

Landsberg, Alison. 1995. 'Prosthetic Memory: Total Recall and Blade Runner'. *Body & Society* 1, no. 3–4: 175–89.

Landsberg, Alison. 2004. *Prosthetic Memory: The Transformation of American Remembrance in the Age of Mass Culture*. New York: Columbia University Press.

Lotringer, S., and P. Virilio. 2005. *The Accident of Art*. New York: Semiotext(e).

Lury, Celia. 2013. *Prosthetic Culture*. New York: Routledge.

Menkman, Rosa. 2011. *The Glitch Moment (um)*. The Netherlands: Institute of Network Cultures.

Mori, Masahiro. 1970. 'The Uncanny Valley: The Original Essay by Masahiro Mori'. *IEEE Spectrum*. https://spectrum.ieee.org/the-uncanny-valley. Accessed 25 September 2023.

Niemeyer, Katharina. 2014. *Media and Nostalgia: Yearning for the Past, Present and Future*. New York: Springer.

Plone. 2020. *Puzzlewood*. Ghost Box.

Prince, Stephen. 2018. *A Year in the Country: Wandering through Spectral Fields*. A Year in the Country. https://ayearinthecountry.co.uk/. Accessed 24 September 2023.

Roy, Elodie A. 2015. *Media, Materiality and Memory, Grounding the Groove*. Liverpool: Ashgate Publishing.

Schofield, Michael Peter. 2018. 'Aura and Trace: The Hauntology of the Rephotographic Image'. Doctoral dissertation, University of Leeds. http://ethe ses.whiterose.ac.uk/22615/. Accessed 23 September 2023.

Weinstock, Jeffrey Andrew. 2013. 'Introduction: The Spectral Turn'. In *The Spectralities Reader: Ghosts and Haunting in Contemporary Cultural Theory*, edited by Esther Peeren, 1–28. New York: Bloomsbury Publishing USA.

Westera, Wim. 2012. *The Digital Turn: How the Internet Transforms Our Existence*. Bloomington Indiana: AuthorHouse.

11

The pandemic and the bomb

Flannán Delaney

I'm writing this in self-isolation in the early days of a terrifying pandemic. Everything has stopped. The streets are empty. The ExCel Exhibition Centre[1] is being converted into an enormous 'Nightingale Hospital'.[2] A few days ago I developed a barking cough, and I haven't left the house since. I'm an anxious person by nature; sudden noises and cartoon violence make me jump out of my skin. And I find the suffering of others difficult to meet with equanimity. At night I dream of friends whose health concerns me; by day, I compulsively read the latest statistics, the infection rates, the numbers signing on for Universal Credit.[3]

And yet, the fact is I'm both calmer and more functional than I've been in years. The paralysing tangles my mind can work itself into have smoothed themselves out. My days at home are filled with activity. I've been organizing with my local mutual aid group; preparing myself to volunteer as a first aider when I'm better; studying patterns for sewing cloth masks to donate to others. As a vegan with an instant pot and a shelf full of dried beans I never really had a need to panic buy. But if I'm honest, since this started, I've not needed to panic at all. My therapist, who I now meet with over Skype, has been startled by the change in my demeanour, I think. What she doesn't

---

[1]The ExCel Exhibition Centre is a large building used for events in the centre of London.
[2]A form of temporary hospital, a number of which were set up in the UK during the pandemic. They were never used.
[3]A controversial form of welfare payment in the UK which notoriously takes a long time to be received after initial application.

understand is that I was ready for this; I've been preparing for it for most of my life.

I went to a small, charming state primary school. The ritual of story time was kept by all classes, regardless of age. Even as ten- and eleven-year-old children, we crowded onto the carpet to listen to the teacher reading to us, though picture books had given way to chapter books and then to 'older children's literature'. This was a category around which there were no firm boundaries, only a vague sense that certain content pushed books from the 'children's' to the 'adult'category – for the most part, depictions of the mechanics of sex, or descriptions of sexual desire. The Juniors' Library was packed with classic science fiction, which had neither description of sex.

Eight years old and hungry for more I read a lot of Arthur C. Clarke and Isaac Asimov, mostly the short stories. There were several generous volumes of these writers on the library's low shelves. Then I moved on to H. M. Hoover and Nicholas Fisk. This was when I began to have a sense of the future on a societal rather than a personal level. The dystopian visions I found in these children's and adults' science fiction stories were intended more as a commentary on the present than as a set of predictions. However, at a tender age I lacked this perspective. As far as I was concerned, fiction merely dramatized the knowledge that was breathlessly expounded in the Juniors' Library's non-fiction collection: in the future, everything would be run by computer programmes, distributed on CD-ROMs; in the future, humans would evolve to have no little toes; in the future, everyone would be a test-tube baby; in the future, authoritarian governments would control every aspect of life; in the future, humans would struggle to find food uncontaminated by radiation and toxic chemicals; in the future, nuclear war was a near certainty.

The Cold War had ended by this point, but it would be years before state school children's libraries reflected this. Having learned all about modern warfare from my extensive reading I fully expected the first Gulf War to result in conscription, rationing and then, of course, 'The Bomb'. I watched every plane that flew over our school playground, convinced that one would contain a nuclear warhead. The template I had been given for nuclear war was an ostensible normality which was suddenly violated by 'The Event'. This mirrored the structure of the public information films, shown on videos that we would watch in class on a periodic basis, in which children who had been careless with fireworks or played on railway lines or climbed electricity pylons to retrieve a lost kite recounted the single instant in which all their reckless optimism confronted reality.[4] Limbless, paralysed, overwhelmed with guilt and grief for their lost friends and burdened families, the

---

[4]There is a history of UK Public Information films, many of which can be accessed via the British Film Institute (BFI) online.

ordinariness of their previous existence now only haunted them. Some of the videos were even narrated from beyond the grave. Many of the children in post-nuclear fiction had begun in this ordinary reality; for others it was a remote history, a fairy tale. For all of them it was a haunting. I began to understand that most of my everyday reality was merely pre-apocalyptic. The cosier it felt, the more dangerous it truly was.

Along with two of my classmates, I went on a children's creative writing weekend in the Lake District. I spent much of the weekend reading Raymond Briggs's *When the Wind Blows* (1982), which I found in the mini children's library the writing coaches had brought with them. It is a graphic novel in which an elderly couple, depicted in the same cosy style as Briggs's *Father Christmas* (1973) and *The Snowman* (1978), are living an everyday life until 'The Bomb' drops. They then spend several weeks attempting to shelter in their poorly prepared house and finally die from radiation poisoning, bald and covered in skin sores.

I was not shocked by the comic, the beats of which were very similar to those of other nuclear literature I had encountered. Nonetheless it coloured my experience of this weekend which had its own strangeness to it. Between writing exercises, we went out for a walk and gathered wild garlic and elderflowers; one of the teachers made a shockingly perfumed cordial. One of my friends cried every night because she was in the middle of a bout of intestinal worms, which would crawl out of her at night and writhe in her underwear.

In the writing sessions we were encouraged to write about our feelings, but I had almost no vocabulary to express mine. An exercise in which we were supposed to pick an emotion and describe it in terms of sensory similes left me in tears of frustration. Finally, I wrote 'My despair is grey, like a used tissue. It tastes like a cold fried egg.'

In Year Six, one of the books our teacher read to us at story time was Jean Ure's *Plague 99* (1989). Although it was not the nuclear literature I knew so well, it was another very familiar story, in many ways a post-Cold War updating of 'Bomb Lit' tropes. It is set in 1999, which seemed both appropriately apocalyptic and plausible for a near-future narrative. It is difficult for me now to imagine our teacher reading the chapters in which Shahid, one of its protagonists, cares for his dying father, who is vomiting blood. Or the moment when we learn that another character's dissociative break with reality is motivated as much by daily harassment by a peadophile, who is one of the last people to still have a functioning telephone, as it is by living for several weeks in the same house as her mother's decomposing corpse; still harder to imagine thirty round-faced, wide-eyed ten- and eleven-year-olds sitting cross-legged on the carpet, wearing royal blue school sweatshirts and listening eagerly. I remember only that we liked the book.

The commonality between the literature of infection and the literature of nuclear war was not located only in societal collapse, but also in bodily disintegration. The promise of 'The Bomb' was never only one of mass death or the destruction of infrastructure, but a physical undoing from the inside, contamination, sickness, mutation. In *Brother in the Land* (Robert Swindells 1984), one of my favourite books, the protagonist looks after his little brother for over a year before finally losing him to radiation sickness. They spend much of that year on a small settlement with some other survivors, but it is already blighted by this bodily unmaking. Crops are twisted and inedible, a baby is born without a mouth, and in one scene which I have never forgotten, the protagonist watches the last painful moments of a mutant butterfly 'flapping its seven useless wings'.

I saw threats of this contamination everywhere. Fairly early in my nuclear literature phase, I watched *E.T.* (1982), but I was unable to understand its narrative except in the terms I had learned from dystopian sci-fi. When Elliott and the Extra-Terrestrial become ill and their house is overtaken by hazmat suited government officials who ask questions about nausea and hair loss, I filled in the gaps and assumed that I was watching the aftermath of a nuclear incident; that they must, somehow, have wandered onto the grounds of a nuclear power plant and received a fatal dose; or perhaps that the culvert in which E.T. is found had been the site of a spill of nuclear waste. I was so upset that I refused to watch to the end. It would be more than a decade before I realized that my interpretation had been wildly incorrect. I have still not watched the entire film, even though I would eventually learn to contemplate the idea of radiation poisoning without disabling terror, although never without dread. I was so convinced that this was an inevitable future that I felt I needed to learn everything I could about it. One day, 'The Bomb' would touch me too; I would vomit, my hair would fall out, my cells would mutate and, like many dystopian protagonists, I would wish that I had not survived.

In later instalments of the '*Plague 99*' series, we discover that the original teenagers'· descendants are living amidst the remnants of collapsed civilization, in various very different communities. Much of *Watchers at the Shrine* (1994), the third in the series, takes place in a community that worships the 'Shrine', which they do not understand is an old, broken-down nuclear power plant that continuously leaks waste. Pregnant women make pilgrimages to spend time near this sacred place, but if their children are subsequently born with birth defects they are understood to have been 'sinful' and are sent away; we later find out that they have been sold into sexual slavery. I read this book when I was eleven years old; it, too, was in the school library. It was, in many ways, a good capstone to the collection. The Shrine itself now seems to me to echo the Juniors' Library's hosting of shelves full of outdated 'Bomb Lit', still pumping out fear and horror even though their original context and purpose had passed.

I don't know when I first learned that the world might not end, after all. What I do know is that I never experienced it as relief. By that time, I, like any apocalyptic protagonist, had learned to prefer the thought of death to its alternative. I did not want 'The Bomb', but I was prepared for it: for a future in which I would scavenge tins and attempt to grow potatoes in the poisoned ground. I was not prepared for a different kind of survival. Even in my cosy, small, charming primary school I had spent the last year crying every night about my social isolation, although at that point I still considered this a failing of others, a failure on their part to appreciate the topics that interested me, a pervasive preoccupation with physical games, fashion, pop music, all subjects which filled me with bafflement and fear. Like the mutants of 'Children of the Dust' (Louise Lawrence 1985), I was comparatively well suited to a post-nuclear landscape, but appeared uncanny and frightening to those used to everyday twentieth-century-style humans. If I was not white-eyed or covered in ultraviolet-shielding fur, I was still adapted to an alien world.

It never really leaves you. I live very near to the former Olympic Stadium in Stratford, now home to West Ham football club. A couple of years ago they began testing the emergency response and crowd control systems. Ever since then, every Friday morning a loudspeaker has repeated, 'Emergency! We are experiencing an emergency! Please leave via the nearest emergency exit! Do not use the lifts!' Because the stadium is open, this becomes a public warning, spreading through the surrounding area and quite audible from within my flat, although the distance gives it an eerie, echoing quality. When I first heard it, I immediately assumed that 'The Bomb', so long-awaited, had finally arrived.

Like a former soldier, I instantly reverted to a mindset of war. The shift into 'Nuclear Mode' was so instantaneous that I did not have time to question the plausibility of my assumption. The main concerns I had were how I was going to rescue my cat, who was playing in the garden, and how to say goodbye to my friends and family, whom I assumed I would be unlikely to see again. It took a few minutes and multiple repetitions of the warning before it occurred to me that perhaps there was another explanation; by that time I was well on my way to taking shelter in the bathroom. Soon after moving in, I'd calculated that this was the best place in the flat to hide out from a nuclear apocalypse, since it is windowless and offers the means to store water.

There was a sort of sickening familiarity when I started to read climatological reports and to understand that the world was once more firmly on a course to end, although more likely by degrees. I feel now that I did not really appreciate the brief window in my life when it looked as if the human species might have a different kind of future. My strange childhood did not make this reality any more tolerable. I was prepared, but still not ready. If anything, it was easier to picture, harder to escape. This is not accidental. Many of the writers of 'Bomb Lit' wanted to make it impossible for people to avoid the reality of the coming apocalypse. Raymond Briggs intended to undermine the government's attempts to make nuclear war seem both extraordinary (and so unlikely to affect ordinary people) and very ordinary (and so not very terrifying). He presented instead a world in which apocalypse was both cosily familiar and terrifyingly strange. I don't think, however, that he intended for his book to be read by the same children who, a few years previously, had read *Father Christmas*, or sung along to *The Snowman* (1982).

Now, in the midst of our own event, it feels like every skill I have is finally revealing its usefulness. When I allow myself to reflect, I am full of fears, but mostly I don't have the time or energy to do so. I'm caught up in an endless stream of activity which feels like the tripping steps of a well-studied dance, or the kick of a duckling's webbed feet. I've often envied my cat for the thoughtless elegance of his movements, their unreflective economy. Now, at my best moments, I approach that; for the first time in my life, I feel not just prepared but well-rehearsed.

Ray Bradbury's 'Embroidery' (1951) was one of the texts we studied in my first year of secondary school and was the culmination of my atomic education. The nuclear fire which undoes everything at the end of Bradbury's story is both frightening and, in its thoroughness, a reflection of human capability: 'At last it found her heart, a soft red rose sewn with fire, and it burned the fresh, embroidered petals away, one by delicate one'. I still remember the secret recognition with which that sentence greeted me. I felt as if I were reading a description of my own death, knowing, as I did, what it was to be both made and unmade by 'The Bomb'.

12

Killing a cow on kids' TV: The case of *Die Sendung mit der Maus*

Alexander Hartley

'Moo, says the cow,' a friendly voice intones.[1] 'In this case it's a female one.' The screen shows us the hefty, peacable animal side-on, with its udders, its bushy tail and clipped horns, its muzzle attached to a dainty rope that dangles offscreen. Then, strangely, the camera pans and zooms sharply to show the ground beneath the cow's feet. We quickly cut to a barn space. The cow is there, along with two men wearing aprons. Suddenly, several things happen at once. One of the men extends his arm, and we glimpse a piston-like contraption in his hand which gleams in the artificial light. A brief and indistinct sound echoes through the barn, the cow's legs collapse from underneath her, and her body crashes down onto the floor. Meanwhile the voice-over, in the same jovial tone as before, explains: 'The cow is slaughtered.' The camera slowly and mercilessly pans and zooms downward to focus on the fresh cadaver as the men walk brusquely around it; we hear the sounds of male voices, distant traffic and the clinking of the chain that will hoist the body in the air for butchering.

---

[1]All translations from the German in this essay, except where otherwise specified, are my own. Where I quote from published translations, for the convenience of readers of German, I have also cited the German original.

This is a description of the first nine seconds of a television spot made in 1972 for an intended audience of under-six-year-olds (Westdeutscher Rundfunk 1972). The remainder of the four-minute spot takes the form of a repeated pattern in which the camera returns to the original shot of the (still living) cow, zooming in on a particular part of its body, before the voice tells us, and the camera shows us, what everyday products are to be made from that part of the cow.

> From the hide you can make, for example, coats. It can be tanned, and then it becomes leather, for instance to make shoes with. A cow has horns and hooves: they're not thrown away, they're collected and made into artificial fertiliser. ... From the bones we make, for example, soap.

The voice might have added that, from the cow as a whole, somebody made a television programme. This raises a question as to how they came to the conviction that this was what children's television should look like?

This chapter considers the programme, *Die Sendung mit der Maus* (The Mouse Show), in which this spot appeared. I will sketch the show's origins in the late 1960s and early 1970s, focusing in particular on ideas about pedagogy and children's entertainment shared by the programme-makers which, viewed in the light of today's expectations, appear shocking and controversial. The show's tagline and original title, *Lach- und Sachgeschichten*, describes its contents: funny stories and stories about things. This essay will focus on the Sachgeschichten (the stories about things).

Though it lacks the globe-spanning ubiquity of its close precursor *Sesame Street*, within Germany *Die Sendung mit der Maus*, which has been broadcast continually for five decades (it celebrated its half century in 2022), is legendary and beloved to an extent that can be difficult to convey to those who have no experience of it. Its reach and longevity is such that the average age of viewers of *Die Sendung mit der Maus*, which is designed for children under the age of six, is thirty-nine (Bäcker 2011). And yet both six-year-old and thirty-nine-year-old viewers of the show today would likely be surprised by both the style and content of the 'Cow' spot, for a steady and profound change to the formal qualities and the subject matter of the Sachgeschichten took place during the 1970s and 1980s, and this analysis will finally place this change alongside changes in the means of production in the rich West during the era of neoliberalism. That's my second purpose here: as well as arguing that *Die Sendung mit der Maus*'s now controversial founding premises may still possess a potentially emancipatory valence, I will show that the programme, and its accessible online archive, can be seen as an index of changes that have occurred in our mediatized and technological lives – packaged up, presented and made visible for the eyes of children.

Stories about things

In the early years of the Federal Republic of Germany, prevailing wisdom held that 'television for small children' was a contradiction in terms.[2] It would simply be inappropriate to introduce children younger than six to the screen, it was felt, not least because – according to the researchers of the influential 'Keilhacker school' – they would be incapable of distinguishing what they were watching from unmediated reality itself (Stötzel 1990, 4). After early experiments, the regional broadcaster Westdeutscher Rundfunk (WDR) increased the minimum target age of their children's programming from four in 1954 to five in 1957 and then to eight in 1958. In 1958 West German production companies justified their decision not to condone programming of Kleinkinder on the grounds of literally symptomatic criticism: doctors had advised them that exposure to television would give infants headaches, sleeplessness and anxiety (Stötzel 1990, 2). It was not long, however, before some programme-makers began to challenge the contention that television was harmful for infants, and a writer working for the WDR drafted a set of ten theses that articulated and defended a particular idea of what TV for young children might look like.[3] The writer, G. K. Müntefering, would go on to be one of the creators of *Die Sendung mit der Maus*. These extraordinary theses give a flavour of the intellectual atmosphere of the late 1960s in Germany:

> Television is not a replacement for reality. We should exploit every means to extinguish the self-forgetting immersion [*Selbstvergessenheit*] of the watching child. In a playful and enlightening way, a critical distance to the technical instrument of the television should be achieved. A children's programme is governed by openness and 'fleeting enchantment'.
>
> WDR children's programming should not be confused with school TV. To place strong didactic demands on this programming would contradict its task to entertain and to inform. (Müntefering, qtd in Stötzel 1990, 31–2)

The injunction against pedagogy was reiterated by the programme-makers again and again. 'We're not interested in school', said Siegfried Mohrdof, one of WDR's editors (Stötzel 1990, 23). 'School isn't our thing.' Müntefering himself, in an article written after *Lach- und Sachgeschichten* had begun, went still further, 'We didn't want a brightly coloured one-two-three, or the

---

[2]In writing about the origins of *Die Sendung mit der Maus*, I am indebted to the work of Dirk Ulf Stötzel, the author of a 1990 media-studies dissertation that remains as far as I am aware the only scholarly monograph dedicated to the series.
[3]A history of WDR that lays emphasis on its progressive ethos can be found in Hickethier 1998.

ABC presented as a kind of intellectual jungle ... We had in mind more a kind of journalism for children' (Müntefering, qtd in Stötzel 1990: 21).

The producers' fears of particolour arithmetic and a Jungle Book alphabet had been realized in a programme that they seized on as the incarnation of all they wished to avoid: Sesame Street, which had first appeared in 1969 (Westdeutscher Rundfunk 2018, approx. 45:25–46:15; see also Stötzel 1990, 191). By the time Lach- und Sacheschichten was developed, during 1971 and 1972, it was oriented against two things: against the idea that TV was intrinsically inappropriate for four- or five-year-olds, and against the patronizing, parochial or schoolmasterly kinds of programme that had up to that point been tried. What did this new programme look like? Some of it took the form of amusing and illuminating stories about human and animal characters. These were the Lachgeschichten. And some of it, the Sachgeschichten, took the form of reported stories that focused on everyday objects. The classical Sachgeschichten are expositions of how their subjects are made (paper, paintbrushes, pizza) or grown (pine nuts, pistachios), how they behave (penguins, parakeets, polar bears) or what their social functions are (popes, princesses, police officers). These stories were reported by journalists who went to visit the factories, zoos, palaces and so on where their subjects could be found, and they were accompanied by a voice-over which helped to explain to the audience what was happening. From the beginning to the present day, many of these voice-overs were conducted by the beloved Armin Maiwald, whose witty and avuncular style has endeared him to generations of Maus-watchers and helps to give a sense of continuity that reaches across many of the individual stories.

A typical example of the Sachgeschichten during the programme's early years is a 1972 story dedicated to beer. (The story can easily be accessed in the Bibliothek der Sachgeschichten listed in the bibliography.) Some aspects of this clip are recognizable to those familiar with more recent Sachgeschichten: the presence of narration accompanying the images; the hint of wryness and humour in, for example, the way the man chugs the beer in an early shot and then again in the closing shot for a little longer than we expect. Other things seem quite unfamiliar – most of all the dizzying camera angles, as in the opening shot where the beer glass is show from below through a glass table, or the shot where the camera pans from the ceiling to the floor of the enormous factory, seeming to descend as it does so and accompanied by a thrumming, percussive foley effect that seems to jokingly suggest a helicopter. These shots, which represent unlikely or actually unattainable perspectives on the objects they depict, bring to mind Müntefering's thesis about critical distance: we are asked to share the perspective not of any human observer but of a somersaulting movie camera and, accordingly, invited to perceive the factory from a position other than that of a worker or consumer. Critical distance is also won by means of alternating of shots from inside the factory with shots in a bare space that show what is going on on a smaller scale. 'That's all you can see of it', says the narrator in the factory. But television's power is to make visible what can't usually be seen, and the apparatus demonstrations seem to me the Sachgeschichte's most potent realization of Müntefering's qualities of 'openness and 'fleeting enchantment'. The child's ability to grasp the connection between the huge factory machine and its microcosm in the bare space is itself a critical faculty. It is honed by repetition. The repeated jumps also have the effect of interrupting the factory narrative: we are very far, formally, from a camera following the liquid through the pipes along its journey through the various stages of the brewing process. And while the teleology of the narrative is not in doubt – we know that what started out as water will eventually have become beer – these interruptions help suggest that the end-product is not paramount, that there is interest and amusement to be found by lingering at the various stages along the way. There is sensual pleasure in the material objects that are depicted in close-ups: beer itself, its frothy head receding; the hard tap of malted grain falling on a table and the crunching noise as it is ground; the jolly clinking of glass bottles moving down an assembly line. A third aspect of the film is textual play, which focuses on the word 'vollautomatisch' ('fully automatic'). The narrator repeats it three times: the first machine is vollautomatisch, the second 'naturally vollautomatisch', the third 'again vollautomatisch'. Then the techno-progressive cry is taken up by an anthropomorphized tin can rolling around and crying like a drunk before being kicked away. The can's cry is a kind of enchantment of reality and creates a winning humour that offsets the technicity of the industrial process. But it is also a kind of commentary: a can that can do its own talking is brought in to talk about machines that can do their own beer-brewing. As a disorderly and critical member of the 'world of things', the can attracts the child's interest and sympathy, but the adult carelessly kicks it away. Finally, when we come to the fifth machine, 'vollautomatisch' is displayed as text at the bottom of a black screen. This is a kind of introductory exercise in referentiality: the relation between the written and the spoken word, the spot is suggesting, in something like the relation between the small-scale demonstration and the factory machine, or indeed between the onscreen representation of the factory machine and the machine itself. And isn't it a wonder, it seems to ask, that all this identification goes on in the child's head, vollautomatisch?

What is at stake in steak

This demonstrates that, if the early Sachgeschichten sought to provide 'journalism for children', they did not adopt a correspondingly dry and factual formal approach. Instead, the programme-makers developed a style full of wit, play and genuine strangeness, one which strove at each moment to achieve an effect of critical alienation (Brecht's Verfremdungseffekt) among its envisaged audience of infants. Faced with a novel challenge – imagining what television for five-year-olds could and should look like – the programme-makers decisively rejected both the patronizing 'Bastelsendungen' (arts-and-crafts programmes; see Westdeutscher Rundfunk 2018, approx. 17:20) and the glossy studio classrooms that had hitherto marked the terrain.

It is in this light that we should seek to understand the 'Cow' segment described at the start of this chapter. In depicting the various things that can be made out of a cow, it satirizes the arts-and-crafts genre: instead of encouraging children at home to accumulate useless homemade objects, its purpose is to provoke children to reflect on the origins of the objects that are already around them. With only a couple of exceptions, the list of objects derived from the mooing cow is scrupulously everyday: coats, soap, oxtail soup, shoes, axle-grease, medicines, dog food. These are not abstract objects, but are linked, again and again, to their origins in the lovable animal whose Christlike sacrifice has vouchsafed the lives of the watching audience. As with the 'beer' spot, the cow sequence is distinguished by its repetitive quality: the successive cuts from the various parts of the living cow to the various consumer products made from it are followed by a recapitulation in which a two-dimensional diagram of the cow is gradually dismembered as the film cuts back to the shots of the various objects and Maiwald's voice narrates the list again.

One way of reading the film's structure would be that that it registers a trauma – the slaughter – which is soothed by a comforting repetition, so that, by the time the camera returns at the very end to the living cow and the audiences hears a final 'moo', the shock of the slaughter has been overcome, even 'worked through', by the structure of the recurring information and even by the comforting presence of day-to-day objects. If this is true, then the film is a document marked by what some writers have called 'anthroposupremacy': it serves to redeem and justify the cow's slaughter on the basis of all the benefits it brings us. Such a reading might seize on one in particular of Maiwald's lines. After showing us the object of 'dog food', illustrated by a Dachshund plopping over to a metal food-bowl to gobble down its meal, the film cuts to a showcase of various cuts of beef together with sausages, mincemeat, garlic, onions and herbs. Strikingly for an early Sachgeschichte, the film makes no attempt to present the meat in a defamiliarizing angle or pose: rather it is styled like a butcher's display, shot frontally as though for the viewer's delectation. 'And this', the voice-over says, 'is eaten by us – the humans'. It reads as though the child audience of *Die Sendung mit der Maus* is being taught to accept and embrace human beings' relationship of mastery over animals, is being given an elementary lesson in the Enlightenment categories of 'human' and 'nature' and the necessary domination of the latter by the former.

And yet even here things are not so clear-cut. The film goes on to show us three scenes of beef as meat for humans to eat. The first is a steak dropping into a pan, sizzling as it touches the hot oil. The third is a man in a woolen jumper munching on a slice of bread topped with beef sausage. But in the second, a pair of hands is shown cutting up cubes of beef to throw into a pan to make goulash. The lid is placed on the pan at an angle, tilted towards the camera, and, as the frame zooms on the handle of the lid, two drops of water fall across the metal surface of the lid. Though the shot lasts only a second, the droplets are unmistakably prominent at the dead centre of the image. It looks quite plainly as though the pan is crying. This jarring moment of anthropomorphism could be put alongside the talking can in the 'beer' spot, except its effect is not to amuse but to accuse: these droplets silently indict the pan, the cook, the narrator and the cow's slaughterers. It is possible to ignore them but not to overlook them. Taken together with the grisly shots of cow bones and organs, and the shock of the initial slaughter, this moment surely highlights the possibility that the film is allying itself with what must have been the impulse of many of its viewers: the impulse towards moral revulsion at the eating of meat. Clearly the 'cow' film is not vegan propaganda, but at the same time its form and content enable it to provide young viewers with information about how much of the domestic economies they inhabit depends on the routinized slaughter of a charismatic and sympathetic animal. By placing no judgement either way on the bovine sacrifice, but using formal means to encourage critical distance and engagement, the film surely hopes that the shock of the cow's slaughter will punctuate the child's unconscious acceptance of their environment and enable them to criticize the assumptions of their parents. The film hopes to kill a few bourgeois sacred cows.

Benjamin's playworld

The makers of *Die Sendung mit der Maus* strove to create a 'journalism for children' that both demystified and enchanted everyday reality by showing children how things worked. Though it was to some extent defined by its scrappy, anti-establishment, low-budget aesthetic, from early WDR experiments in children's TV one can adduce a coherent and sophisticated aesthetics – an aesthetics that obviously differs from both the 'entertaining' and 'pedagogical' flavours of modern children's TV and one that was sometimes controversially willing to transgress viewers' expectations of appropriate subject matter and presentation for children. I have already noted the influence of Brecht on Müntefering's theses and his approach to *Die Sendung mit der Maus*. Still – as Peter Wollen wrote in a set of notes recently published posthumously – 'Brecht never developed any detailed programme for cinema as such' (2022: 81). To understand the television 'programme' of *Die Sendung mit der Maus*, it is necessary to turn to the writing of Brecht's friend and arguably the first writer to develop a recognizably critical theory both of the audiovisual medium and of child's play: Walter Benjamin. I am turning to Benjamin not because a direct line of influence can be shown between his writings and the early Sachgeschichten, but because of something that amounts more to an elective affinity. It is clear that the '68ers who conceived and created the programme echoed, consciously or not, Benjamin's own philosophy of childhood, a philosophy that saw revolutionary potential in the child's mode of interacting with the world.

In the 'At the Corner of Steglitzer and Genthiner' section of the *Berlin Childhood around 1900*, Benjamin recounts visits to his Aunt Lehmann's apartment:

> Hardly had I entered, in fact, than she saw to it that someone set before me the large glass cube containing a complete working mine, in which miniature miners, stonecutters, and mine inspectors, with tiny wheelbarrows, hammers, and lanterns, performed their movements precisely in time to a clockwork. This toy – if one can call it that – dates from an era that did not yet begrudge even the child of a wealthy bourgeois household a view of workplaces and machines. (*SW*, 3:358–9; *Gn* 2019, 1:576)

What gives this passage its feeling of trepidation? Perhaps the fact that this model of the mineshaft is one of those toys that adults impose on children out of a mistaken assumption of what children want. (In the 1967 theses, Müntefering would write: 'The image of [children's] entertainment ought … not only to be shaped by the memories of adults and from their wish-fulfilment' (qtd in Stötzel 1990, 31).) This reading is encouraged by the turn of phrase []his toy – if one can call it that'. What, then, does deserve the name of toy? Benjamin wrote explicitly about toys, by my count, at least four times: in two versions of his review of Karl Gröber's *Kinderspielzeug aus alter Zeit* (*SW*, 2:113–16 and 117–21; *GS*, 3:113–17 and 127–32), both in 1928; in an article, 'Russian Toys', published in *Südwestdeutscher Rundfunk Zeitung* in 1930 (2007, 107; *Gn* 2006, 75) and in the two-part radio presentation 'Berlin Toy Tour' (2014, n.p.; *GS*, 7:98–111). Thinking through toys was also a living practice for Benjamin. Scholem recalled, 'In the twenties he was apt to offer philosophical reflections as he brought forth a toy for his son' (1981, 37; *Gn* 1997, 51–2).

In his writing on toys, in particular the programmatic second review of Gröber, 'Toys and Play', Benjamin begins to outline something like a philosophy of play. It is repetition that, in Benjamin's understanding, vouchsafes play. 'The law of repetition', he writes, is 'the great law that presides over all the rules and rhythms of play' (*SW*, 2:120; *GS*, 3:131). This is a particular kind of repetition: 'Not a "doing as if" but a "doing the same thing over and over again", the transformation of a shattering experience into habit – that is the essence of play'. And it is different for children from that for adults: 'An adult relieves his heart from its terrors and doubles happiness by turning it into a story. A child creates the entire event anew and starts again right from the beginning.' Jeffrey Mehlman, in a book-long essay on Benjamin's radio broadcasts for children, takes 'Toys and Play' to be arguing that 'the toy is ... above all that wherein the child negotiates the imposition of an adult agenda' (1993, 4). It is clear that the young Benjamin in his aunt's parlour is negotiating an adult agenda of sorts; equally clearly, a child watching the 'Bier' Sachgeschichte is negotiating an adult agenda: a drink that is forbidden to children, factories they are not allowed to go to. Repetition helps to neutralize the threat of the word, vollautomatisch, that has a positive valence in the world of adults but a negative one in the world of children. Repetition may help to tame the shock of seeing a cow slaughtered in front of you when afterwards the products of its slaughter are processed in front of you repetitively. One thing that distinguishes a television programme from a film is the fact that in television, a given format is established and then repeated (in this case weekly). Television is thus generically well equipped to offer children an opportunity for the kind of repetition Benjamin is talking about in 'Toys and Play', and a recognition of this is, I think, detectable in the 1967 theses, with their evocation of 'fleeting enchantment' (Stötzel 1990, 31). The Sachgeschichte's obsession with physical objects may then be less about the 'redemption of physical reality' (in the phrase of Benjamin's contemporary Siegfried Kracauer) than about the toyification of human-made reality. It is Benjamin himself who suggests, elsewhere, that the child's relationship with a toy is made lively by the child's ability to understand how the toy is made.

> If only our artisans would not so often forget when doing this [producing 'primitive' children's toys] that it is not the constructive, schematic forms that appear primitive to the child, but rather the total construction of his doll or his toy dog *insofar as he can imagine how it is made*. This is just what he wants to know; *this first establishes his vibrant relationship with his things* [Sachen]. (Benjamin 2007, 107; *Gn* 2006, 75; my emphasis)[4]

Toys are made by adults, and an understanding of how the toy is made is an understanding of how adults create a world that children inhabit and inherit; playing with the toy is the repeated act of grappling with both the adult-made-ness of the world and the ability of children to repurpose things made by adults for their own uses. This, in the end, is what is frightful about

---

[4]Esther Leslie's published translation reads: 'his vibrant relationship with his toys'.

the mineshaft in Tante Lehmann's apartment: it is overdetermined, and like any overly complex, delicate and lifelike toy, it resists the young Benjamin's attempts to play with it.

We can complete the arc of Benjamin's thought by linking the repurposing of adult agendas in child's play to the wider repurposing – or, in the Brechtian term Benjamin adopts, Umfunktionierung – of art, and by extension of physical reality, made possible by photographic technology in his most famous essay:

> *It might be stated as a general formula that the technology of reproduction detaches the reproduced object from the sphere of tradition. By replicating the work many times over, it substitutes a mass existence for a unique existence. And in permitting the reproduction to reach the recipient in his or her own situation, it actualizes that which is reproduced.* These two processes lead to a massive upheaval in the domain of objects handed down from the past – a shattering of tradition which is the reverse side of the present crisis and renewal of humanity. … The social significance of film, even – and especially – in its most positive form, is inconceivable without its destructive, cathartic side: the liquidation of the value of tradition in the cultural heritage. (*SW* 4:254; *GS* 1:477–8; emphasis in original)

The potential and the stakes of the kind of reproduction, the kind of repetition, enabled by photography is, of course, dramatically sketched in the juxtaposition of communism and fascism at the end of the essay's first and third versions (*SW* 4:270; *GS* 1:508). Here, in another passage written at the peak of Brecht's influence on him, Benjamin expands on that comment to consider what revolutionary possibilities committed writers should try to exploit in their work.

> Does he [the intellectual] succeed in promoting the socialization of the intellectual means of production? Does he see how he himself can organize intellectual workers in the production process? Does he have proposals for the *Umfunktionierung* [repurposing] of the novel, the drama, the poem? The more completely he can orient his activity toward this task, the more correct the political tendency of his work will be, and necessarily also the higher its technical quality. (*SW*, 2:780; *GS*, 2:71)

Doesn't the world of the Sachgeschichte have the potential to be one in which children and adults can grasp the contingency of manufactured objects, and thus understand the ways in which they might be repurposed? Isn't play a kind of rehearsal for revolution?

This, at least, is the suggestive premise of an intriguing text written by Benjamin around 1929, unpublished in his lifetime, which lays out a 'Program for a Proletarian Children's Theater'. Like the fascists against whom he was already fervently writing, Benjamin had grasped the immense revolutionary potential of children's education, which derived both from their ownership of the social future and from their immunity to cant ideological phrases (which 'have no power over children', *SW* 2:201; *GS* 2:763). The child's impulse towards play manifests here, in what amounts to Benjamin's most extreme conception of it, as a desire to dominate and command reality: 'the child inhabits his world like a dictator' (*SW* 2:204; *GS* 2:766). And it is precisely this will to power that, in dialectical fashion, provides child's play with its liberatory power, its potential to remake reality. This is why Benjamin's proscription for a socialist pedagogy for children between the age of four and puberty is based on repeated play-acting. 'What is truly revolutionary', he concludes, 'is not the propaganda of ideas, which leads here and there to impracticable actions and vanishes in a puff of smoke upon the first sober reflection at the theater exit. What is truly revolutionary is the secret signal of what is to come that speaks from the gesture of a child' (*SW* 2:206; *GS* 2:769).

Umfunktionierung

Though *Die Sendung mit der Maus* survived the cultural and economic ructions of the 1970s and 1980s, the radical antipedagogy, the nonconformism and, above all, the dependence on image and repetition of the early Sachgeschichten did not. Instead, the Sachgeschichte genre was itself umfunktioniert throughout the 1970s and 1980s. Stötzel writes:

> While at first it was primarily visual perception that was addressed, the pace of speech and the complexity of sentence construction increased continuously up to 1988. ... By 1988 we find that sentence construction is almost exclusively hypotactic, with the text determining the pace of the cuts and governing the film, while the images largely have a commentary, referential and supporting character. (Stötzel 1990, 134)

We can speculate about the reasons for these changes. Müntefering was succeeded as lead producer of the programme in the mid-1970s by Enrico Platter, who adopted a more favourable view of the determining possibilities of the voice-over: 'the text can be very helpful', he commented (Stötzel 1990: 42). In stark contrast to Müntefering's original programme for children's television, later theses developed by WDR in the 1980s became explicitly pedagogical, as well as mentioning the importance of the voice for training children to watch television (Stötzel 1990, 32). And even beyond the change of personnel, perhaps the Sachgeschichten were bound to succumb to the cultural pressure to align with other children's programming as well as with TV for adults, and to adopt a more overdetermined, didactic and 'entertaining' narrative mode.

Not only has the form of the Sachgeschichten changed, but as industrial production has been increasingly automatized within the rich West (when not delocalized entirely), this has been reflected in the content of the stories. This amounts to an unusually clear example of what Marx referred to as the relationship between economic base and societal superstructure. To see how the older Sachgeschichten compare with more recent ones, we can compare the two films that have shown the production of paintbrushes, one made in 1977 and the other in 2012 (the latter is the Bibliothek der Sachgeschichten, the former not available online in its entirety). It is easy to see how much more important the spoken text is in the later spot. It drives the action, introducing and narrating each set of images; in 1977 voice and image had been on a much more level footing. The earlier Sachgeschichte is organized according to a logic of workers, with the camera picking out each individual worker to emphasize how many steps are necessary to produce a single paintbrush. By contrast, the more recent film is organized by the narration into the three parts that together form the product – three stages that are not visually but verbally demarcated. The structure is no longer repetitive and episodic; Armin Maiwald's narrating voice, and the frame narrative of his painting of Cologne Cathedral, unifies the Sachgeschichte into a diegetic whole, whereas if you were to watch the 1977 Sachgeschichte you would not even know what the Sache was until you had deduced it. The viewer is less likely to consider the strangeness and abstraction of the components and processes that make a paintbrush in the 2012 Sachgeschichte, partly because technological developments have automated most of the process, but in large part also because those components and processes are much more firmly embedded in a narrative whose protagonist is now the commodity itself, and no longer the people by whom or even the objects out of which it is made. As if to demonstrate the point, when the 1977 paintbrush story was rebroadcast a few years ago, it was prefaced by a new speech to camera by Maiwald laying out what the viewing audience was about to witness, and the introductions of each individual worker were cut out of the video (Westdeutscher Rundfunk 2019).

As such the Sachgeschichten, taken in their entirety, are a reflection both of changing methods of production and of the changing way in which production has been made visible to children. In the 1970s, the programme gave names to the workers it depicted, showing them as experts in their individual roles; in the 2010s, the product moves serenely through the various stages of its production as the voice explains the technical and scientific considerations that determine how it is made. In this Umfunktionierung of a once radical narrative mode, the workers have quite literally left the factory, and with them the early Sachgeschichten's striking potential for aesthetic emancipation. What remains, encased within layers of closed and soothing voice-over, is the commodity. We can see this, baldly enough, as neoliberalism silently indexed within, haunting, kids' TV.

Abbreviations

GS: Benjamin, Walter. 1972–89. *Gesammelte Schriften*. Edited by Theodor W. Adorno and Gerschem Scholem. 7 vols. Frankfurt: Suhrkamp.
SW: Benjamin, Walter. 1996–2003. *Selected Writings*. Translated and edited by Michael W. Jennings, Marcus Bullock, Howard Eiland and Gary Smith. 4 vols. Cambridge, MA: Belknap Press.

References

Bäcker, Marcus. 2011. 'Klack, Klack, Klack'. *Frankfurter Rundschau*, 7 March. https://www.fr.de/kultur/klack-klack-klack-11436619.html. Accessed 25 September 2023.

Benjamin, Walter. 2006. *Walter Benjamins Archive: Bilder, Texte und Zeichen*. Edited by Ursula Marx, Gudrun Schwarz, Michael Schwarz and Erdmut Wizisla. Frankfurt: Suhrkamp.

Benjamin, Walter. 2007. *Walter Benjamin's Archive: Images, Texts, Signs*. Translated by Esther Leslie. Edited by Ursula Marx, Gudrun Schwarz, Michael Schwarz and Erdmut Wizisla. London: Verso.

Benjamin, Walter. 2014. *Radio Benjamin*. Translated by Jonathan Lutes with Lisa Harries Schumann and Diana K. Reese. Edited by Lecia Rosenthal. London: Verso.

Benjamin, Walter. 2019. *Berliner Chronik/Berliner Kindheit um neunzehnhundert*. Edited by Burkhardt Lindner and Nadine Werner. 2 vols. Frankfurt: Suhrkamp.

Hickethier, Knut. 1998. *Geschichte des deutschen Fernsehens*. Stuttgart: Metzler.

Kracauer, Siegfried. 1960. *Theory of Film: The Redemption of Physical Reality*. New York: Oxford University Press.

Mehlman, Jeffrey. 1993. *Walter Benjamin for Children: An Essay on His Radio Years*. Chicago: University of Chicago Press.

Scholem, Gershom. 1975. *Walter Benjamin: die Geschichte einer Freundschaft*. Frankfurt: Suhrkamp.

Scholem, Gershom. 1981. *Walter Benjamin: The Story of a Friendship*. Translated by Harry Zohn. Philadelphia: Jewish Publication Society of America.

Stötzel, Dirk Ulf. 1990. *Das Magazin 'Die Sendung mit der Maus': Analyse einer Redaktions- und Sendungskonzeption*. Wiesbaden: Otto Harrassowitz.

Westdeutscher Rundfunk. 1972. 'Die Geschichte der Kuh'. https://www.youtube.com/watch?v=RFBwJyjT_Fo. Accessed 25 September 2023.

Westdeutscher Rundfunk. 1972–. *Bibliothek der Sachgeschichten* [database]. https://www.wdrmaus.de/filme/sachgeschichten/a-bis-z.php5. Accessed 25 September 2023.

Westdeutscher Rundfunk. 2018. *Gert K. Müntefering im Gespräch mit Klaus Michael Heinz*. https://www.ardmediathek.de/video/wdr-geschichte-n/

gert-k-muentefering/wdr/Y3JpZDovL3dkci5kZS9CZWl0cmFnLWVkYzF
lZjA5LTI5NmItNDA2Ny1hZTg0LTZmNzIxOTQ5ZDJkNg. Accessed 25
September 2023.
Westdeutscher Rundfunk. 2019. 'Ein Pinsel aus Tierhaaren' [rebroadcast]. https://
www.youtube.com/watch?v=JOrco8b8_qs. Accessed 25 September 2023.
Wollen, Peter. 2022. 'Brecht in L.A.: A Few Footnotes'. *New Left Review* 136
(July–August): 71–81.

13

Confronting ghosts: The inherited horrors of the Kent State Shooting

Elizabeth Tussey

Before I could read, I used to sit on the floor of the basement near the bookcase and deliberately scare myself by looking at the covers of my father's books, a collection of horrors – terrestrial and imagined. His books lined the basement on wired shelves smelling faintly from a combination of enamel dust and the assorted snacks and antacids he carried in his plastic moulded lunchbox.

My father worked first shift in the enamel mill at a company called American Standard for over forty years. He could devour an entire book in a workday if the mills ran slow, and I recall the steady rotation of paperbacks stuffed into the dusty contents of his lunchbox. *Watership Down* was one of the few books I ever saw make a return appearance. The cover art of my father's paperback copy depicted a simple drawing of a rabbit set within a compass – the unassuming image a departure from the grotesque covers of pulp horror and war novels that filled my childhood home.

I took a great interest when my father would talk about *Watership Down*. He quoted from it readily – repeating Richard Adam's imagining of anthropomorphized rabbits and their epic quest across the English countryside, and the Prince with a Thousand Enemies. Based on the reverence and depth of feeling my father expressed towards this book, I figured it must be even more frightening than something like Stephen King's *Night Shift*, a book I was incapable of reading at the time. It horrified me, nevertheless, when I considered the cover art of his edition of a bandaged hand covered in unblinking human eyes.

A collection of books dealing with The Kent State Shooting also lived among the horrors of my father's bookshelf. The covers of these books were similarly foreboding with black and blocky capitalized text, and thick spines. I knew about the events of 4 May 1970 before I could read, and much like the covers of the horror novels, the pictures within his Kent State collection filled my young mind with a more immediate, and real sense of terror. An hour or two before The Ohio National Guard fired a deadly volley of bullets into a crowd of unarmed Kent State University students and anti-war protestors, a photographer named Howard Ruffner captured the image of a crowd. They were watching members of the same Ohio National Guard (ONG) conducting an exercise in a field near the centre of campus. Earlier that week, President Nixon announced the expansion of the Vietnam War into Cambodia, resulting in widespread protests across the country. Kent State University and the surrounding community of Kent, Ohio, became the site of unrest and, following an inflammatory speech by Ohio governor James Rhodes, the ONG was dispatched to maintain order. Ruffner's photograph depicts a group of students standing in front of one of the dormitories with a group of soldiers and an army Jeep in the foreground.

My young father is in the background of Ruffner's photograph. His brows are furrowed and his mouth is slightly open. The expression can be read a number of ways – shock, confusion, dread. Somewhere beyond the scope of Ruffner's camera, my mother, also a Kent State student, stood in line at the campus credit union. The tension intensified over the course of the weekend and on the morning of 4 May, my mother decided to leave campus and either accompany my father to his mother's home in Pittsburgh, Pennsylvania, or find a way back to her mother and father's home in Canton, Ohio. Less than an hour later, the ONG shot and murdered four Kent State students: Jeffrey Miller, Sandra Scheuer, Allison Krause and William Schroeder. A different photographer, John Filo, captured perhaps the most well-known image from this event: a black and white photograph of a young man face down in the Taylor Hall, his face turned away from the photographer; a trail of black blood runs away from his still body. Fourteen-year-old Mary Ann Vecchio kneels at his form. Her left hand grips the arm of a man standing next to her while her right hand reaches out, palm open towards the sky; her mouth yawns in a perpetual scream.

Over fifty years later, the series of events leading to that deadly moment remain clouded by years of government suppression and the gradual fading of memory. To this day, no one has been held directly accountable for the shooting. Apart from a vaguely worded 'statement of regret', a formal apology or restitution, or any form of restorative justice remains absent. I never found any images of my mother's face among the crowds, despite searching through hundreds of photos from that weekend. Only my father remains in these records; his haunted face is forever part of the visual telling of the Kent State Shooting.

Our family scrapbooks hold photographic evidence of trauma beyond the horrifying images captured in my father's Kent State books. In a photograph of my mother and father sitting together in my grandparents' home during the summer following the shooting, my mother's face is gaunt and hollowed. My father attempts to smile at the camera, but his eyes are downcast and there is noticeable tension around his jaw. My mother was twenty-two years old and my father was twenty-one years old in 1970. They were young and in love, and the events of 4 May permanently and fatally altered the trajectories of their short lives.

I cannot say if my father's love of horror, ranging from pulp to the pastoral, emerged in the immediate aftermath of the Kent State Shooting or if it was a genre that he had always embraced. Regardless of the timeline of his own fascination with the macabre, he saw it fit to begin exposing me to the world of horror in fiction and film at an early age. My first initiation was watching the animated film version of *Watership Down* when I was three or four years old.

The horrors lurking in Martin Rosen's imaging of *Watership Down* are both pastoral and hallucinogenic. One unsettling feature of this film is the abrupt shifts in animation style between various chapters of the story. The film opens with a crudely drawn vignette describing the violent and destructive creation myth that guides the characters in the film through their adventures. At the conclusion of this chapter, the animation style shifts. We see a hyper-realistic shot of the main character, Hazel's face – the details so precise that one can count his whiskers. In one of the first examples of this shift, Hazel's brother, Fiver, has a prophetic vision of the impending destruction of their warren by a real estate developer. During this hallucinatory sequence, Fiver watches in horror as the field before him runs red with blood that only he can see. Heeding this psychic vision, Fiver, Hazel and a number of their friends flee their homeland in search of safety. Following the destruction of their warren, the lone survivor of the massacre recalls the traumas visited upon their warren. As he recounts his story, the animation shifts from realistic watercolour representations of animals and their surroundings to a nightmare realm of bleeding suns, monochromatic rabbit corpses and inverted colour schemes.

As a child, I understood all these shifts had a place within the story, and no representation of reality was necessarily truer than the other. The nightmare realm of trauma existed in tandem with the realistic, pastoral world. This sensation was compounded by a scene late in the movie where these worlds and their associated animation styles coalesce in one of the film's most haunting scenes. After Hazel, the main character, is shot and wounded by a farmer, two of his friends return to their warren to inform Hazel's brother, Fiver, that they believe Hazel has been killed. Lurking behind the two rabbits is a third form, appearing in the shape of a black, disembodied rabbit head with glowing red eyes. Fiver immediately recognizes this form as the Black Rabbit of Inle, a frightening mythic figure known to call rabbits to their deaths. Fiver is not frightened by this appearance and follows the Black Rabbit towards his wounded brother. Throughout this short scene, accompanied by a lilting and melancholy Art Garfunkel tune, the various styles of animation swirl together into a dream-like sequence, grounded in the reality of trauma and horror. At one point Fiver pauses for breath beneath a row of power lines. He gazes up at them as they shift into caressing hands. He stares at the setting sun which becomes a goblet of spilling blood. The crude shadow form of the Black Rabbit of Inle eventually leads him to Hazel, who is wounded but still alive. The animation style returns to hyper-realism as the figure of the Black Rabbit fades out. I used to rewind this scene and watch it over and over again. I felt like I was learning some truth or peeking behind the veil. If I kept watching this scene, I would understand something that I couldn't quite name.

I suspect my father found a similar expression of truth in the book and film he loved so dearly. Perhaps that is why he saw it fit for me to see such a horrifying movie so young. I also saw these attitudes reflected in the way he parented me – some people would call it 'tough love'. My father made sure to point out ugly, and even frightening, truths to me. Many of these were communicated through examples in the natural world.

I was five or six years old and had recently experienced my first family death when my maternal grandmother unexpectedly passed away. I was confused and hurt and terrified in the wake of her passing. I was in the car with my father on our way to Pittsburgh to visit his family. My father had been the one to tell me what happened to my grandmother, and he made it clear to me that her body was just a shell. We passed a bloated deer at the side of the road, its abdomen swollen and all four feet sticking out at grotesque angles. My father pointed to it and asked me if I knew why the corpse was in such a state. I told him that I didn't. He proceeded to explain to me the process of decomposition, deconstructing the sickening image of the decaying deer into a series of scientific processes.

The horrifying can be natural and a part of the working world, he conveyed to me. Death and rot are not inherently evil, or even things to be feared. At my young age, I could not put these ideas into cogent words, but I understood my father was teaching me something very complicated, but also very necessary. This was the same sensation I felt during repeated viewings of *Watership Down*. I felt fear with every watching, but also a strange comfort and the sense that this knowledge was essential to understanding the natural world.

My mother and father carried their trauma apart from each other, and in remarkably different ways. Their shared experience at Kent State bonded them, yet it also drove them away from each other. I was born the day after their fourteenth wedding anniversary in October 1985. My parents had been a childless couple for almost twenty years when I came into the world, and my arrival complicated and widened the gulf between them. My father was an avowed agnostic and he detested pseudoscientific beliefs. My mother, who was raised without religion, converted to Catholicism a year or two before I was born. When I asked her why she decided to embrace religion as an adult, she vaguely answered that she knew massive changes were coming in her life and she needed something transcendental to guide her through them. My childhood home was a safe and loving one but was also deeply complicated. My father developed a binge drinking problem and was prone to explosive fits of anger and despair. He never lost his job or acted violently towards my mother and I but spoke and behaved with cruelty when in the grasp of these episodes.

When I was in high school, my father spent his days off in the bar, returning drunk in the mid-afternoon. He often stumbled into my room on the verge of tears and would mumble his worries and fears to me. My memories of those years are faded and suppressed, but the common theme of these encounters was my father's accounting of his impending death, despite his young age and good health. He implored me to take care of my mother when he was gone. This litany of imminent death and abandonment was repeated to me through the haze of my father's inebriation so often that I came to understand it as prophecy. As a teen girl listening to my father tell me that death was coming for him, I understood Fiver and his fields filled with blood.

I cannot remember the first time my parents told me about the Kent State Shooting, but I recall asking my mother where the students had fallen when she took me with her to enroll at the satellite Kent State branch in our hometown of Salem, Ohio. I was four or five and my mother was attempting to finish the degree she abandoned after the shooting. I was so young that I couldn't understand that we weren't at the same location. However, at this point I had seen the image of Jeffrey Miller, face down in the Taylor Hall parking lot. I asked my mother if their ghosts were still there. My mother, unnerved by my questions, assured me that we weren't in the same place. But she did not answer my question about ghosts.

Much like my memories of the Kent State Shooting, ghosts were part of my life from the time I was an infant. My mother believed I saw and waved to the spirit of my great-grandmother who died the day before my baptism. The same week, she felt a hand grasp her shoulder while she stood at our kitchen sink and turned to find no one behind her. I was raised on these stories and many more from deeper in my family history – my grandmother dreaming of the Four Horsemen of the Apocalypse right before her death, my coal miner ancestors foretelling disaster. More often than not, this genealogy of ghosts almost always came in tandem with thinly veiled references to undiagnosed mental illnesses.

As a child of the late 1980s and early 1990s, I grew up with a host of horrifying television programmes to buttress these family legends. Most Americans who came of age in the 1990s can readily recall the foreboding image of Robert Stack standing in a trench coat amid the swirling fog of liquid nitrogen as the synth-heavy opening track to *Unsolved Mysteries* pulsated in a minor key. Stack would complete his introductory monologue with the phrase: 'Perhaps you could solve a mystery', inviting the viewer, if not directly tasking them, to assume a bit of ownership of the horrors he was about to recount. I spent countless hours sitting a few feet from my mother and father's cabinet TV in the chill of our wood panelled basement watching the show. *Unsolved Mysteries* featured a series of vignettes ranging from unsolved crimes to miracles and to the supernatural. As Stack narrated the weekly mysteries, actors dramatized Stack's words. A young Matthew McConaughey even appears in one of the early episodes. While the stories Stack told were grounded in truth, the recreations provided the viewer with a nice cushion of unreality.

Unsolved Mysteries unnerved me but the episodes never truly frightened me. The programme *Sightings* is less remembered than *Unsolved Mysteries*. Both programmes aired on American television in the late 1980s and early 1990s. Episodes of *Unsolved Mysteries* are easy to find on the internet and are readily available on streaming services in America. Netflix rebooted the series in 2020 and retained the same creepy synth music as the original and delivered an eerie tribute to Robert Stack in the form of a brief flash of his transparent image in the opening credits.

Conversely, media related to *Sightings* has been almost impossible to track down. *Sightings* followed a format similar to *Unsolved Mysteries*: an intensely creepy introduction sequence, a dour host and a series of stories ranging from true crime to the supernatural. The major difference in the programmes by my reckoning is that while *Unsolved Mysteries* provided me with some fun thrills, *Sightings* terrified me to my very core. As a child who thrived on a steady diet of Stephen King books, horror films and really any creepy form of media I could get my hands on, I was not easily frightened. *Sightings* was the exception and was one of the few horror programmes to cause me to sleep with my lights on.

My memories of the programme are dim. I cannot remember what specifically frightened me so badly about *Sightings*. I was not able to revisit the episodes like I might with episodes of *Unsolved Mysteries*. As an adult, I've searched for years for a DVD copy or YouTube evidence of *Sightings* episodes and always come up empty-handed, until recently I procured an old VHS copy of a collection of all of the ghost episodes from *Sightings* on eBay. After dragging an old TV/VCR combo up from our basement, I popped the tape in and gleefully revisited the terrors of my youth. After watching the first two episodes I became very aware of why *Sightings* was so frightening to me as a child. *Unsolved Mysteries* grounds the narrative of each episode in the same structure as a campfire tale; *Sightings* grounds the narrative in a sort of journalistic investigation. Like *Unsolved Mysteries*, *Sightings* not only featured recreations but also heavily relied on professional investigation, featuring professors from Oxford who dabbled in the paranormal, or creepy, dark-lit interviews with witnesses who preferred to remain nameless. The other revelation I gained from this viewing was that the realistic tone of *Sightings* matched the ghost stories that my mother told me – they were grounded in terrifying reality.

When my beloved maternal grandfather took his own life in 2001, the tension and dread that haunted my childhood home became unbearably palpable. I was fifteen years old and his suicide came just seven months after the death of my paternal grandmother. Her death threw my father into a tailspin and his binge drinking and outbursts haunted that era of my teen hood with increasing and awful intensity. This was the state of our house when my mother found her father's body. She found him in his garage during a weekly visit in August 2001, less than three weeks before 9/11, and never recovered from the shock.

The events of 9/11 compounded the terrors unfurling in the microcosm of our chaotic and grief-laden home. In 2002, following a steady year of grief and national terror, my mother saw her first and last ghost. It came to her during a sleepless night. After turning over in her bed, my mother saw a tall, black figure standing in the corner of her bedroom. At first, she thought it was me, pulling what would have been a cruel prank by shrouding myself in black fabric and standing in the corner of her room. She put on her glasses, sat up in bed, and prepared to yell at me. When her eyes adjusted and the full view of the thing came into focus, she could only think of the term, 'shade'. Not a ghost or demon. A void. She told me it was almost flat, dimensionless, a figure peeled from the shadows. It lacked any distinct form but was tall and had the general outline of a two-dimensional human form draped with a black that swallowed any ambient light in the room. The boundaries of this thing rippled at the edges and began to gain form. She told me that it grew an arm, flat and black and empty as the rest of it. The arm waved back and forth as if to beckon her to pay closer attention, to warn her of something. Before it could completely take form, she fled the room. She told me she knew if she paid it more attention those edges would sharpen and a face would emerge out of the shadow. I never asked her whose face she expected to see.

I spent the rest of my teen hood terrified of that room. Whenever I walked down the hall towards my own bedroom, which was adjacent to my mother and father's room, I would put my hand up to my face to guard my peripheral vision from catching even the slightest glance of a shadow.

The dread of that house never fully lifted and, while I loved my parents and their company, I yearned for independence. Despite the horrors my parents experienced on 4 May 1970, they were adamant that I attend

Kent State University Main Campus following my high-school graduation. In August 2004, I moved into my dorm at the KSU honours college. As part of our orientation, we were shuttled into the campus KIVA to watch a documentary about the shooting. I recall shifting uncomfortably in my seat, as I watched something I knew intimately in the presence of strangers: the source of my father's drinking and my mother's panic condensed into an hour-long documentary.

Every day I crossed through the Taylor Hall parking lot and passed the burning beacons that marked where each student fell. Countless times I saw those haunting lights glowing in the still night like will-o-the-wisps as I made my way back to my dorm after a night of drinking in downtown Kent. I endured my own trauma while at Kent State when my first boyfriend nearly ended my life in a dorm room in Koonce Hall.

I recovered as best as I could from the experience. My abuser left campus the following year. Despite my own trauma, and the ghosts of my parents' trauma, I went on to live the best years of my life at Kent State. Away from the oppression of my family home, I grew into myself. I felt less haunted, less of a ghost and, following my own brush with an early death, a living, whole person. The entire campus became a memento mori to me and those constant reminders pushed me to fill my life with all the joys and wonders offered by youth. The only shadow that lingered was a constant worry for the health of my parents, whose habits only worsened as they aged. My father's prophecy of an early death, repeated to me endlessly throughout my high-school and college years lived in my mind as I became an adult. As I neared the end of my twenties, his prophecy came true. My parents' lives ended twenty-two months apart. They met their deaths with the dignity and bravery of people who saw their own ends coming decades away. Or as people who lived the final quarter of their lives haunted by an act of senseless state violence. My father departed first, suddenly and in a rush of chaos. He retired in 2014 after a gruelling forty years of mill work. I saw him truly happy for the first time in my recollection and thought perhaps I would get to experience him as a healed, relaxed adult.

He developed a cough and a fever on Christmas Day of 2014, only nine months following his retirement. What appeared to be the flu led to a hospital stay. The first night my father spent in the hospital he turned to my mother and told her that the room was filled with people. The man I knew to be the ultimate sceptic began seeing ghosts. He wouldn't tell her who was in the room with him, only that she couldn't possibly imagine who was in attendance at this courtly, ghostly gathering at his bedside. In the flurry of medical testing and my father's rapid decline, only one doctor would speak the horrible truth to my mother and me. While the tests had not come back yet, he suspected my father's kidneys and liver were failing and there was cancer throughout his body. My father passed on a freezing cold day in January 2015. I sat vigil at his bedside for the last twelve hours of his life.

I left briefly to return home for a shower and breakfast, and, as if he'd been waiting for me to leave, he passed five minutes after I left his room. When I returned to his still, peaceful form, I felt such joy for him. Not for the ending of his recent suffering, but for his release from a life plagued with trauma and sorrow and fear. In life I never saw my father look as restful as I did in those moments following his death.

When my mother fell ill fifteen months later, I waited for the ghosts to arrive. Like my father, her illness first manifested as a lingering cough that rapidly turned into something worse. Unlike my father's swift passing, my dear mother fought lung cancer for eight months. That final year of her life was full of terror. But these were the terrors my mother and father both prepared me for. I did not fear the grotesqueries of the cancer ward, or the horrors of a body as it fails.

I moved in with my mother and cared for her. Because I was acquainted with the macabre, the ravages of cancer did not prevent me from fully connecting with my mother during those final months. We continued to laugh and joke and remained ourselves in the face of her impending death. When she entered hospice care, we both agreed that she could remain in her house with me as a full-time caregiver. The hospice social worker assigned to us remarked at how unusually strong our bond remained, and how she knew we would manage this final journey together just fine.

Using my father's experience as a benchmark, I expected an exponential response from beyond the veil as my mother neared her end. In late November, her health rapidly declined. She remained in her bed in the room where, fifteen years earlier, a shadow beckoned to her. I found myself entering and re-entering the room that terrified me so, and felt that yet another prophecy had been fulfilled. Perhaps it was me she saw all those years ago, my form shadowed by a future not yet realized.

In her final hours, I sat with my mother in that room, waiting for ghosts to appear. On the Christmas morning of 2016, I held my mother's hand and told her it was Christmas Day. As many times before, I told her I loved her and that it was okay to let go. No ghosts arrived from the past, present or future. My mother held on throughout the day and into the evening. Like my father, she waited to pass until I was absent. When I returned to her dreadfully silent room, I kept my back to the corner where the shadow issued its vague warning to her. I opened the window to the dark of Christmas night so that her soul could pass unobstructed into the ether of the other side.

I returned to Kent State on a research trip during the summer of 2022. I was there to do research on the much-maligned May 4 Memorial – a university-sponsored project established amid much controversy in 1990. I hadn't been back since my mother died. It had been years since I ventured beyond the library and student centre. I walked to Taylor Hall in the early morning. Intersession had ended and the campus was empty except for a lone dog walker. The memorial consists of four faceless granite monoliths each positioned on the opposite side of Taylor Hall, beyond the view of the parking lot where four students lost their lives. While I was standing amid those blank stone blocks a memory returned to me.

It is 1998. My parents are showing me around Kent State for the first time. It is a hazy summer morning and my mother and father stand amid the massive oak trees that sprout from the hill behind Taylor Hall. My father wanders down the hill, looking up at the trees. When my mother asks what he's looking for he tells her he's trying to find the tree that he carved their names into the year before the shooting. He wants to see if their names are still there.

In 2022, I wander down the hill, my eyes scanning the tree bark for their names, for a crude heart with Robert + Danielle Forever, or whatever wish my father carved all those years ago. I wander away from the anemic May 4 Memorial, and the glowing beacons, and the site of death to find this carved memory of my parents. I scan the gnarled bark of these old trees but find nothing. It is 2022 but it is also 1969. My mother and father are in the old student centre, just around the corner from Taylor Hall. Their hearts and minds are whole, the trajectory of their lives bends upwards, and they are in love. My father loads quarters into the jukebox and dances with my mother to their song, 'Everlasting Love'. This is the version of their ghosts I choose to carry, and the narrative I give them ends with hope.

14

Creeping dread in *The Singing Ringing Tree*: East German cinematic fairy tale as children's tea-time entertainment

Wayne Johnson

No one of a certain age would ever forget the fear they experienced during the weekly viewing of a three-part serial first shown by the BBC in 1964. This serial, *The Singing Ringing Tree*, would psychologically scar a generation. The series was taken from a feature-length movie, (*Das Singende, Klingende Bäumchen*, dir. Francesco Stefani, 1957) as part of an East German tradition of the *kinderfilme* (children's film). Although originally released in glorious Agfacolour as a film to be screened in European cinemas, it is its cultural relocation via the BBC's serial syndication in the 1960s which is of primary focus here. While the original film is now regularly shown in cinemas around the world as part of the art-house circuit and on various film festival tours, its presentation as a quaint curiosity in historical cinema belies the very significant impact it had on children growing up in 1960s Britain. For audiences watching on a different media and in a significantly different version via its serialization, it was 'one of the most frightening things ever shown on children's television' (Hudson 2002). Similarly, for that same generation, watching the film now, as it was originally made, is to experience a charming love story; a fairy tale of good versus evil, a transformation of a princess, a didactive moral piece, in fact. But, to view that same cultural artefact as it was originally broadcast by the BBC in 1964, reduced down into three, 25-minute segments, and shorn of its dazzling Agfacolour into stark, binary monochrome, is to view something quite different, and quite extraordinary in the collective consciousness of that first generation. In the words of Rosemary Creeser, it cast 'a spell over British audiences' (Creeser 1993, n.p.). It was like nothing ever seen on TV before, with its 'power to disturb and to evoke terror', in its horror and threat in both characters and images (Callow 2019, 64). As this chapter will demonstrate, the series truly haunted a generation. It was in effect *Twin Peaks* for children, or, as Rosemary Creeser has called it, 'Cocteau for Kids' (n.p.). This chapter will examine, then, how an adaptation, from cinema to TV, and from colour to monochrome, could lead to this collective, traumatic haunting, through an analysis of the fairy-tale content and the social and political contexts of the film/series. Furthermore, it will serve as a consideration of the powerful medium that once was television, as well as an evaluation of the many-faceted processes of hauntology and finally, an exploration of reliable and unreliable memory (I think).

Although an original tale, the film was part of the *Marchen*/fairy-tale films produced by the East German state-controlled company DEFA (Deutsche Film-Aktiengesellschaft), which was founded in 1946. It was filmed in the German Democratic Republic (DDR) state-controlled studio located in Potsdam, Brandenburg. The project would have been authorized and overseen by the Minister of Education, Hans-Joachim Laabs, and the director of the children's film department, Hellmuth Hantzsche, who believed that children's films should have an identical and pedagogical 'outlook and have the same grounding in socialist realist aesthetics' as films made for adults (Callow 2019, 69). Only twenty-five fairy tales were made there from the 1950s to the late 1980s. The film project was only achieved as a result of the creative collaboration between the DDR writer Anne Gellhaar (1914–1998) and the West German director, Franco Stefani (1923–1989). It was described as being 'among the DDR's most enduring cultural achievements' (Callow 2019, 62). The series, or rather the original film, operated within a range of cultural and political anxieties, just as the film 'managed to circumvent and transcend the suspicions and stereotypes fostered by the Cold War' (Callow 2019, 63). Indeed, from another perspective, the film could be interpreted not through its role in traumatizing a generation of British children, but rather as part of a larger body of work by DEFA 'that foreground[s] cinema's role in negotiating and reworking what were in fact the profound contradictions and tensions in GDR's state socialism' (Bergfelder 2002, 5). Similarly, just as the film must be located within the context of the post-war reconstruction, socialist renewal and political realignments of Germany, so the film, adapted as a BBC series, must also be placed within the specific environment of the post-war world of Britain in the 1960s. In reality, *The Singing Ringing Tree* was simply just part of a crop of series imported from Europe by the BBC and dubbed into English (*The Magic Roundabout* (1965–77), *Hector's*

House (1966–70), *The Flashing Blade* (1967), *Belle and Sebastian* (1967–68), *Heidi* (1959), *The White Horses* (1966–67)). But, as Jon Towlson states, television of this sort performed a dual role; both in reconnecting audiences with pre-modernism 'fulfill[ing] a similar function in the UK during a difficult period in industrial capitalism', and also in 'exert[ing] a profound influence on children's television, negotiating childhood anxieties of premodernity as horrific and threatening' (Towlson 2023).

On the surface, the film can be seen as a simple fairy tale, where beauty must be sacrificed in order for true love to flourish. The film title is an amalgam of two of the Grimms' tales – *The Juniper Tree* and *The Singing, Soaring Lark*. More accurately, though, the story is an amalgam of a number of fairy tales, including *Beauty and Beast*. When a prince (Eckhart Dux) visits a castle to win the hand of a vain princess (Christel Bodenstein), he is rejected until he can bring her a singing, ringing tree, planted in a Magic Kingdom. Having failed to win the hand of the princess, the prince travels to the Magic Kingdom to find the legendary tree, which is ruled by a malicious 'dwarf'. The prince is turned into a bear by the evil 'dwarf' when he fails to win the hand of the princess. The bear then kidnaps the princess and she is taken back to the Magic Kingdom, and subsequently the princess is transformed into a grotesque figure by the cruel 'dwarf'. While initially displaying cruelty towards the many animals she meets, a further transformation gradually occurs, as the princess begins to care for the animals (including freeing a goldfish, who gets trapped by the wicked 'dwarf', and freeing a white, antlered horse who gets trapped in a snowstorm). (Given the episodic nature of the original story it lent itself very well to the serial-style airing that would follow.) It is in the realization of the healing power of cooperation and kindness, that, finally, love eventually wins through. With every act of kindness, the princess regains her beauty, and she is rescued by the animals she has helped, learning to care for them rather than focusing on her own vanity. Beauty is sacrificed in order for true love to flourish. Despite the 'dwarf's' interference, the couple finally overcome the 'dwarf', with the support of the animals. Ultimately, it is the love of animals which liberates the protagonists. Humanism triumphs with the transformation of the bear back into the prince, as the tree has begun to sing, and the couple's eventual return to the castle. Indeed, the stressing of the humanistic over the magical was a normal feature of DEFA fairy tales. And unlike a number of other such tales, the chief protagonists 'shed passivity or dependence on magic' through virtuous hard work (Shen 2015, 248), so that magic, then, is 'replaced by … self-confidence and self-agency' (249). The princess is 'converted from a person with a bourgeois, aristocratic attitude to a loving, virtuous, and working person, a desirable product of socialist education' (Shen 2015, 134).

As Silberman states, the TV fairy tale adheres to a 'quintessential model of child-oriented programming that aimed to please the "naive" imaginative capacities of young viewers by means of reductive, simplifying narratives, and visual strategizes' (2010, 108). As for DEFA, so also for the BBC. *The Singing Ringing Tree* was shot in *Bilderbuch*, in other words, in the style of a picture book, where the characters move across the screen, although unlike in a picture book they move from right to left, not left to right, and notably the princess's kingdom is in the east and the Magic Kingdom is in the west. With its surreal mise en scène, it was unlike anything seen in the UK at the time. According to Zipes, these fairy-tale films are often 'diminished by kitsch aesthetics and stereotypical characterization' (2011, 343). However, clearly there is a mysterious otherworldliness to the drama with its obvious 'foreignness', its brief and abrupt staccato dialogue and its eerie, early synth-style music. The bizarre papier mâché sets give it a 'psychedelic lustre' too, according to Hudson (Hudson 2002). This nightmarish vision, in whatever iteration of the work, has, therefore, a great deal to do with its uncanny visual, as well as sonic, aspects. The special effects were created by Ernst Kunstmann and his daughter, Vera Kunstmann (1898–1995); the former best known as the cinematographer for *Metropolis* (dir. Fritz Lang 1927), *The Testament of Dr. Mabuse* (dir. Fritz Lang 1933) as well as working with F. W. Murnau, and with Leni Riefenstahl on *Triumph des Willens* (1935) and *Olympia* (1938). After the war, he became the head of special effects at DEFA until his retirement in 1963. The variant stylizing of the cinema/series holds important clues as to the significance of its various transmissions.

In order to fully assess the impact of the series when first shown in the UK and its essential oddity, it is necessary to draw attention to the 'weird' physical location of the television set itself, existing in the corner of the living room; a seemingly benign effigy to Harold Wilson's 'white heat of technology' speech, given in Scarborough at the Labour Party conference in October 1963, in which he hoped to accelerate opportunities to those working people previously excluded from normal outlets, through the insertion of science and technology into public life, thereby ending the corrosive cycle of dominance 'by men whose only claim is their aristocratic connections or the power of inherited wealth or speculative finance' (Wilson 1963). Even earlier, in a speech in Glasgow, Wilson spoke about how he wanted to end 'educational segregation' by utilizing the technologies of radio and TV for the purposes of bringing education to a wider community. The Open University, the 'University of the Air', became a direct descendant of this spirit, created in April 1969, and using television as its main communication channel. For many growing up in the dull and monotonous working-class world of the 1960s and 1970s, TV became their cultural and sociopolitical school and 'university', its 'golden age' coverage offering a comprehensive education to compensate for a comprehensive school experience (open). It is, therefore, in the 'living quality' of television, particularly for that generation witnessing the heyday of the medium, that it has such a special resonance. Although physically dormant when switched off, when 'on' the TV set could present wondrous images of other worlds, cultures, civilizations, realms and ages. However, for Sconce, among others, television was 'alive ... living, real, not dead' (Sconce 2013, 246). For the generation having to contend with the mighty presence of that 'box' sitting in the corner of the living room, and an electronic presence at that, any programme had some kind of magical impact. Indeed, Sconce further reflects on 'the media's awesome powers of animated "living" presence: the delusional viewer who believes the media is speaking directly to him or her' (247). And for those growing up in the 1960s, as Silberman correctly states, television 'fulfilled the task of substitute babysitter' (2010, 106). In a way, then, all TV programming was 'discursively "live" by virtue of its instantaneous transmission and reception' (246). It is as if, according to Sconce, 'the media assumes[s] a particular sentient quality, figuring as a seemingly candid and intimate interlocutor engaged in a direct contact with its ... audience' (247). Marshal McLuhan compared media technology to being an extension of man's nervous system, while Raymond Williams's concept of 'flow', with the interweaving and the indistinguishing of the media form from its audience, includes, to Sconce, 'the "flowing" imagination presents the possibility of analogous exchanges' (Sconce 2013, 248, 251). The television therefore, whether on or off, was at that time a potential, or actual, window into the world of wonder and in this case, sinister fascination, as well as repellence. Other technologies could offer similar trauma, such as the half-hour radio programme, *Sing Something Simple*, broadcast on Radio 2 at 7 pm on Sunday evenings (the ominous prelude to bedtime for children). It was a long-running, yet mournful singalong show, featuring popular, yet somehow ancient spectral tunes transmitted across the air waves from a bygone age, and sung by the Cliff Adams Singers; it had the same daunting effect on that generation, and served as a desperate presage to preparation for school on Monday, when homework would remain undone, and one conjured up foreboding for the inevitable sinister scenarios to be acted out in the playground the following day. A simple refrain from that show can instantly resurrect the same unsettling dread.

In his discussion of Freud's 'The Uncanny' (1919), Coverley refers to the way in which the uncanny, or more appropriately for this piece, its more literal translation, as the 'unhomely' (and for our purposes we can extrapolate a sense in which a media technology lies in situ, in the living room), while conveying an alternative realm, holds the potential to produce a feeling in the audience which represents 'a residual trace' of a mythic past (the home of fairy tales), an earlier more instinctual, primitive stage of development, or rather, as Coverley suggests, 'as a manifestation of infantile or arrested development' (2020, 76). This would have adhered more closely to Freud's original intentions, sans Derrida's extrapolations. In this way, we can interpret the haunting as a vague, even traumatic memory from childhood of magical and alien apparitions or presences (something which would haunt H. P. Lovecraft's work). For Freud, these were ancient 'remnants of animistic mental activity', which might be reawakened with the right (or maybe, wrong) apparition (Coverley 2020, 77). Similarly, and in relation to this concept, Fisher remarks upon the 'unhomely' as if it concerns a 'fascination for the outside, for that which lies beyond standard perception, cognition and experience' (2016, 8). In relation to the – on the surface – banality of the physical 'presence' of the TV set, in the living room, this analogy is appealing. The TV remains dormant in the corner of the room, and functions as a curious item of furniture, a 'black mirror'. And for Fisher, this fascination usually involves a certain apprehension, 'perhaps even dread' (8). Furthermore, and in connection to *The Singing Ringing Tree*, the Agfacolour original may have appealed to those sharing and participating in the gloss and vivid, psychedelic colours of 'Swinging' London in the 1960s, but it would have had no resonance with those audiences in the hinterlands, experiencing the authentic realities (in the case of my own experiences) of the industrial North Midlands, where the bleak monochrome hit home with a far more powerful force. As Callow states, 'the transference to monochrome [led] to a heightened sense of atmosphere, with the exaggerated play of light and shade inducing a heightened sense of fear and foreboding' (94). For example, when the 'dwarf' creates an ice storm, in the original Agfacolour version, the ice disperses, whereas in monochrome, the storm appears 'to hold the valley in [its] grasp until the final scenes and the breaking of the bewitchment by the princess' (Callow 2019, 94). The lingering vapours from the billowing smoke or steam, oozing from factory chimneys, bottle kilns and smelting sheds, could be brought to mind here, alongside the memories of the cathode ray tube television, like something from a James Whale studio set for *Frankenstein* (1931), with its component parts, of filaments, coils, electrical signals transformed into patterns of light, and the heat and phosphorous smell of burning dust from the tube and the back of the TV cabinet; a kind of miniature foundry, a technology straight out of Wilson's white heat revolution, but yet belonging to an earlier, analogue, time.

The role and significance of television is currently undergoing a profound transformation, and as a result of streaming services and the realities of technological convergence, commentators have recently theorized on the way it has created a hybrid genre (TV/film), yet its profound importance as a media technology has long been one of perpetual transformative continuity. Indeed, the *Tales from Europe* series (1964–69) must be placed within the realm of modification and adaptation, since the series can only be seen as 'a tale mediated by Peggy Miller's subtle and sympathetic reshaping' of the original filmic narrative (Callow 2019, 94). So the very process of 'translation' too must also be considered here, from film to serial format, and then from TV to the audience. The series was also an early champion of an adaptation/translational/transnational format of broadcasting, as the BBC collected cinema films from not just Europe, but also Russia and Mongolia, such as *The Tinderbox* (1959). As Zipes has pointed out, 'translation is always concerned with our conscious and unconscious ties to the past and the present'. He goes on: 'However, the past is problem full because we both need it and need to transcend it.' As he further states, 'appropriation always involves translation of some kind' (2011, 11–12). In a divided Germany, 'television was simply not in a position to present for children imaginative scenarios that were in some way connected to the postwar physical and psychological reality' (Silberman 2010, 108). There were no such restrictions in Britain where the film premiered at the Edinburgh Film Festival in 1958. The BBC purchased the film, and Peggy Miller (1919–1993), who was Assistant Foreign Films, Children's Programmes, decided to slice the film up into three, 25-minute episodes, to be shown in black and white in the autumn and winter of 1964 (although it was frequently repeated up to 1980), accompanied by a rather stilted narration by Tony Bilbow. It was shown in a 'tea-time slot', at 5.30, on Thursdays, and after the legendary children's magazine show, *Blue Peter*, alongside three other folk tales, as part of a series *Tales from Europe*. Peggy Miller, who selected the film for serialization on the BBC, believed that East Europe was a more open source for folk tale in the medium of film, and clearly more authentic than the Disney's output. For Callow, Miller

> seems to have been committed to encouraging the development in children of a feeling for a pan-European culture that bridged Cold War divisions and propaganda, and which stood in conscious opposition to the consumerist ideals, rampant individualism and often subliminal violence that characterised the dominant cultural values and studios outputs of the United States. (92)

This looking eastwards by the BBC must be seen, as Callow suggests, 'as a bulwark – to the dominance of North American popular culture with its emphasis upon the individual and the cloying commodification of the genre by the Disney corporation' (64). This would also follow the atmospheric fallout caused by Richard Hoggart's landmark work *The Uses of Literacy*, published in 1957, in which he condemned the imposition of a 'top-down' mass culture dominated by Hollywood 'entertainments' and a distinctly American sheen, which he saw then as eroding authentic local, popular, class culture. The series must therefore be seen as an adaptable alternative, with its focus upon community and cooperation against evil forces. In this sense, however, it is a transnational and 'accented' screen product, and as such, subversive (Naficy 2018, 43).

In its 'accented' look, then, it was a Gothic nightmare vision of cruel, enclosed entrapment and utter helplessness. Antlered horses, a giant goldfish, a narration over but not hiding the more forthright German dialogue. It was a nightmare fairy tale unlike anything seen previously on British television. But then, British TV in the 1960s and 1970s 'got down to the nitty-gritty of scaring the living daylights out of the kids' (Towlson 2023, 231). A feeling of claustrophobia permeated the whole series; bizarre considering the fairy-tale setting, the bright lighting and the papier mâché sets. Something clearly was amiss. The studio setting of the kingdom seemed to increase the feeling of claustrophobia, 'rendered in a queasy palate of jade greens, sunburst yellows and atomic puce gave the nightmare fable a feverish sheen as enervating as it was compelling' (Norman 2015, 52).

Yet to see those images in grim monochrome was to intensify the feelings of enclosed, airless oppression. In transmitting the East German fable, and in black and white, Monica Sims (1925–2018), then head of the children's department (and future Controller of BBC Radio 4), was clearly testing the limits of what was acceptable on children's television.

Key to the whole experience, however, was the truly terrifying performance by an actor of restricted growth, played by Richard Kruger, as the malevolent ruler of the Magic Kingdom, who constantly undermines the prince and princess. Indeed, the sense of the Gothic is typified through the character, who scuttles around the papier mâché set, displaying a dark evil that truly 'horrified' the viewing children.

The 'little man' of the Magic Kingdom would cause vivid nightmares of an unprecedented nature, mainly due to his very ubiquity, as he emerged from underground, and from behind every stone; he appears in clouds, from inside shells, from under the ground, where he is constantly observing and listening in on the couple, and interfering in their plans of cooperation, with his evil magic, his spells and his tricks, ready to thwart them at any opportunity; he freezes a waterfall, for instance, thus entombing a giant goldfish, which the princess then frees, at danger to herself, or destroying their shelter. He haunted the set and for that reason, the 'wicked dwarf' could be re-imagined by children in their real lives, coming from under the bed, out of a wardrobe, up from the floor, down from the ceiling. It is the nature of the effect which the 'dwarf' had which has haunted that generation. Responses to a questionnaire undertaken by those present at a later National Film Theatre screening, as well as later interviews, and collected by Creeser, all testify to the dark malevolence of the evil 'dwarf' who 'leaps out at you from all sorts of nooks and crannies' … 'a "dwarf" of such terrifying malevolence that he still turns up in my dreams … there was this sort of malevolence and this little scuttling creature' (n.p.). The many and varied responses to this may be related to personal and subjective trauma. This nightmare vision would be used later to memorable effect in Nicolas Roeg's *Don't Look Now* (1973), where he recognized and visualized the potency of the grotesque 'dwarf' figure.

Zipes has pointed out that 'the present has no essential meaning without our conscious reflection and knowledge of the past' (2011, 12). To Zipes, we as an audience must be alert to the 'anachronistic features that weigh upon us' (12). This can include TV series which have lingered in our consciousness, for whatever inexplicable reason. In her study on haunted television, Helen Wheatley suggests that programming can 'act as a classic Derridean specter, with an ethical and political potential to confront a traumatic history' (2020, 70). For del Pilar Blanco and Peeren, 'to be traumatized … is to be possessed by an image or event located in the past' (Pilar and Peeren 2013, 11). To be possessed, 'gripped indefinitely by an anachronistic event – also describes the condition of being haunted' (11). This can be true when dealing with a type of trauma, or a recurring figure. Wheatley considers a continuing 'sensory relation to the dead' whereby through the medium of television, the hauntings and the memory can keep returning, via television flows (Wheatley 2020, 71). Television can, therefore, be interpreted as a 'medium of posthumous entertainment' (Wheatley 2020, 74). Here, Derrida's hauntology can be seen as both literal and metaphorical, in that 'the works of the Brothers Grimm were brought within an explicitly socialist pedagogy, and how official Marxism attempts to comprehend and refashion folk and fairy tales "for a modern audience"' (Callow 2019, 62). And for a television audience for that matter, exposed to the bizarre Gothic nightmare of *The Singing Ringing Tree*.

Looking down on the Lancashire town of Burnley is a physical Singing, Ringing Tree, a three-metre steel construction designed by Mike Tonkin and Anna Liu and created in 2006. It is a sound sculpture of pipes which, when infused by the Pennine wind, sings an evocative, but truly horrifying discordant song; a haunting legacy for a de-industrialized age. If, as Callow suggests, the sculpture and the film have

> become divorced from their original ideological and national contexts and subsumed within a wider fabric of folklore, family entertainment and pedagogy then it is testimony to the adaptability of the fairy tale as a genre and its ability to present that which is new and challenging as timeless and palliative. The recourse to the fairy tale in times of marked uncertainty, in this case against the backdrop of both the reconstruction of a war-ravaged East Berlin and a post-industrial Lancashire, is singularly arresting. (63)

The 'memory' of TV is ultimately of critical importance here, as well; residual hauntings of images and even the reinterpretation, or re-imagining, of action which in reality perhaps did not occur. They are adornments, supplied by a faulty (or traumatized) memory, one which has overplayed the original narrative, but has overlaid it with other, more identifiable and even personalized images. Lozano states that 'television memory is always linked to a socially-shared televisual past' (2013, 131). But it can also be deeply personal and inimitable. The resuscitation of *The Singing Ringing Tree* in its original filmic version, both as a DVD release in 2011, and as recurring cinematic screenings 'represents a ghostly resurfacing of unprocessed trauma from the past' (Anderson 2022, 45).

But what of the nature of the genre itself? To Mark Fisher, the weird and the eerie 'were to be found at the edges of genres' (8). In this case, it could be horror, fantasy and fairy tale; but maybe also comedy. Admittedly, *The Singing Ringing Tree* could be unintentionally funny in places; it inspired humourous re-adaptations too, such as in the comedy sketch series, *The Fast Show* parody in 1997 (*Ton Swingingen Ringingen Bingingen Plingingen Tingingen Plingingen Plonkingen Boingingen Triee*). This can adhere to Fisher's remarks upon the 'strange – not the horrific'; although this is not to malign the many genuinely creepy moments in the film/series (2016, 8).

What of memory itself? For Zipes, 'the past weighs like a nightmare on the minds of the living' (2011, 12). It is as Pilar and Peeren state, 'the haunting of the present by the past that emerges as the most insistent narrative' (2013, 11). And as Merlin Coverley has recently reflected, 'in the face of what may appear as a growing obsession with excavating and examining the cultural detritus of our recent past, hauntology is often viewed as a little more than a new form of nostalgia' (2020, 12). So, the resonance of the haunting may very well be caught up with the nature of nostalgia itself, with the 'reassuring rhythms of one's childhood' (Boym, quoted in Coverley 2020, 12). The internet has become another platform, and it has breathed new life into the nostalgic haunting of the film and the series of *The Singing Ringing Tree* – where people on social network sites share personal recollections and have collective memory exchanges. This transcends simply a construct of memory itself; it becomes a site where an emotional response and memory meld. But is the film/series best left in the vaults of occasional recollection as opposed to its recurring resuscitation? Memory often dilutes the original or even conjures up images that were never there; as Mark Pilkington states, 'hauntology may be a thing of the past, but this of course means that it will always be with us' (quoted in Coverley 2020, 7). Originally, and as envisioned by Derrida as a reflection of the political reverence of Marx in 1993, and as further transcribed by thinkers such as Mark Fisher and Merlin Coverley, the mapping of hauntology offered a critique of late-capitalism (which was as applicable in Britain in the 1960s as it was to East Germany in the 1950s where *The Singing Ringing Tree* was born), and *The Singing Ringing Tree* was a perfect vehicle for both contexts. Both Fisher and Coverley incorporate the influence of technology in this hauntology, in this case television, which 'allowed us to capture and control time, bringing the past back to life and allowing us to revisit it at our leisure' (Coverley 2020, 12). And this manifested in our homes, with the visitation of the 'unhomely', for as Lozano states, 'we cannot overlook the social importance of television memory' (2013, 142) which provides for a 'residual haunting' (Coverley 2020, 12). Could it have been the physical presence of the television set itself, located in a corner, in our homes, and yet transmitting? Whatever it was, *The Singing Ringing Tree* was unlike anything else seen on children's television before or since, and it is both its unnerving eerie style, and its recirculation now in the digital sphere, which tether it still to viewers who originally witnessed its creeping, scuttling dread.

References

Allan, S., and S. Heiduschke. 2016. *Re-Imagining DEFA*. New York: Berghahn Book.

Anderson, J. 2022. 'Return, Remembrance and Redemption: Hauntology and the Topography of Trauma in The Virtues and This Is England '88'. *Journal of British Cinema and Television* 19, no. 1: 45–66.

Bergfelder, T. (ed.) 2002. *The German Cinema Book*. London: BFI.

Callow, John. 2019. 'An Enduring Enchantment: The Fairy Tale in the DDR, from Brothers Grimm to the *Singing Ringing Tree*'. *Twentieth Century Communism* 16: 62–102.

Coverley, M. 2020. *Hauntology: Ghosts of Futures Past*. London: Oldcastle Books.

Creeser, R. 1993. 'Cocteau for Kids: Rediscovering *The Singing Ringing Tree*'. In *Cinema and the Realms of Enchantment: Lectures, Seminars and Essays by Marian Warner and Others*, edited by D. Petrie, 111–24. London: BFI.

Davidson, J., and S. Hake. 2018. *Framing the Fifties: Cinema in a Divided Germany*. Oxford: Berghahn.

DEFA Film Library, University of Massachusetts. https://www.umass.edu/defa/peo ple/938. Accessed 27 April 2023.

Del Pilar Blanco, M., and E. Peeren (eds). 2013. *The Spectralities Reader*. London: Bloomsbury.

Fisher, M. 2012. 'What Is Hauntology?' *Film Quarterly* 66, no. 1: 16–24.

Fisher, M. 2016. *The Weird and the Eerie*. London: Repeater Books.

Hudson, M. 2002. 'Return of the Teatime Terror'. *The Daily Telegraph*. 30 March. https://www.telegraph.co.uk/culture/tvandradio/3575363/Return-of-the-teatime-terror.html. Accessed 2 May 2023.

Lozano, J. 2013. 'Television Memory after the End of Television History?' In *After the Break: Television Theory Today*, edited by M. de Valck, 131–44. Amsterdam: Amsterdam University Press.

Naficy, H. 2018. *An Accented Cinema: Exilic and Diasporic Filmmaking*. Princeton, NJ: Princeton University Press.

Norman, P. 2015. *A History of Television in 100 Programmes*. London: HarperCollins.

Sconce, J. 2013. 'Haunted Media: Electronic Presence from Telegraphy to TV'. In *The Spectralities Reader*, edited by M. Del Pilar Blanco and E. Peeren, 245–55. London: Bloomsbury.

Shen, Qinna. 2015. *The Politics of Magic: DEFA Fairy Tale Films*. Detroit, MI: Wayne State University Press.

Silberman, M. 2010. 'The First DEFA Fairy Tales: Cold War Fantasies of the
    1950s'. In *Framing the Fifties: Cinema in a Divided Germany*, edited by
    J. Davidson and S. Hake, 106–19. Oxford: Berghahn Books.
Towlson, J. 2023. '"To Traumatise Kids for Life": The Influence of Folk Horror
    on 1970s Children's Television'. In *The Routledge Companion to Folk Horror*,
    edited by R. Edgar and W. Johnson, 227–35. London: Routledge.
Warner, M. 1995. *From the Beast to the Blonde: On Fairy Tales and the Teller*.
    London: Vintage.
Wheatley, Helen. 2020. 'Haunted Television: Trauma and the Specter in the
    Archive'. *Journal of Cinema and Media Studies* 59, no. 3 (Spring): 69–89.
Wilson, Harold. 1963. Glasgow speech. https://www.open.ac.uk/library/digital-arch
    ive/download/1963WilsonGlasgow.pdf. Accessed 12 June 2023.
Wilson, Harold. 1963. Scarborough speech. https://web-archives.univ-pau.fr/engl
    ish/TD2doc2.pdf. Accessed 12 June 2023.
Zipes, J. 2011. *The Enchanted Screen: The Unknown History of Fairy Tale Films*.
    London: Routledge.

15

'May cause drowsiness': A (false) memory of weekday morning television in the mid-1970s through the filter of prepubescent illness and sedation

Jez Conolly

It was all very well to say 'Drink me', but the wise little Alice was not going to do that in a hurry ... for she had read several nice little histories about children who had got burnt, and eaten up by wild beasts and other unpleasant things, all because they would not remember the simple rules their friends had taught them.

LEWIS CARROLL, *ALICE'S ADVENTURES IN WONDERLAND AND 'THROUGH THE LOOKING-GLASS AND WHAT ALICE FOUND THERE'*, 1865

In March 1973 I spent a whole week without television. This was an enforced depravation: I had been diagnosed at the age of seven with pneumonia and had to be taken into hospital in order to recover. While I was fortunate to have a room to myself, at that time there were no bedside TV sets to be had on the ward. I don't even recall a communal viewing lounge in which to sit and suffer the three-channel programme choices of others. So for the seven days of my stay, in between visits from my parents and battles with the nurses over the disturbingly cloche-covered meals, by way of distracting entertainment I had to make do with the limited range of radio stations available through the wishbone-shaped plastic earphones hooked to the hospital bed frame. Frankly I don't know how I survived. Without television.

Once I returned home from the hospital I had to remain 'off school' and was under strict orders to stay largely indoors through until at least Easter so as to fully convalesce. Who would have thought that forty-seven years later we'd all be doing exactly that? Anyway, it was during this time that I first experienced something close to a form of domestic incarceration born of kindness; while I'm not suggesting that a Munchausen's by Proxy scenario played out, I can say that my parents were so concerned about my health and the ill effects that exposure to any chills or draughts might have that they practically kept me captive, wrapped in thick blankets during the day, downstairs in the front room positioned on the settee in front of the box. For those living south of my home town of Cleethorpes in the 1970s the latter part of that sentence should read 'downstairs in the *lounge* positioned on the *sofa* in front of the *television*'.

Over the course of the next five years or so, despite their best efforts to protect me from germs, I succumbed to every chest infection that happened to be doing the rounds, which led to repeated periods of illness and further time away from my lessons. The days of recuperation were routinely spent in front of the television, especially in the mornings when my parents were working. They came to rely particularly on morning television to keep me 'occupied' while I gradually got better.

These were the days of 'linctus', 'lozenge' and 'Lucozade'; I remember the consumption of an awful lot of the kind of milky antibiotic jollop that you had to keep in the fridge, but the blur of time was mainly made more so by the effects of the ruby-red cough syrup that was repeatedly spooned into me. It was the kind of mixture normally reserved for bedtime due to its sleep-inducing effects but, given its efficacy, my parents in their infinite wisdom decided to dose me up with it morning, noon and night. This meant that I would spend the better part of several days in a semi-comatose state, at the mercy of the televisual content parading before me. 'May cause drowsiness' warned the label on the cough medicine, 'do not drive or operate heavy machinery'. As I was some years off gaining even my provisional licence and as the only forklift truck I owned bore the word 'Corgi' on its underside, I wasn't too concerned about these latter cautions, but '*may* cause drowsiness'? I never knew it not to. Combine this with some of the accidentally or deliberately illusory television images of the time and the result was like a junior school Charles Dodgson on opium, except without the written record (until now).

Possibly in an attempt to ameliorate the separation anxiety, around the time of my return home from the hospital my parents acquired their first colour television, and I can vividly recall that the first programme that I saw on it was an episode of the animated pre-early evening news five-minute filler *Crystal Tipps and Alistair*, a programme as vibrantly colourful and fleetingly gratifying as the contents of a packet of Mackintosh's Tooty Frooties and, for all I know, about as carcinogenic. My parents seemed to favour German-made TV sets; Grundig, Blaupunkt, Telefunken, which now sound like the attacking midfield of the West Germany national team that won the 1974 football World Cup. That was where the similarity ended, the televisions certainly did not possess anything like the levels of quality, durability and reliability one associates with one of the greatest football teams of the decade. That first colour set lasted about a couple of years before it gave out. It's possible that this was due to my father's insistence on keeping the colour setting at near maximum; I think he thought he was getting his money's worth by doing this but sometimes it felt like we were forced participants in an experimental acid trip. Whatever the cause of death was, this seemed to be a decade of televisions with rather short lifespans, the inevitable demise of each preceded by a visit from the Radio Rentals repair man who, with sideburns, Chelsea boots and body odour, administered the last rites over the course of twenty minutes, on his knees with his toolbox by his side, before delivering the ominous verdict: 'your tube's gone'.

As suggested earlier, I still refer to televisions of today as 'the box', which is dimensionally absurd when one considers that the modern screen is about as boxy as an after-dinner mint. Not to mention being as big, rectangular and cataract-inducingly bright as a wall-mounted sun bed. The sets of the 1970s (and our first colour TV was no exception) were like foursquare tea chests by comparison; mock walnut veneered crates deep enough on top to place an ornament, a bowl of fruit or possibly a vase of flowers, with a ventilated cover at the back hiding the delicate parts of the cathode ray tube which one could just about glimpse through the casing slots, glowing with a fascinating and mysterious orange warmth. They also gave off a subtle but incredibly evocative aroma, like someone in the house next door slightly burning some toast, equalled only as an olfactory memory trigger by the dusty, radiant valves of my father's Dansette mono record player.

It's worth contemplating that this was an era when home entertainment, including television sets, needed a few moments to 'warm up' when you first switched them on. Within this awakening, when both picture and sound would gradually emerge from the silent murk of the sleeping set, we find a replication of consciousness, something 'waking', something seemingly sentient, something … eventually … *on*. When the television was *on*, and once I had been suitably lubricated with 'Dr. Mum's Sleepy Cough Balsam', I harboured a mini-neurosis that as I was watching *it*, it was watching *me*. Not only could it see what I was doing, it could also tell what I was thinking. As such it provided my parents with the ideal 'nanny', designed to keep me both placated and sedated, literally (as far as my imagination was concerned) keeping an eye on me while they were out or busy. They probably thought it was providing me with some diverting company to help me get better, but it simply left me feeling like I was under surveillance. The TV was less a comforter, more a captor.

Some earlier viewing matter set me up to feel this way. For several months before my illness and hospitalization I bore witness to *Romper Room*, a daily preschool programme of nursery play, milk and biscuits and 'I'm a Little Tea Pot' rhyme-singing hosted, in my ITV region at least, by 'Miss Rosalyn'. There was a regular point in each programme when 'Miss Rosalyn', a bouffant disciplinarian with the combined matriarchal heft of a Hartnell-era companion and a recently lapsed nun, looked into her 'magic mirror' (a hoop-shaped empty hand-mirror frame), straight down the camera at the audience at home, and at me in particular, perhaps exclusively me, in order to determine who among the viewers had been a 'good do-bee' or a 'bad do-bee'. If you're wondering, 'do-bee' referred to Mr. Do-Bee, a hymenopteric glove puppet on the show, any relation to 'doobie' marijuana cigarettes being purely coincidental. We'll leave that jive to Serge Danot and Ivor Wood.

> Romper, bomper, stomper boo,
> Tell me, tell me, tell me, do.
> Magic Mirror, tell me today,
> Did all my friends have fun at play?

'Miss Rosalyn' would always follow her rhyme by calling out the names of little boys and girls in 'television land' while maintaining her fixed glare at the camera: 'I can see David, and I can see Sally, and I can see Jonathan' and so on. I presume now that the idea was to instil hope in children that their names would be called out for being good, but for the young me the experience was traumatic. The very thought that 'Miss Rosalyn' could actually see me through the television filled me with sheer terror. This wasn't a fun thing at all, this was like trying to avoid being picked by Irma Grese to play for her school football team. It also explains why I'm now very nervy about Skype, FaceTime and the host of other apps that rose to prominence during the Covid-19 lockdown.

This early feeling of being under critical observation set up my relationship with the television, specifically its term-time weekday morning content, so that when my sentence of protracted and intermittent illness-related incarceration began in 1973 I had already developed a mild dread of being left on my own in the room in my semi-incapacitated state with just 'the box' for company. I'll account for a comparison to poor little Heather O'Rourke in *Poltergeist* later. This was a cut-down homespun version of

Bentham's Panopticon; there was just enough doubt in my young mind to believe that this 'nanny' was somehow keeping its eye on me, and when that apprehension was mixed with the somnifacient effects of the chesty cough medicine that was administered to me each time that I succumbed to a bronchial infection (which was three or four times a year for several years after that first bout of pneumonia) I felt powerless when placed before its unblinking gaze, a slave to the logic of mild paranoid dread that it precipitated. And this is before the content of the weekday morning programming during those poorly years inveigled its way into my mind.

From time to time the spell being cast would be briefly broken with a relative entering the room with a hot drink and asking in passing 'What are you watching?' On occasion, if their appearance with refreshments should happen to coincide with something on screen that, out of context, was silly or peculiar they would apply emphasis to their question: 'What *are* you watching?' to which my enfeebled reply would either be the metacryptically vague 'this' or the existentially obtuse 'nothing', the effort of anything more loquacious being beyond my torpid disposition and the capacity of my afflicted lungs. The 'this' I was watching in my tranquillized state was highly likely to be something from the ITV 'Independent Programmes for Schools and Colleges' smorgasbord of educational content interspersed with a blast of BBC 2 morning content by way of light relief. The change of channels between ITV and BBC 2 usually represented my exercise for the day, if your concept of 'exercise' constitutes a slow slither of lethargy out of my swaddling wraps and off the sofa followed by an ineffectual commando crawl across the carpet towards the television.

The buttons on the front panel of the set required a very firm push if you wanted to actually change channels; none of your touch-sensitive technology, 'turning over' between 'stations' required a very firm shove that elicited a loud gunshot click percussive enough to rattle the ceramic shire horse ploughing its lone furrow on top of the telly. This was one reason, apart from the comparative lack of choice, why one tended not to channel-hop so much in the early 1970s – doing so typically required a concerted run-up. Or in my drugged-up state a languid squirm of a few feet. Added to which the only people with TV remote controls in those days probably also had a breakfast bar and a bidet. We had central heating installed before we had a TV with a remote. I knew of one relative who stuck with a black and white portable television for many years – a GEC Junior Fineline if my memory serves me correctly – on the refrigerator in his kitchen no less, so you can imagine the amount of ambient cooking fat it picked up on its outer casing. He was never one to favour highbrow content, which was evident from the layer of dust that had settled on the BBC 2 button and the fact that grooves had worn smooth on the now-shiny ITV button.

So with this need for adjacent proximity to the set in order to change channels, a certain amount of time was necessarily spent crouching down or sitting directly in front of the set with one's nose almost pressed to the screen in order to see what was on 'the other side' (sign up here for your 'Through the Looking-Glass' hauntological tour, minus Dinah the cat). There I would be, depressing the knobs or fiddling with the volume, contrast and brightness dials and unavoidably looking very closely at the myriad of RGB dots that formed the picture. More than once while nestling at the feet of the set I inadvertently sneezed or coughed onto the screen, sending out a small shower of moisture droplets that affixed to the vitrified barium glass and magnified the coloured dots in a most pleasing pattern of globular clusters. Forget two metres, I was barely two inches from the screen.

As with much TV output in the 1970s, one might be mistaken for thinking that the makers of the 'Programmes for Schools and Colleges' took many of their content and editorial decisions through some means of Druidic divination. How else might one account for the curiously muddy, meditative weirdness of much of what was broadcast, if it was not directed by a process involving hazel twigs or the reading of tarot cards? While BBC 1 produced its fair share of programming for the school audience I suspect there was something in its public service remit that prohibited it from putting out daytime morning educative content that might crop up years later in a psilocybin flashback. They reserved this for their teatime children's programmes. In the mornings the torch was firmly carried by ITV's schedule.

Barely a morning passed without some fresh horror seemingly designed to lodge itself in my doped subconscious for the rest of my childhood. Not wishing to state the obvious, but what possible reason did the makers of *Picture Box* have when featuring the musical number 'Maneche' by Jacques Lavry as the theme tune – described in one pithy YouTube comment as sounding 'like a paedophile's ice cream van' – other than to stoke some terror in the hearts of minors? And then they play this piece of music, knocked out as it was on the trusty cristal baschet (an instrument fashioned in Hell if ever I saw one) over blurred footage of a rotating red velvet lined musical box, followed by a cut to an extreme close-up of presenter Alan Rothwell's face, fading in like a nightmarish mash-up of *1984*'s Big Brother and the huge, green, disembodied head of the Great and Terrible Wizard of Oz.

Pause.
'Hello.'
Pause.

Hello Alan. Go away please Alan. It was bad enough witnessing this sitting cross-legged on the herringbone parquet flooring of the school hall among the fidgety throng of your classmates, it was a whole other ball game when faced with that huge inescapable face glaring at you, on your own at home with nowhere to hide. Added to which, think how disturbing this would be when experienced with a clear head, then imagine what it was like to absorb it under the influence of the soporific medication.

Another programme that fed briefly into this pre-lunch dreamscape was *Seeing and Doing*. On the face of it, it was an innocuous enough affair, gently educative in a 'things to make and do' kind of way. Judging by the acoustic equivalent of Oxford Bags that was the signature tune it was probably put together by a production team made up largely of gap-toothed traditional folk singers called 'Maggie' who used the sleeve of a Wishbone Ash LP to rest on when rolling their liquorice paper cigarettes. It was presented by *Play School* alumnus Toni Arthur, who had a previous conviction for spreading folksy weirdness in the shape of her 1971 album *Hearken to the Witches Rune* recorded with her unfeasibly whiskered husband Dave, which foreshadowed the one particular edition of *Seeing and Doing* that led to a recordable spike in my tucked-up anxiety levels. It was a Halloween-themed episode that opened with a montage of shots featuring Toni dressed as a witch, but mounted in such a creepy way that it made the Spirit of Dark and Lonely Water look about as frightening as *The Sooty Show*. It was *really* frightening, I mean wake-up-screaming-in-a-cold-sweat-in-the-middle-of-the-night frightening. To make matters worse, it was common practice for programmes to be repeated during the same week, so after its first airing on a Monday or Tuesday that witchy episode was shown again on the Thursday or Friday. Did I avoid it after being so terrified by it the first time? Of course, I didn't, because that was the thing about my groggy state; I just didn't have the strength to battle the inertia and so found it difficult to avoid these repeat performances. It was rather like being tethered to a trolley and wheeled at glacial speed through Madame Tussaud's Chamber of Horrors, then wheeled round again on a terrifying 'lap of honour', all the while with my eyelids pinned back in the manner of Malcolm McDowell in *A Clockwork Orange* just to be sure I don't miss anything.

Amid all of this trauma it's easy to forget that the primary purpose of these programmes was educative, designed to help young people learn and make sense of the world. Yet even when the output adhered closely to more formal pedagogic classroom or textbook content it still possessed qualities that, when consumed in the limbo between wakefulness and the arms of Morpheus, would lead to lingering preoccupations. Take for example the work of educational film producer (and programme narrator) Jack Smith, known principally as creator of the austere science lesson series *Experiment*, so slavishly and affectionately aped by Robert Popper and Peter Serafinowitz in the first series of *Look around You*. Smith also shot and produced two other series for Independent Programmes for Schools and Colleges, the on-location 'nature notes' styled *A Place to Live* and *Pond Life*. All of Smith's work betrayed a quite specific dry, dull pacing with a conspicuously spartan, utilitarian colour palette and drab, flat lighting together with Smith's very precise 'severe side parting and split-frame spectacles' commentary track, all of which combined to elicit a lulling yet somehow alluring ennui that fuelled the 'dislocation of time' aspect of my bewilderment. In among the perception-challenging longueurs one experienced the incongruity of shifts between super-normal laboratory conditions and the experiments themselves which often seemed to involve proving the existence of the nervous system in a captive invertebrate such as a locust through the application of electrical wires to the poor creature's soft parts. In another context such footage could easily pass for the back catalogue of one of those blood-letting Austrian video artists.

While Smith stuck with his Mengele-esque sterility approach to the world of science, that area of biology generally reserved for awkward one-sided parental conversations was taken care of in the schedule by *Living and Growing*, an inevitably controversial programme designed to convey the basics of sex education, and one that wound up being screened late night on Channel 4 in the 1980s for the delectation of post-pub adult viewers. The era of the programme that I saw was written and presented by Stanley Mitchell, a white-haired Scot with an austere yet creepily transgressive air, imagine a Presbyterian minister combined with Dr Alex Comfort. This was indeed basically *The Joy of Sex* for junior school children, and in a way just as well I saw it when I did, because subsequent school lessons on the subject of procreation seemed to focus heavily on the reproductive organs of plants and rats, which I suppose made a change from birds and bees. Of course there was the one school biology lesson later on that led to knotted-stomach anticipation, the one featuring the projection of some worn cine film depicting childbirth, a grainy, gaudy spectacle, shown with curtains drawn and lights out like a baptismal rite-of-passage with production values and mise en scène borrowed from *The Texas Chainsaw Massacre*. This aside, I learned a lot from watching *Living and Growing*, admittedly at a slightly earlier age than was strictly appropriate, and despite receiving the information from Stanley Mitchell, the kind of man likely to have a bag of sweeties in his glove compartment and the promise of some puppies back at his bedsit who we were frequently warned about through a number of public information films. This reception of *Living and Growing* also explains why I still find fairly amateurishly rendered pencil crayon animation to be mildly pornographic.

Either side of the 11 am broadcast of *Play School* on BBC 2 would be the daily limbo of Test Card F. Like a retinal scar, this hypnotizing temporal stasis represented some kind of threshold, a brink between the reality of the room I was in and the unknown pleasures or pains of the realm inside 'the box'. Even with a clear head, the eternal lack of resolution to this game of noughts and crosses between child and clown could feel like the only thing stopping all that we know from sinking irreversibly into a diabolical black hole. This was a game destined never to progress beyond the first two moves, although there's Carole Hersee with her Alice band poised to make her mark and thereby thwart the evil game plan of Bubbles, that pint-sized Punchinello approximation of Death from Bergman's *Seventh Seal*. Will she ever put her second cross in the bottom right square, as she appears to be about to do?

As an aside, looking at the state of play after two moves, frankly neither player has applied sensible tactics. Page one of the golden rules of noughts and crosses states that, when playing first, claim a corner square instead of the centre square, and when playing second, claim the centre square if the first player did not. With a cross at left middle and a nought at top middle, Carole and Bubbles have therefore both already committed signal failures in this respect.

If this fixed spectacle wasn't strange enough, add in the effects of the medicinal intoxicant and the very concept of the passage of time would be brought into question. Was Carole destined to spend her entire life in this prepubescent state? She didn't seem to grow up any during the many years I kept an eye on her. Heavens knows I looked for signs of change, it came to feel like a kind of vigil, convinced as I was that this poor girl was being forced against her will to not only never grow up but also remain as still as a statue so that viewers up and down the country could adjust their sets to the right colour balance. I would find myself in a state of near-unblinking scrutiny of the image, because hold on – and prove me wrong here – I could have *sworn* Carole just moved! What's worse, I think Bubbles is now *looking at me*!

Despite the palpable inescapability of the all-seeing eye combined with the lead boots and perceptual bewilderment visited upon me by the medication, I still managed on most days to tear myself away from the television, most likely driven by hunger or simply by improving health that led me to be more mobile. This meant that I would manage to break the spell and actually switch the set off. It should be said that there was a small but memorable experiential reward when the time came to switch the television off. And by 'off' I really do mean *off*. There was no such thing as 'stand by'; this was the decade of the public information film, shown at the end of the programme schedule, that advised viewers to not just switch their televisions off before they go to bed, but to be extra safe and switch the power off at the wall *and* completely unplug the set from the mains socket. That reward for complete shutdown came in the form of an invisible 'lawn dew' of static electricity that would cover the TV screen. This could be discharged or 'wiped off' with one's hand, leading to a most pleasurable prickly, crackly tingle, probably the sort of audio-haptic phenomenon that would leave ASMR YouTubers reaching for their webcams today.

The pattern of school absence and semi-hallucinatory sedation as part of recuperation continued for around five years, right up to my final weeks at junior school in June 1978, at which time a particular event put a cap on matters and jolted me into a woke adolescence that simply didn't have room for such juvenile fripperies as staring unavoidably at a screen for hours on end (although over forty years on that is exactly what I find myself doing a lot of the time, along with almost everyone else). One early evening I had good reason to watch the regional ITV teatime news bulletin *Calendar*; my half-brother, a folk musician of some renown, was appearing on the programme to discuss and play some of his music. This being some years prior to my family's ownership of a video recorder, I decided to tape the moment for posterity using my dad's portable audio cassette recorder. I'll wager this was a not-uncommon pre-VCR practice in many households; how many of us still have perfect recall of gags from mid-1970s Morecambe and Wise Christmas Shows thanks to some rattly tape cassette recordings that we made at the time of broadcast, complete with family members laughing in the background? The practice involved holding the small black plastic microphone attached to the recording device close to the television speaker in order to capture the audio at close quarters and, fingers akimbo, depressing the PLAY and RECORD buttons simultaneously, then attempting to stay as silent as possible.

The interview ran, the taping concluded. For quality control purposes I rewound the cassette and gave it a listen. Mid-way through the recording, in one short breath-space during the conversation between my brother and the interviewer I heard what sounded very much like a third male voice, just once, utter a single sound.

'Errr.'

Not a word, more of a descending exhale. I heard it on the tape and in a sting of hot anxiety I rewound a few seconds in order to replay it, just to be sure that I hadn't imagined it. There it was again:

'Errr.'

I knew it wasn't me making the sound, partly because I was absolutely certain that I hadn't spoken once during the recording, but mainly because this was a fairly deep male voice – being twelve years old at the time my own voice hadn't broken. I played it back several more times, but no matter many times I listened I simply couldn't account for it. What made it all the more eerie was that I could tell from the noticeable difference between this voice and the voices on the television that the microphone had picked it up, not from the speaker, but *in the room*, and at very close proximity. When this penny dropped I rapidly switched off both television and cassette player, left the room and proceeded to the back garden in order to kick a football around for a while, in the hope that this fairly mindless and repetitive activity would help to blot out thoughts of what Yvette Fielding would no doubt call the 'EVP' on the tape.

I'm afraid to say that I have absolutely no idea what happened to that cassette, so I'm unable to provide any proof of what I heard. I suspect my sister taped over the recording with the following Sunday's Radio 1 Top 20 countdown with Simon Bates. The year 1978 was a long time ago now, and when the autumn of the year came along, and the traumas of moving to senior school rapidly crowded out a great many of the childhood neuroses that held me in their illusory fugue state for most of that decade, I only seemed to salvage as many memories as I could carry out of the house fire that was the transition to my teens. Somehow the thought of that voice on the tape seemed to fade. Only a random assortment of mostly silly micro-freak-out moments survived, like the time I took apart the plastic component inside my Laughing Bag toy to reveal a tiny vinyl record within, which naturally I flipped over and played, only then discovering that it contained a recording of birdsong. Not spooky at all.

With the onset of puberty my rate of chest infections diminished quite rapidly, only to be replaced by terrible hay fever, which played havoc with my exam results in my mid-teens and called for the consumption of strong prescription antihistamine medication that was powerful enough to put a glass eye to sleep, but that's another story, one involving laying on my bed for hours, staring at the ceiling while wearing stereo headphones and listening to loud music. I don't mind admitting that on the odd occasion during my adult life, when a bronchial malaise has set upon me, I have reached for the bottle of sleepy linctus, not just as a cough suppressant, but also as a rabbit hole down which one may again experience those almost, *almost*, nostalgic feelings of juvenile captivity.

16

Bleak adventures in Kenneth Johnson's *V*

Keith McDonald

The TV miniseries, *V*, began in 1983 as an ambitious, challenging and disturbing dystopian allegory developed by Kenneth Johnson. Initially intended for adults, the first miniseries was swiftly followed by a second miniseries *V: The Final Battle*, in 1984, partly in response to significant audience figures. It ended in 1985 as a somewhat diluted, formulaic and latterly child friendly adventure show, failing in terms of ratings and ambition. However, *V* is remembered by a generation who, as children, caught sight of this compellingly adult show. This chapter will focus on *V* and *V: The Final Battle*, these aligning most neatly with its creator's original intentions. Within these texts, Kenneth Johnson used science fiction (SF) as an extrapolative medium entwining with arresting narrative moments.

For audiences in Britain this was another glimpse of a form of broadcasting from overseas; families who were also enjoying a diet of TV including for adults, *Dallas* (1978–91) and *Dynasty* (1981–89) and for children *Knight Rider* (1982–86) and *The A-Team* (1983–87). Aesthetically, *V* combined these elements while integrating a highly polemical, deeply paranoid and fundamentally unsettling conspiracy narrative. The television landscape in the UK in the 1980s was significantly different from that today. Television consisted of four channels, and the latest had only been in existence since May 1982. Limited choice, plus the novelty of families being drawn together for a new manner of consuming television, made *V* compulsive viewing. In the United States the first two parts were broadcast on 1 and 2 May 1983 and *V: The Final Battle,* was shown in May 1984. In contrast and in the UK, *V* was broadcast over five nights in summer of 1984 on the commercial terrestrial ITV network. The first two-part series was shown on Monday and Tuesday with the three-part V: *The Final Battle* following on Wednesday, Thursday and Friday on ITV as a part of a counter-programming strategy to the BBC's broadcasting of LA Olympic Games. So, we have a situation where we see a highly polished, utopian vision of the United States on the BBC and a dystopian version of America in crisis on its rival station. This is, essentially, a clash between two forms of 'event television', but with *V*, it is the seductive and salacious aspects of the programme that perhaps cause it to rest in the collective memory.

> US television is 'event-driven' insofar as it takes a Challenger disaster, the Ollie North hearings, an earthquake in San Francisco, the fall of the Berlin Wall, or a Gulf War, in order for the beast to spring into action, in order for it to deploy the 'electronic sublime' of global omnipresence. (Elsaesser 2005, 286)

V is an early example of this form of programming where politicized themes sit uneasily next to reptilian conspiracy theory and body horror. The novelty of the programming brought a family audience to a show aimed at adults. In addition, it is notable that the body genre is both emerged and evolved in cinema. The fascination with the grotesque body can be seen in films as early as Tod Browning's *Freaks* (1932) and the unsettling effect of human/animal amalgam is mined in SF in Kurt Neumann's *The Fly* (1958). In relation to *V* and historical cultural context, *David Cronenberg's* remake of *The Fly* (1986) is considered a key text in the canon of the body horror boom of the late 1970s and the 1980s (Huckvale 2020). It is also notable that body horror is often political in nature, as it acts as a malleable narrative conduit for discussions concerning the body in society, the body politic and the national body (Meeker and Szabari, 2012). The haunting legacy of the programme can be seen in online forums and Amazon reviews of the DVD box set, 'Had to be bought if you were a kid in the 80's. Watched this at the time and it scared the pants off me as it did many adults of the time.' Although what scared the adults and what haunted the children may not have been the same thing.

   V most clearly functions as a tale about totalitarianism and draws heavily on holocaust imagery and Nazi propaganda. It falls between two trends of 1980s American popular culture: the SF boom which began with the unparalleled success of *Star Wars* (1977) and quickly made its way into TV, and the renewed interest in body horror narratives popularized by film-makers such as David Cronenberg and John Carpenter.

   In a world where conspiracy theories have proliferated through digital culture, the notion of a reptilian hidden race infiltrating and coercing the populace is commonplace. Conspiracy theorists such as David Ike have chosen to make shape-shifting 'lizard people' central to their theories of a corrupting elite of leaders as far back as 1999; a narrative that is viewed by many as being fuelled by thinly veiled anti-Semitic undertones. (Ronson 2001, Cox, Sutcliffe and Sweetman 2017). Back in 1983 though, the concept of a reptilian race disguised as humans was not a common conspiracy trope. The notion of an intelligent, reptilian and antagonistic force was present in popular culture and subsequently filtered into the collective consciousness. Robert E. Howard (creator of *Conan the Barbarian*) is credited for invoking the idea of a malicious reptilian species in his short story 'The Shadow Kingdom' in 1929 for *Weird Tales*. *Weird Tales* was an influential publication, in that it provided a platform for H. P. Lovecraft to develop, among other things, the Cthulhu mythos (Mitchell 2001, 12). This in turn worked as a sandbox for other authors writing of humans' violent interactions with antagonistic species. That is not to say that young viewers of *V* (or indeed any viewers) would be familiar with *Weird Tales* or the work of H. P. Lovecraft, but rather that the trope of a reptile, antagonistic race was not original. Suyand Tryamback Joshi (1995) states that Lovecraft's 'imaginary cosmology was never a static system but rather a sort of aesthetic construct that remained ever adaptable to its creator's developing personality and altering interests' (165). *V*'s creator, Kenneth Johnson, took this opportunity and used it to full effect, adding viscerally impactful and memorably affective villainous force to the SF television format, which, looking back, acts as a forebear of the conspiracy theory narratives that are so prevalent today. Johnson made a significant mark on the canon of American SF television, particularly in the late 1970s through to the late 1980s, where he was a producer on *The Six Million Dollar Man* (1974–78), created *The Bionic Woman* (1976–78), wrote on shows such as *The Incredible Hulk* (1977–82) and produced the TV adaptation of *Alien Nation* (1989–90).

The original miniseries of *V* tells a story where fifty saucer-shaped 'motherships' appear and hover over Earth (a well-worn SF motif that had already appeared in multiple 1950s SF films and would later be used to great effect in the hugely successful *Independence Day* (1996)). Rather than reveal themselves to be violent aggressors, the aliens communicate that they 'come in peace' and seek to attain some vitally needed minerals from Earth to save their planet in return for providing access to their advanced technology. World governments agree to this trade and what follows seems amicable, yet we soon see their leader and his second in command, Diana (Jane Badler), begin to exert their influence upon policy and international politics. From thereon in, we see an invasion not through direct attack, but through insidious propaganda; a scheme recognized by one of the characters, Abraham Bernstein (Leonardo Cimino), who is suspicious of the visitors' intentions; Abraham is a Holocaust survivor who sees parallels between the visitors' behaviour and the Nazi regime. Viewers are encouraged early in the narrative to see such parallels too; the uniforms worn by the visitors are distinctly militaristic and their flag displays a symbol closely modelled on a swastika. The visitors understand the power of the media and begin to covertly control it, homing in on a campaign to discredit scientists in particular. Aino-Kaisa Koistinen notices that in the 1970s and 1980s, Holocaust metaphors were not uncommon, and *V* clearly evokes recent history. However, *V* takes this into new territory when Abraham Bernstein's grandson, Daniel, joins the 'youth programme'. John A. Riley notices that in SF, hauntology, with its focus on spectral traces and uncanny discontinuities, can fix our attention on these moments and help us to determine how they are relevant to our ongoing sociopolitical moment (18). This spectral aspect is amplified in *V* as it does not simply evoke the spectres of past atrocities and systematic cruelty but makes direct correlations with contemporary practices and the wilful ignorance of the populace. What is most striking is how it portrays adolescents as the most gullible or perhaps even duplicitous. This nihilistic tenor, we must remember, resonated through 1980s popular screen culture and is evident in the rhetoric of many films (*Wall Street*'s (1987) 'Greed is good.' epitomizes this). There were also popular cult films where the young were not to be trusted, and this powerful anxiety was used memorably in such films as *Heathers* (1988) and *The Lost Boys* (1987). To a younger audience allowed to stay up later than they were normally allowed for this televisual event, this is a dark portrayal of what lies ahead in their immediate future.

V's conspiracy narrative included some grotesque imagery akin to the popularized body horror that ran alongside the more child-friendly cultural zeitgeist of the time. Dan Copp states that

As many of us who grew up in the 1980s can attest, *V* had a tremendous impact on our childhoods. But what our elementary brains didn't realize then was that Johnson's landmark miniseries was a lot more than colorful battles and spaceships … In essence, the original *V* two-parter is a political commentary in the guise of a sci-fi film depicting the rise of fascism in America. (6–12)

A crusading journalist named Mike Donovan (Marc Singer) is one of the guides who help reveal the visitors' secret identities and via that their real intent. He gains access to an alien ship and sees that beneath a synthetic skin, the visitors are reptilian creatures and, in one of the most iconic scenes in the franchise, sees Diana eat a live rodent. This scene, with its 'cost effective' effects, remains notorious, as we see Diana's jaw dislocate and a large gerbil lowered into her throat, wriggling and writhing before being digested. Donovan and others uncover a plot whereby the visitors aim to harvest a docile human race as food. Donovan eventually joins a resistance group, and the rebellion narrative is established. This image, of Diana throwing her head back and lowering a rodent into it is of course unsettling and works on a narrative level in revealing not only the ruse that the invaders have enacted, and their cruelty and inhumanity, but the visceral nature of their horrific consumption. To a young audience, this scene takes *V* in a vastly darker direction than they may have expected, and symbolically draws attention to the conservative economic and social environment they find themselves coming of age in. Certainly, this audience may have seen the grotesque appetite of Jabba the Hutt in *Return of the Jedi* (1983) or the extreme body horror imagery of Nazis having their faces melted in *Raiders of the Lost Ark* (1981). However, in an era where there was still low take up of video cassette recorders and such SF horrors were often confined to the cinema, this image appeared directly within the home.

This is television in the 1980s, where viewers were rarely confronted with such graphic or shocking images, yet the use of prosthetics (which may look dated now) made it possible to see the rodent writhe as it slips down Diana's throat. Mark Derry writes that in terms of abject horror, the mouth has a particular potency. He writes,

> Certainly, the mouth, as the biggest breach in the body's integrity, holds its own terrors: What's this big hole in the middle of my face?! What if something falls out? What if something falls in? Not for nothing has the face of mythic horror been a slavering maw (*Alien*), a toothy portal welcoming you to the afterworld. (*Jaws*, 205).

The visual image of Diana unlocking her reptilian jaw to consume a live gerbil as a shocked Donovan covertly watches on and the ripping of the prosthetic skin of the leader to reveal his lizard form do visually what dialogue cannot, and these images remain iconic to this day, in that they were also transgressive and brought this adventure show, and with it its young audience, into the realms of body horror (Karkulehto, Koistinen and Varis 2020, 34). Kelly Hurley attests to the power of the image in body horror and its potency in presenting the view with the potent symbiosis of revulsion and pleasure:

> Body horror seeks to inspire revulsion – and in its own way, pleasure – through representations of quasi human figures whose effect/affect is produced by their abjection, their ambiguation, their impossible embodiment of multiple, incompatible forms. Such posthuman embodiments are liminal entities, occupying both terms (or rather, existing in the slash between them) of the opposition human/not human. (1995, 203)

This liminality is key in the wider narrative of *V*, through the realization that these visitors appear human and beautiful yet are in their natural form very much non-human and grotesque. This reveals that all that they promise (youth, beauty, health, etc.) is a lie and part of a conspiracy. The placement of this image is jarring as Diana epitomizes a Western vision of glamour, intelligence and success, yet takes great pleasure in the repulsive act of consuming a live animal. This image, then, explodes the veneer and plunges an adolescent viewer into the realm of grotesque spectacle. This serves to elevate the show, broadening its boundaries and possibilities, which to a young audience may be deeply entertaining as it adds an 'adult' pleasure/abjection to what is up to that point a highly polished adventure show.

Mikhail Bakhtin draws attention to the carnivalesque spectacle that blurs boundaries between the rational and the corporeal, stating that the body 'is not separated from the rest of the world. It is not a closed, completed unit; it is unfinished, outgrows itself, transgresses its own limits' (1982, 26). Mary Russo elaborates on this, drawing attention to the transgressive nature of such displays:

> The grotesque body [is] exuberantly and democratically open and inclusive of all possibilities. Boundaries between individuals and society, between genders, between species, and between classes were blurred or brought into crisis in the inversions and hyperbole of carnivalesque representation. (1994, 79)

Up until this point in the narrative of *V*, the visitors present themselves as exceptionally uniform, physically fit and the very opposite of the alien other. Certainly, in the text itself the public are drawn in by their cleanliness, beauty and their promise to eradicate disease, which from a Bakhtinian point of view, is a reminder of our animal nature. The visitors, for the most part, resemble an Aryan ideal blended with 'true American' beauty currency. We see the public cautiously approach them and marvel at their uniforms and (in their non-lizard state) idealized form. Daniel, the grandson of Abraham, the alarmed Holocaust survivor, is seduced by such allure and joins the 'Visitor Youth', another direct link to the successful propaganda machine of these Fascists.

There is also a distinctly sexualized element; Diana is a strong and domineering character, who seems to typify the 1980s notion that a certain version of beauty and power are achievable ideals in the context of 1980s post feminism on screen. The revelation of her grotesquery (her lizard-like skin, her appetite for live flesh, etc.), would, one would think, explode this notion. However, the opposite is true. The iconic scene of her dropping a live rodent into her throat is of course repellent, but shrouded in sexual connotations and pornographic imagery, enhanced by Donovan witnessing it while hiding in a vent, viewing it through what compensates for blinds, thereby completing a voyeuristic fantasy that blends desire and disgust in a distinctly Cronenbergian moment.

The memory of this moment figures heavily in recollection. Even the most cursory scans of forums and review shows that the mention of one of the alien creatures (in human disguise) eating a live rodent whole, and revealing their lizard-like form, is the image which invokes the strongest recollections of recoil and fascination. This iconic moment separated *V* from its televisual contemporaries, in that it added an element of horror and disgust to an otherwise conventional SF narrative and in doing so heightened the spectacle of the whole show itself, by foreshadowing horrors yet to come. This was something that cinema had been doing successfully for a number of years. David Buckingham asserts that 'many people find violence on television shocking, frightening or disgusting – although they may also find it exciting, enjoyable or even funny' (1994, 6). This is the draw of such viscera, its magnetic effect. The 'disgusting' element of this particular scene, in terms of young viewers, made *V* a compelling illicit pleasure. Buckingham dispels the notion of children as innocent viewers of television, illiterate to the modes of adult entertainment forms. Rather, he states that we should acknowledge the 'diverse ways in which they make sense of what they watch; to the kinds of knowledge they bring to television, and the critical skills they develop in relation to it' (6). This pivotal moment in *V* may have sent many children to their beds and nightmares, but to others it supercharged the viewing experience and added the thrill of what they anticipated would follow, not realizing how dark the show would become.

Adjacent to the family friendly SF which thrived in the early 1980s, there was also a wave of body horror SF which is evident in *V*. Marty Roth contends that Philip Kauffman's *The Invasion of the Body Snatchers* (1978) and Carpenter's *The Thing* (1982) were a part of a 'seriously infectious' screen virus and SF body horror texts would flourish during the decade (2000, 103–4). Each of these films is deeply paranoid and involves alien invasions in very different ways. *The Invasion of the Body Snatchers* is perhaps more narratively similar to *V* in that the aliens walk among the populace, hiding their true identity and replacing humans as can be seen in *V*. However, *The Thing* is perhaps most memorable for its stunning visual gore aesthetic which came to epitomize the body horror that *V* brought into families' living rooms.

Subarna Mondal contends that in body horror, the skin plays an important role in that it draws attention not only to our fragility, depicted in the ease with which it is penetrated and torn, but also in how it demonstrates mutability. She states that in body horror skin can 'dislocate and render fluid the idea of a human body and … reinscribe itself as constitutive in the construction of socio-cultural identities and its variances' (2021, 13). This concept of the skin illuminating the malleability of the body and therefore fixed identity, beauty and defence runs through body horror but flourishes in 1980s in films such as *The Fly, Society* (1989) and *Hellraiser* (1987). In terms of the social body, Kauffman's version of *Invasion of the Body Snatchers* uses the notion of the doppelgänger and the animal imagery of shed skin to great effect, using the imagery to illustrate a paranoid fantasy of a non-violent invasion and takeover of America. This notion is also evident in John Carpenter's *They Live* (1988). *They Live* depicts a scenario in which a wandering protagonist finds that in looking through specialized sunglasses, he can see a growing alien population that has infiltrated Earth and by using media, encourages its alien invaders to breed and take over a docile population. To return to Bakhtin's notion of the carnivalesque and the grotesque (despite our outward beauty we are united by our blood, our bile and our faeces), *V* illuminates another element in its conspiracy theory which reinforces Johnson's parallel Holocaust allegory and on reflection makes *V* an even more nihilistic tale. To the visitors, we are all food. The scene of Diana eating a live rodent is but an aperitif to the feast that is at the core of their mission. Our dehumanization comes from their understanding that we are all flesh, and the bovine servitude depicted by the masses in *V* is deeply disturbing.

As the series continues, the instances of the reveal of the aliens' true identity become a refrain. In a further pivotal scene, a human worker is saved from an accident in a factory by clumsy and loveable alien Willy (Robert Englund) who himself forms a tentative and ultimately unrequited relationship with the human Harmony Moore (Diane Cary). This somewhat unusual and tender love story was set against the relationship between the adolescent Robin Maxell (Blair Tefkin) and the visitor youth leader, Brian (Peter Nelson). This narrative thread is unsettling on a number of levels. Initially it is the corruption of Robin at the hands of Brian. Robin believes she is in love with the Aryan youth leader, while we are privy to the machinations of Diana who gives Brian the 'mission' to impregnate Robin; the echoes of human experimentation are clear. Robin has adolescent dreams of a relationship with her handsome boyfriend. Although we know that in this case in particular his looks are literally skin deep. Robin is lied to and thus, while unstated in the context of viewing this in the mid-1980s and perhaps opaque to the adolescent viewer, this is a disturbing rape narrative. There is more than a passing connection between this and cinematic teen narratives which gained popularity in this period; consumption is once again at the heart of this, the consumable 'item' this time being virginity: a critique, perhaps, of the framing of virginal characters in teen narratives from slasher to comedy. There are echoes of *Rosemary's Baby* (1968), *Demon Seed* (1977) or *The Incubus* (1982); none of these films intended for family viewing. *V* is not a subtle series, and its metaphors are clear and direct. For a youthful audience the prospect of the development from adolescence to adulthood is presented as dark and threatening.

Prior to this troubling narrative line body horror has been made safe – after all, it happens to the alien visitors. We are repulsed by the uncanny quality afforded by their disguises but from the moment Diana eats the rodent we know what lies beneath. The pregnancy storyline changes this and turns the body horror back to the human and something recognizable and real. The nightmare for Robin continues as she begs resistance leader and doctor Julie Parrish (Faye Grant) to terminate the pregnancy. It is revealed that the threat to Robin's life is too great, and she will need to see the pregnancy to term; the programme makers allow her no quarter.

> In this most sinister of sub-plots … Robin's traumatic pregnancy culminated in the birth of a baby girl; a baby girl with a FORKED TONGUE! The shocks didn't stop there though, as moments later, to the utter horror of all present, a twin emerged: a green, slimy baby lizard twin, whose horrific visage was the subject of the shock freeze-frame ending to *V: The Final Battle*'s second episode. (Mitchell 2019, 175)

This is the very essence of Barbara Creed's notion of the monstrous feminine (Creed 1993). Robin harbours something literally alien within her which has the potential to be the downfall of humanity.

> 'These images of reproduction as unstoppable signal fear of something excessive about birth itself. The anxiety of wombs gone wild, spewing (rather than birthing) countless offspring, generates nightmarish images of hordes of insect-like babies or monstrous aliens taking over the planet or the entire universe.' (Oliver 2012)

Robin is left to deal with all aspects of this on her own; her family and the resistance offer support, but they are incapable of anything significant by way of intervention. In *V: The Final Battle*, Brian is captured by the resistance who are developing a poison to use against the visitors. Robin takes her child to visit Brian, who is being held in a Perspex cell; it is unclear at this stage what her intentions are. True to his character, Brian spins a story about the three of them living 'happily ever after'. In recognizing the ongoing duplicity, Robin's progression to adulthood is complete; she rejects patriarchal mythmaking, not motherhood. She uses the as yet untested weapon on Brian, and we witness his writhing death as he tears at his human disguise, revealing the reptile beneath.

A generation of young people, sitting in suburban British homes with their parents, were anticipating a thrilling week of viewing. Exciting spaceships and high adventure coexisted with political allegory and stories of betrayal as the series developed an increasingly dark view of adulthood rooted in abjection. It's perhaps no wonder that comments are still being left on YouTube clips and online forums by a generation haunted by the visitors.

References

Bakhtin, M. 1982. *The Dialogic Imagination*. Austin: University of Texas Press.

Buckingham, David. 1994. 'Television and the Definition of Childhood'. In
    Children's Childhoods Observed and Explained, edited by Berry Mayall, 79–96.
    London: Routledge.
Copp, D. 2017. *Fascist Lizards from Outer Space: The Politics, Literary Influences
    and Cultural History of Kenneth Johnson's V*. Jefferson: MacFarland.
Creed, Barbara. 1993. *The Monstrous-Feminine: Film, Feminism and
    Psychoanalysis*. London: Routledge.
Derrida, Jacques, Catherine Porter and Philip Lewis. 1984. 'No Apocalypse, Not
    Now (Full Speed Ahead, Seven Missiles, Seven Missives)'. *Diacritics* 14, no.
    2: 20–31.
Dery, M. 2012. *I Must Not Think Bad Thoughts: Drive-By Essays on American
    Dread, American Dreams*. Minneapolis: University of Minnesota Press.
Elsaesser, Thomas. 2005. 'British Television in the 1980s through the Looking
    Glass'. In *European Cinema: Face to Face with Hollywood*, edited by Thomas
    Elsaesser, 278–98. Amsterdam: Amsterdam University Press.
Foucault, M. 2014. In *Are You Not a Man of God? Devotion, Betrayal, and Social
    Criticism in Jewish Tradition*, edited by Tova Hartman and Charlie Buckholtz,
    127–60. Oxford: Oxford University Press.
Holdsworth, A., Rachel Mosely and Helen Wheatley. 2019. 'Memory, Nostalgia
    and the Material Heritage of Children's Television in the Museum'. *Journal of
    European Television History and Culture* 8, no. 15: 111–22.
Howard, R. E. 1929. 'The Shadow People'. In *Weird Tales*, edited by F. Wright,
    16–24. Stoneleigh: Rural Publication Company.
Huckvale, D. 2020. *Terrors of the Flesh: The Philosophy of Body Horror in Film*.
    North Carolina: McFarland.
Hurley, K. 1995. 'Reading like an Alien: Posthuman Identity in Ridley Scott's *Alien*
    and David Cronenberg's *Rabid*.' In *Posthuman Bodies*, edited by J. Halberstam
    and I. Livingston, 203–24. Bloomington, IN: Indiana University Press.
Joshi, S. 1995. *Miscellaneous Writings by H. P. Lovecraft*. 1st edition.
    Wisconsin: Arkham House.
Karkulehto, Sanna, Aino-Kaisa Koistinen and Essi Varis. 2020. *Reconfiguring
    Human, Nonhuman and Posthuman in Literature and Culture*.
    London: Routledge.
Lewis, S. 2021. *It Can't Happen Here: A Novel*. Prabhat Prakashan.
Meeker, N., and A. Szabari. 2012. 'From the Century of the Pods to the Century
    of the Plants: Plant Horror, Politics, and Vegetal Ontology'. *Discourse* 34, no.
    1: 32–58.
Mitchell, C. 2001. *The Complete H. P. Lovecraft Filmography*.
    New York: Bloomsbury.
Mitchell, Neil. 2019. '*V: The Mini-Series*, *V: The Final Battle*, *V: The Series* (ITV, 24
    episodes, 1984–1986'. In *Scarred for Life, Volume Two: Television in the 1980s*,
    edited by Stephen Brotherston and Dave Lawrence, 173–80. Liverpool: Lonely
    Water Books.
Mondal, Subarna. 2021. 'Destruction, Reconstruction and Resistance: The Skin
    and the Protean Body in Pedro Almodóvar's Body Horror *The Skin I Live In*'.
    Humanities 10, no. 1: 54. https://www.mdpi.com/2076-0787/10/1/54. Accessed
    24 September 2023.

Oliver, Kelly. 2012. *Knock Me Up, Knock Me Down: Images of Pregnancy in Hollywood Films*. New York: Columbia University Press.

Robertson, D. 2017. *UFOs, Conspiracy Theories and the New Age: Millennial Conspiracism*. London: Bloomsbury.

Rogers, A., Noel Castree and Rob Kitchin. 2013. 'Biopolitics'. In *A Dictionary of Human Geography*. Oxford: Oxford University Press.

Ronson, J. 2001. 'Beset by Lizards'. *The Guardian*. https://www.theguardian.com/books/2001/mar/17/features.weekend. Accessed 13 October 2023.

Roth, M. 2000. 'Twice Two: "The Fly" and "Invasion of the Body Snatchers"'. *Discourse* 22, no. 1: 103–16.

Russo, M. 1994. *Female Grotesque: Risk, Excess, and Modernity*. New York: Routledge.

Seed, D. 2013. *American Science-Fiction and the Cold War: Literature and Film*. New York: Bloomsbury.

Stevenson, R. L. 2007. *Dr Jekyll and Mr Hyde and Other Stories*. London: Vintage.

17

Don't turn tail from horror: Using eco-horror in the secondary-school classroom

Hollie Adams

Historically children and horror have often been regarded as a genre and audience that do not fit together. Lester states that 'the idea of the child spectator of horror has long been the object of anxiety and tension' among adults (Lester 2021, 3). After all, the genre 'evokes feelings of loathing, repugnance, aversion, dread, and outright terror', emotions adults attempt to shield children from (Rust and Soles 2014, 509). Despite this, children will still seek out horror, whether as an act of rebellion against protective adults or as a thrill-seeking experiment to embody bravery to friends. In a discussion with my class of thirty-two Year 7 students (eleven–twelve-year-olds), I asked what genre of book they were reading as part of their literacy programme. Twenty of them announced they were reading 'horror'. When asked why, students' answers ranged from 'curious', 'less boring' to 'enjoying a scare'. For my class, the horror genre was used as part of a thrill-seeking experience or something to stifle their boredom and nurture their curiosity. They were not the only children to seek out a thrill as can be seen from the experience my father who, at age fifteen, decided to watch *The Exorcist* while alone one sunny afternoon. Halfway through the film, rapt in terror, he opened the curtains and the back door (for a quick exit) and was sitting on the arm of my grandfather's chair. The memory of this lives with him still. That afternoon my father sought out, like many children before and after him, the thrill that horror can bring. However, thrills and rebellion are not the only reason children are drawn to horror. As sociologist Margaret Kerr notes, there are a number of reasons. Firstly, horror triggers a part of our brain that releases 'endorphins, serotonin, oxytocin, and dopamine', giving the viewer a euphoric feeling upon being scared (Kerr 2015). Secondly, there is some form of empowerment to watching horror. Although we are aware that a movie cannot harm us, having finished the horror movie and surviving people feel as though they overcame adversity and feel empowered by this. For children, experiencing simulated horror at a distance that is safe to engage with provides them with control and a way to feel in charge of their lives. Thirdly, for children who love horror, it can be 'a place for them to feel strong, to engage their imaginations in a way that feels empowering to them, endlessly fascinating or thrilling, and just generally a positive experience' (Ernst 2019). Here, horror as a tool of empowerment is important when it comes to education, especially since education often seeks to empower students to have an impact on the world and communities around them. It is this that raises the question, why not use horror as an educational tool? If it is empowering and interests children, it has the potential to be an influential topic in the classroom. After all, horror can commentate on present-day societal, cultural and historical events or issues, and with horrific events happening every day, 'it is only natural that these events find their way into our collective imagination', making them contemporary and relevant to use in the classroom (Rust and Soles 2015, 509). Alongside this, 'horror is one of the most enduringly popular film genres', mainly due to the possibility to express anxiety and fear, or experience horrific events in a simulated, safe environment (Vinney 2022). With its ever-increasing popularity and ability to commentate on real-world issues, horror is a multifaceted genre that provides real opportunities for discussion, exploration and understanding. When treated sensitively and used in a safe setting, it can expose viewers to a multitude of real-life issues that need to be addressed now.

In this chapter, I discuss methods in which horror, specifically eco-horror, can be used in the classroom. Beginning with the well-established context of eco-pedagogy, this chapter proposes activities that teachers could use to teach about the environmental crisis through eco-horror. These activities and tasks will be based upon three key texts that can be introduced in the classroom: tv series *Animals of Farthing Wood* (1993), novel *Scary Stories for Young Foxes* (2019) by Christian McKay Heidicker and movie *The House* (2022).

Eco-pedagogy

Soles and Tidwell state that 'we live in ecohorrific times' (Soles and Tidwell 2021, 1). The earth is dramatically changing and we, alongside other species, are suffering. We live in a time where phrases such as 'global climate change, the sixth extinction, and environmental injustice' are part of everyday media rhetoric (Rust and Soles 2015, 509). Across the globe, biodiversity is declining and coral reefs are dying, and we are now facing a mass extinction event (Soles and Tidwell 2021, 1). In 2022, the human population saw the effects of climate change with record-breaking heatwaves across Europe, spreading wildfires and freak weather events (1). In response to this, young climate activists have been fighting against socio-environmental injustices and preparing to become 'the environmental leaders of tomorrow', rallying the younger generations to prevent further environmental damage or reverse damage already done (Alhendawi and Lambertini 2019). While older generations can help by changing habits and protesting themselves, they can also help the young generation of climate activists through teaching eco-pedagogy – a branch of Paulo Freire's critical pedagogy, a pedagogical approach that 'enables students to explore the possibilities of what it means to be critical citizens' while examining and challenging power structures and inequality in society (Giroux 2010, 715.) Freire was not the founder of eco-pedagogy as, sadly, he passed before further writing could be completed; however, he did lament 'the predatory cultures that oppressed the planet and insisted on the need of a planetary citizenship and ecopedagogy as a model to defend the planet, a most oppressed entity' (Misiaszek and Torres 2019, 464).

The main goal of eco-pedagogy 'is for students to critically understand how environmentally harmful acts lead to oppressions for humans (*anthropocentric aspects*) and all else that makes up Earth (*biocentric aspects*), the politics of the acts, and how to problematize the acts to end socio-environmental oppressions' (Misiaszek 2018, 3). Eco-pedagogy has a 'commitment to the coherence between theory and practice'; it is not solely teaching about environmental injustice but also about practising the theory and using new methods learned in order to have a positive impact (Gaard 2009, 332). These methods do not have to be large protests or boycotts and instead could be small changes such as using recycled materials in the classroom after discussions about plastic pollution or using digital resources instead of paper after learning about deforestation (332). These methods would then fulfil the main purpose of eco-pedagogy which is to guide students' 'environmental actions through their reflection' of the understandings they take from the teaching of environmental injustice (Misiaszek 2018, 4).

There are many ways in which to bring theory and practice together in eco-pedagogy but the one in which I will discuss and use in this chapter is the six 'boundary conditions for an ecopedagogy of children's environmental literature', developed by Greta Gaard (Gaard 2009, 332). Firstly, there is praxis: the environmentally friendly choices students can make to test and synthesize their classroom knowledge. Secondly, there is 'teaching ABOUT the social and natural environment', where teachers use texts, media, and other resources to highlight environmental issues, how they occur and strategies to respond (333). Then there is 'teaching IN the social and natural environment', where excursions can be used to experience the natural world (333). These excursions may go from admiring the natural environment to litter picking and discussions of industrialization. Following this, there is 'teaching THROUGH the social and natural environment' where classroom exercises, projects, and instruction put theory into practice (333). The litter picking from the previous boundary may lead to an abolishment of plastic in the classroom, or a slight change to the way a student's sandwich is wrapped for example. Penultimately, there is 'teaching the connections of sustainability', which 'illuminates connections and system-flows as simply "the way things really are"' and that 'divisions between human and nonhuman animals are just more ways of promoting hierarchy and domination (333). Finally, there is urgency. As sighted earlier, the natural world is facing a crisis *now*. The use of eco-pedagogy in the classroom provides an opportunity to direct students into thinking of solutions, strategies and methods to help slow down or eradicate climate change so there is no longer an urgency.

'What about the curriculum?' Some may ask, and herein lies one of the limitations of eco-pedagogy. In the UK secondary-school context, teachers are provided with a curriculum in which topics are outlined that students are required to learn in each subject. Oftentimes, these topics are what may appear on the SATS (UK National Curriculum Tests) or GCSE (General Certificate of Secondary Education) exams, leading to teachers turning to a 'teaching to the test' mentality, in which teachers focus more on test preparation to ensure students' and school's exam successes (Sellgren 2017). However, in the UK's National Curriculum of Key stages S3, Y7, Y8 and Y9 (age eleven–fourteen) students have more freedom with no state examinations during these years of study. This freedom can be seen in The National Curriculum (UK) for English in KS3 – pupils should be 'reading a wide range of fiction and non-fiction, including in particular whole books, short stories, poems, and plays with a wide coverage of genres, historical periods, forms and authors' (Department for Education 2014, 15). They should also be 'making inferences and referring to evidence in the text' and hypothesizing 'the purpose, audience for and context of the writing and drawing on this knowledge to support comprehension' (Department for Education 2014, 15). Specific texts are not identified in the curriculum, leaving room to explore environmental, eco-horrific texts. Students could use these to identify environmental themes, how they are presented and inform student's knowledge of socio-environmental injustices. In terms of subject, eco-pedagogy can be used in every subject's classroom. For example, in maths, percentages and statistics could be taught by discussing population growth, land loss, biodiversity loss and so on. There are, however, some issues that could arise within a school. School budgets may not allow for trips to teach 'in' the environment or make radical changes within the school.

However, Greta Gaard's boundary conditions outlined earlier are not to be treated as a checklist and, instead, are possibilities for using eco-pedagogy. Accompanying this, eco-pedagogy does not require radical changes to our habitats and lifestyles. Even the smallest change can make a big impact and therefore, small ethical swaps and choices still put the theory into practice. Finally, teachers must take into account the diversity of socio-economic backgrounds. Some students may be unable to make radical changes that other students can, potentially causing conflict within the classroom with students questioning dedication to the cause. The class must learn to value each other's opinions and negotiate strategies and methods they may disagree on and the teacher must be prepared to delegate other methods and create equity within the classroom. Before using eco-pedagogy, it is important to acknowledge these issues so that they can be resolved to focus on the real matter at hand – educating about the environment.

Eco-horror

Horror is a diverse media with many sub genres. In this chapter, I discuss a sub-genre that came to light in the 1960s and 1970s – 'Eco-horror grapples with the troubled relationship between humanity and the natural environment' (Ajani 2022). Eco-horror features a range of ecological disasters from humans being 'attacked by natural forces … that have been altered or angered by humans in some way' to 'mad scientists, creatures, or animal attacks' (Soles and Tidwell 2021, 2). Oftentimes in these narratives, nature fights a human oppressor. Animals attack humans because they encroach on or destroy habitats, mutated creatures seek revenge on the humans who created them, and the earth itself fights back as a response to humans' impact upon it. In these narratives it is not unusual to witness 'far-reaching events or processes such as pollution, species extinction, or extreme weather', as the genre is used as a social commentary on the environmental crisis (2). This genre is diverse and features anything from animal attack to allegory to black comedy. An early eco-horror narrative can be found in Daphne Du Maurier's 1952 short story 'The Birds', adapted by Alfred Hitchcock in 1963; an animal-attack narrative that features nature fighting back. An allegorical film would be *Annihilation* (2018) which depicts Earth as a patient with the humans being a disease who have ravaged its body (Goldberg 2022). Then there is the black comedy eco-horror, *The Toxic Avenger* (1984). This film 'uses the negative repercussions of toxic waste for comic effect' but it comments on the battle against consumerism in a stark, environmental message (Murray, 2017). Interestingly, a reboot of *The Toxic Avenger* was announced in 2020. Rated R, the reboot has been likened to popular anti-hero, *Deadpool* and while it may appear to evoke only hilarity, there is an underlying environmental message in context of 'larger climate change-related issues' (Soles and Tidwell 2021, 2). Soles and Tidwell state that 'contemporary eco-horror narratives can be read as a response to real-world environmental fears' and while they provide the opportunity for viewers to witness the destruction of Earth or environmental fight-back narratives in safe spaces, they also provide an opportunity for audiences to realize that the events of the film could happen and that we need to take action now.

The texts central to the analysis herein were chosen for a variety of reasons. Firstly, all three texts explore different aspects of the environmental crisis and do so in a way that can be seen as disturbing or even violent by viewers. Secondly, with the exception of *The House* (2022), the texts are suitable for children aged nine and above, which means they are suitable for teaching in secondary schools. Thirdly, the texts vary from TV series to novel to movie, allowing children to explore different interpretations of environmental issues through different mediums. Finally, while not all are formally identified as 'eco-horror', they do all project important lessons about the environment in eerie, sinister or even gruesome ways. For example, *Animals of Farthing Wood* (1993) depicts a multitude of environmental themes from humans destroying habitats, hunting and animal cruelty. A show that is colourfully animated, features whimsical music and fuzzy animals does not scream horror; however, in just thirty-nine episodes, twenty-four animals are killed. This excessive death can be likened to a 'slasher' film with characters being bumped off one by one (Jones 2016). Meanwhile, Christian McKay Heidicker's novel *Scary Stories For Young Foxes* (2019) features a den of fox cubs, listening to scary stories. These stories involve vicious humans and hunting, and focuses on the foxes' tale of survival. With horrifying commentaries on trapping and conservation, this novel features some 'eco-horrific' topics. Finally, *The House* (2022) is an animated, stop-motion anthology horror with three stories in which I will focus on parts II and III. With an age categorization of twelve and above, the film is darker and more complex than the previous two texts as it focuses on deeper environmental themes such as greed, materialism and anti-capitalism. Overall, the three texts depict harsh environments with the threat of species extinction, pollution and an obvious commentary about humans' impact upon the environment that mirrors traditional eco-horror narratives.

Animals of Farthing Wood

Animals of Farthing Wood was first broadcast on CBBC in 1993, a time when other environmentally conscious children's series were on air including, but not limited to, *David the Gnome*, *Captain Planet and the Planeteers* and *The Smoggies*. Aimed at children aged four–ten, these shows focused on fantastical characters, cleaning up human destruction. In contrast, *Animals of Farthing Wood* featured animals the British public may have grown up with whether from childhood tales or from viewing them in the wild. The fact that the viewer may have a connection with these animal characters is vital as it provides an emotional investment into the animals' struggles. This emotional investment is then key to teach the audience about their impact upon the environment and possibly inspire them to make environmentally conscious changes to their lifestyles.

Throughout the series, the key commentary is biodiversity loss and how humans have enforced this. This can be seen through the graphic deaths of thirty-nine beloved characters. The deaths of these animals highlight that man versus nature is a fight that humans often win. As human viewers, we can rationalize why the human characters behave in such a way, understanding the necessity for housing, parking and so on. However, we do not often think beyond our species and about the consequences our actions have upon other creatures. This is something the show provides us – an insight into humans as monsters, ravaging the environment. In the show, humans are depicted as sinister, ruthless, unfeeling and faceless; humans are only ever seen behind glass, as a shadow, or down the barrel of a gun. With this, the human becomes a mysterious, faceless entity with a desperate need to devour animals. Therefore, in this series, the human becomes every horror nasty from monster to bogeyman to mindless killer. They become the terror, the slasher, the ghoul, filling the viewer with dread.

In season 1, episode 5 – 'Snare of the Unwary' – the animal protagonists come across a farmhouse, occupied by humans. Here, the 'bumbling, loveable' pheasant couple meet their end to a faceless farmer, who aims down his shotgun and shoots the female pheasant (Jones 2016). In the scene, the human is off-screen and instead, the gun is aimed down the camera, making the viewer the hunter's prey. Here, the gun is anthropomorphized, staring with its 'cold, uncaring eyes' (Jones 2016). Not only does this scene make the viewer the prey, it also connects the viewer with the victims as the male pheasant displays the human emotion of grief through sobbing. This is an emotion all humans recognize but may not associate with animals. Soles and Tidwell state that 'emotion is crucial to eco-horror' (Soles and Tidwell 2021, 4). There needs to be grief, anger and other such emotions for people to feel the urge to take action and perhaps this is why the series writers and Colin Dann killed so many beloved characters – to shock, horrify and upset, in the hopes that humans realize the harm they cause.

Further in the scene, the viewer is shown the pheasants cooked. This moment forces the viewer to acknowledge that meat comes from living creatures, a topic that is all too often avoided in children's media. In the classroom, the teacher is provided many opportunities with this scene. This allows for the opportunity for the teacher to ask questions about the pheasant's death and the whys and the how's of this happening. These questions could then lead into an exploration of 'socio-historical oppressions', such as colonialism and patriarchy, and how these 'create, sustain, and/or intensify socio-environmental ills' (Misiaszek 2020). This scene provides opportunities for students to analyse using the lens of colonialism, looking at power dynamics of humans versus non-human. By analysing this way, students can understand the context behind how environmental ills occur. Leading from this, a debate could be facilitated about hunting and veganism, looking at stereotypes and controversies. With the debate, students could complete research about the politics of the two lifestyles, making them more knowledgeable about the whys and hows of the lifestyles. Post-debate, the classroom could become a hive of activism. Classes should decide what they would like to see changed and turn this into activities such as campaigning for vegan options, writing to councils opposing hunting, making posters or art installations in the school to help promote whole-school activism, alongside many other activities.

Eco-horror is 'not defined solely by human fear of non-human nature' but also by the 'human fear for nonhuman nature' (Soles and Tidwell 2021, 5). These texts emphasize harm caused by humans in order to 'prompt sympathy for the creatures', leading to guilt or anxiety about our responsibility to the future of the world (6). In *Animals of Farthing Wood,* as the protagonists get closer to the utopian haven, 'White Deer Park', they must overcome one last hurdle. So close to their goal, the viewer is lulled into a false sense of security and as we are shown the busy motorway, the 'human fear for nonhuman nature' is triggered. In the scene, a hedgehog couple curl up in terror on the road; inevitably, both are crushed by a large, articulated lorry. Again, the viewer is put in the position of the victims as the wheel comes screeching towards the camera. In eco-pedagogy, it is imperative that eco-pedagogues 'teach students to deconstruct and thus unlearn ideological "reasoning" that produces unattainable environmental violence done for some populations' benefit' (Misiaszek 2020). Thus, with this scene, pupils could unlearn the ideological reasoning behind car usage. These reasonings range from lack of public transport, rural living, importance of cars for day-to-day life and the argument of 'where would we be without cars'. These reasonings are vital to acknowledge and so, the teacher could make pros and cons lists based on research. With the lists, students would then look into 'who benefits and who suffers' and explore the 'oppressive effects' these have upon populations, such as non-humans (Misiaszek 2020). While this would all be facilitated in the classroom, there is also the opportunity to teach IN the environment. Ensuring all students feel safe and are not triggered by the idea of animal–vehicle collisions, the teacher could take the class to a local road, dependent on the location of the school. Viewing the road allows the students to see the threats and how nature and the human world collide. This may then inspire students to enact change. Teachers could show students 'wildlife under- and overpasses', especially those in Florida, Mexico and the Snoqualmie Pass in

Washington State (Vartan 2019). By highlighting how these have been created in other places, we should ask 'then why not here?', leading to a launch of a school-wide campaign to talk to council members or government officials to create these under- and overpasses. Supported by the American research, students can demonstrate how to use statistics and facts in their campaign and all subject areas in the school could become involved, leading a whole new cohort of planetary citizens. This 'ecopedagogical literacy nurtures the kind of deepened and widened understanding for action that can emerge from critical theorising (i.e., praxis), rather than environmental pedagogies that centre on quantitative environmental knowledge' (Misiaszek 2020).

Other texts

Scary Stories for Young Foxes by Christian McKay Heidicker is a children's horror novel, inspired by horror greats such as Bram Stoker, H. P. Lovecraft and Edgar Allan Poe (2019). The novel features eight interconnected stories about two fox cubs who are separated from their litter and find themselves in terrifying situations. The story begins with the foxes begging for a story 'so scary our eyes fall out of our heads', paralleling the human child's fascination with horror (Heidicker 2019, 1). The storyteller then tells them eight stories, the one discussed here will be the third story, 'House of Trix', a subversive tale about conservationist and author, Beatrix Potter.

This story begins with fox kit, Mia, and her mother travelling through the wilderness until they come to a road. The mother immediately states, 'we must leave this place. Now', leaving the reader feeling uneasy (77). Upon wandering further, the danger is revealed as the mother is stuck in the 'silver jaws' of a trap and a human appears (78). The human is described as monstrous, having 'no fur on its face or paws', 'loose skins' and 'two legs', painting a sinister, disgusting image of the human as monster with the potential to scare the child reader (82). Anything related to the human can be associated with danger in this tale such as the human's cabin, where 'no crickets chirped. No frogs croaked. There were no scuffles in the underbrush', implying that humans bring silence, death and danger (85).

Ironically, despite the villainous portrait painted of the human, the human calls foxes 'villains' for 'murdering innocent ducks, and mouses', leading to the potential for a classroom discussion on the irony of this comment and the reality of environmental injustices (86). Furthering the irony is the fact that the trapper in the story is a subversive version of Beatrix Potter. Famous for her animal stories, conservation efforts and work as a natural scientist, Potter could be used as a case study to teach *about* environmental injustices and strategies to prevent or fix them. Students could lead research projects about what it means to be a conservationist, why conservation is necessary and its benefits. However, it is also vital to look at the negatives of conservation, which this mutinous idea of Beatrix Potter highlights. For example, in the cabin, a rabbit tells Mia that 'she keeps us in these cages, feeding us nothing but oatmeal until our fur loses the smell of the forest' (90). In this quote, the rabbit implies that by being taken away from the wilderness, the animals are losing pieces of themselves. This is further displayed when Mia is faced with some of Potter's most famous characters, 'a bullfrog, a bunny, a squirrel' but 'they weren't behaving like animals. They stood upright on their hind paws and wore extra skins just like a human' (92). The rabbit states that 'Miss Potter doesn't like animals the way they are' and so she 'makes them more like her' (92). This could lead to a dialogue about anthropomorphizing animals and how it takes away from their natural being. However, as this story focuses more on conservation, it is perhaps more pertinent to start with a conversation of sustainability. Here, students should discuss how/ why conservation could be detrimental to wildlife, leading to stories about SeaWorld, famous zoo escapes or attacks and so on, which would link to the animal attack narrative in eco-horror. The teacher could ask students how zoos promote hierarchy and domination in the fact that animals must rely on the human for protection, food and general needs. The aim of these conversations would be for students to decipher ways in which we could make conservation more sustainable in which there is no such hierarchy and domination and then working to make campaigns for their actions to work. By being part of a campaign, students are at the centre of their learning and are in charge of the outcomes of their education, which is vital in creating inspired, enthusiastic learners.

The third and final text to analyse is the 2022 Netflix stop-motion animation *The House* by Enda Walsh. *The House* 'showcases three short films set in different worlds, at different times, but they all take place in the same house' (Botts 2022). According to Botts, the stories' themes, which range from materialism to self-delusion to accepting reality and moving on, can be 'taken in the context of climate change' and 'tell a story deeply critical of humanity' (Botts 2022). The film is an anthology with three parts, and while part I shows the devastating consequences of materialism rotting the soul of a family, it is parts II and III that have a more eco-horrific feel with creatures taking over and an uneasy sense. In part II, the audience are introduced to a house developing rat who is desperately trying to flip a house before the buyer can notice any of its issues. The developer is portrayed as irritable, hostile and downright unpleasant. He is constantly phoning his contracting company, complaining about incompetence, lying and, eventually, harassing his own dentist (Botts 2022). The house itself is grim. Some parts are nice, such as the lighting and gleaming countertops, but deep down, the viewer can see the garbage in the corners, the bug infestation throughout and the rat in charge. The house and the developer are allegories for 'our need for more and newer things' leading 'to growing piles of waste until we find ourselves trudging through a world littered with the old and discarded' (Botts 2022). 'We build homes that displace other creatures, and then we work relentlessly to fight off infestation of pests and vermin' (Botts 2022). The truth of the story is that we are the pests, and we, as humans, are what cause the problems. This is exemplified further in the ending, when the developer is released from hospital only to find his property is infested with bugs and a freeloading family of rats. Our last view of the developer is him scuttling through a tunnel, reduced to nothing but the vermin he was so desperate to once eradicate. Before showing the entirety of part II, it could be beneficial to pre-teach the connotations and symbolism of rats and explore the potential of connections to humans and socio-environmental injustice. Following from this, students could be required to note down anything that seems 'odd' about the house and the developer's behaviour. With this, ideas could then be collected about what is wrong with the house and a character profile created about the developer. The character profile could then be used to explore the reasoning behind his behaviours and why he wants the house flipped so quickly, looking at what benefits he receives for selling. This could then turn into a criticism of greed and the materialism of humans and an examination of how we as a class could be less materialistic. Some fun ideas here would be listing the most recent things we had bought or wanted to buy and placing them in columns of 'need' and 'want'. Students could then see how many of their 'wants' and 'needs' are necessities or materialism at work. Other ideas for these classes could be explorations into what students could live without and why/why not, which could be furthered into a discussion of capitalism and materialism. With the right guidance, these investigations then lead to students putting theory into praxis, attempting to be less materialistic, looking at sustainability and ethical choices regarding purchases. Classes could make a pact together on items they would purchase or how often they would purchase unnecessary items, the results could be checked monthly and the teacher or students could research the positive impact these little changes are making. While there is a sense of urgency with eco-pedagogy and climate change, there is also a need to inspire and celebrate the little achievements. One thing that we do not want to see from students is a feeling that they cannot make a change, a feeling of disillusion and being disheartened. Students need to understand that simply by showing their understanding of socio-environmental injustices, creating strategies and implicating some form of change, they are being planetary citizens.

Part III displays a post-apocalyptic world, flooded and taken over by swirling mists, something that can most definitely be imagined in relation to climate change. In this part, the protagonist, Rosa, is a kind-hearted landlady, who desperately wants to improve her house, making it sustainable for her and her guests. Throughout the tale, Rosa begs her tenants to pay her with real money rather than fish and crystals. She denies the horrors that have destroyed the world and is adamant that things can go on as they were before. For example, when Jen mentions that 'the water took the whole garden', Rosa does not reply, prompting Jen to ask, 'Why don't you ever talk about the flood?' Rosa this time does reply with 'there's nothing to talk about', showing her true denial of the issues at hand. In this, Rosa 'is a stand-in for people blind to the realities of climate change' (Walsh 2022). Instead of facing the issues, Rosa's deep obsession with the house is her attempt at finding normalcy in the devastation around her. This is the true horror in this story, there are no bugs or visual nasties; instead, there is an unsettling, eerie sense about Rosa's state of mind, which we fall into as viewers. Unlike the other parts though, this one has a happy ending. When Jen's friend Cosmos arrives, he agrees to fix the house in exchange for lodgings (Botts 2022). However, Cosmos lives in the post-apocalyptic mindset and his idea of fixing the house is by fixing it into something useful, such as a boat. Devastated and delusional, Rosa becomes angry with her friends. She refuses to believe that Cosmos is 'only here to help' her 'move on' (Botts 2022). That is until the mist causes her to hallucinate her friends as 'monstrous and terrifying' visions (Botts 2022). These lead her to have the realization that she must 'see through those obscuring mists, the lie of materialism and status from within', she must 'accept that the world she knew is gone' and she must open her eyes and believe in the dangers of climate change (Botts 2022). This part of the film would be fun to use to discuss fake news and the way socio-environmental injustices are recorded. Looking at news stories about climate change from varying news outlets, students could be divided into groups to debate about the truth behind climate change. One side would use news stories (mainly fake news) to disregard climate change, while the other would argue, using credible sources, that climate change is real. This would support students in distinguishing fact from fiction and in identifying credible news sources, a skill vital in the social-media-run world today. To support this activity, students could then do artwork, posters and presentations, using credible news sources to display climate change facts around the school, ensuring that fake news is not spread through propaganda. Other class groups could create a student newspaper or write for existing student papers with facts found from credible sources. The main skill they should be able to take from this is being able to distinguish between credible sources and discredited sources as this is a vital skill that will be needed to challenge climate change and reporting.

Eco-anxiety

Using horror in the classroom could prove to be a safeguarding nightmare, especially if children are sensitive and get scared easily and this is further fuelled by the term 'eco-anxiety'. This term, while not a diagnosable mental health condition, describes the symptoms occurring from a deep-seated fear and anxiety about what is happening to the world around us (Camden et al. 2022). While 'not considered a pathological problem', eco-anxiety can cause 'genuine distress' and lead to mental health symptoms (Camden et al. 2022). Due to this, researchers have suggested that eco-anxiety should be 'placed on a spectrum' with two ends – one end has strong emotions that may empower people to 'change their habits and help the planet', the other 'may lead to debilitating paralysis when facing the immensity of the problem' (Camden et al. 2022). Thus, 'knowledge about climate change can lead to an increase in pro-environmental behaviours, it can also lead to paralysing anxiety and denial' (Camden et al. 2022). For children, they are 'growing up in an uncertain world, where messages of 'doom and gloom' about climate change often dominate the public discourse' (Camden et al. 2022). It is important that instead of torturing children with the doom, we fill them with some form of hope. Instead of children simply learning about climate change, they could learn about the changes they could make and put them into practice, which is what they would do in an eco-pedagogical classroom. Children should be involved in discussions about climate change, especially if they are always hearing the doomsday discourse from the media. Parents/carers and educators should open conversations and allow the child to be at the centre of these, asking the questions they need answering and be provided with some form of hope to ease the anxieties within.

To repeat Tidwell and Soles once more, 'we live in eco horrific times'. It is vital that the urgency of this matter is demonstrated, and what better way to do this than through the genre of horror – a genre that strikes fear and anxiety into viewers and when used as a social commentary may be a dire plea to fight injustices. Eco-horror specifically is imperative as it focuses on environmental injustices and is used as a social commentary on the fears, anxieties, threats and carnage that the environmental crisis could cause. However, it could promote eco-anxieties. But to alleviate this, the eco-pedagogical classroom – a classroom focusing not solely on the context of environmental injustices but also on strategies and responses to reduce, reverse or eradicate – should be a safe space, where children may deliver their fears and anxieties, and even face them in the form of eco-horrific texts. Teachers should allow for meaningful, complex conversations that ideally deliver a solution, a strategy, a method to combat the negativity, the anxiety, the fear being discussed or observed. Teachers must choose eco-horrific texts sensitively for their class dynamic and socio-economic backgrounds. Throughout this chapter, I have outlined three eco-horrific texts that could be suitable for secondary classes and have provided ideas for tasks that could be used to support students make environmental choices and create global, planetary citizens. It is my hope that by exploring different facets of horror and children's horror, schools will not only adopt more horror in their curriculums but will also use it eco-pedagogically or view it through lenses, such as colonialism, gender studies, queer theory and so on. If it is a genre that children enjoy, why not use it to benefit society? After all, 'if you turn tail from the horror and don't stay till the end, then the darkness of the story can swallow all hope' (Heidicker 2019, 9).

References

Ajani, Ashia. 2022. 'The Evolution of Eco-Horror'. Atmos. Last Modified 27 October 2022. https://atmos.earth/the-evolution-of-eco-horror-jordan-peele-halloween/.

Botts, Eric. 2022. 'The Ticking of Clocks'. The Other Folk: Articles, Essays, Stories & Poems about Horror in Media and Life. Last Modified 9 March 2022. https://www.theotherfolk.blog/dissections/the-house.

Camden, Chantal, Terra Leger-Goodes, Catherine Malboeuf-Hurtubise, Trinity Mastine, Melissa Genereux and Pier-Olivier Paradis. 2022. 'Eco-anxiety in Children: A Scoping Review of the Mental Health Impacts of the Awareness of Climate Change'. *Frontiers in Psychology* 13 (July): 1–3.

Department for Education. 2014. *The National Curriculum in England: Key Stages 3 and 4 Framework Document.* United Kingdom.

Ernst, Jackie. 2019. 'Why Children Love Spooky, Dead Things'. Romper. Last Modified 10 October 2019. https://www.romper.com/p/why-children-love-spooky-dead-things-19199976.

Gaard, Greta. 2009. 'Children's Environmental Literature: From Ecocriticism to Ecopedagogy'. *Neohelicon* 36, no. 321: 332–3.

Giroux, Henry Armand. 2010. 'Rethinking Education as the Practice of Freedom: Paulo Freire and the Promise of Critical Pedagogy'. *Policy Futures in Education* 8, no. 6 (December): 715.

Goldberg, Matt. 2022. 'Annihilation Explained: Unpacking Alex Garland's Brilliant, Trippy Sci-Fi Horror Film'. Collider. Last Modified 1 November 2022. https://collider.com/annihilation-movie-explained/.

Heidicker, Christian McKay. 2019. *Scary Stories for Young Foxes.* New York: MacMillan, 1–92.

Jones, Wil. 2016. '*The Animals of Farthing Wood*'s Most Traumatic Deaths' Den of Geek. Last Modified 25 October 2016. https://www.denofgeek.com/movies/the-animals-of-farthing-woods-most-traumatic-deaths/.

Kerr, Margee. 2015. 'Why We Love to Be Scared'. Psychology Today. Last Modified 7 October 2015. https://www.psychologytoday.com/us/blog/why-we-scream/201510/why-we-love-be-scared.

Lester, Catherine. 2021. *Horror Films for Children: Fear and Pleasure in American Cinema.* London: Bloomsbury Academic, 3.

Macmillan Publishers. 2019. 'Scary Stories for Young Foxes.' Macmillan Publishers. https://us.macmillan.com/series/scarystoriesforyoungfoxes.

Misiaszek, William Greg. 2018. *Educating the Global Environmental Citizen: Understanding Ecopedagogy in Local and Global Contexts.* New York: Routledge.

Misiaszek, William Greg. 2020. *Ecopedagogy: Critical Environmental Teaching for Planetary Justice and Global Sustainable Development*. London: Bloomsbury Academic.

Misiaszek, William Greg, and Carlos Alberto Torres. 2019. 'Ecopedagogy: The Missing Chapter of Pedagogy of the Oppressed'. In *The Wiley Handbook of Paulo Freire*, edited by Carlos Alberto Torres, 463–89. New Jersey: Wiley-Blackwell.

Murray, Robin. 2017. 'Laughter and the Eco-horror Film: The Trauma Solution Part I: The Toxic Avenger'. Ecocinema, Media, and the Environment. Last Modified 29 June 2017. http://ecofilmmediaenvironment.blogspot.com/2017/06/laughter-and-eco-horror-film-troma.html.

Rust, A. Stephen, and Carter Soles. 2014. 'Ecohorror Special Cluster: "Living in Fear, Living in Dread, Pretty Soon We'll All Be Dead"'. *Interdisciplinary Studies in Literature and Environment* 21, no. 3 (Summer): 509–12.

Sellgren, Katherine. 2017. 'Teaching to the Test Gives Hollow Understanding'. *BBC News*. 11 October 2017. https://www.bbc.com/news/education-41580550.

Soles, Carter, and Christy Tidwell. 2021. 'Introduction: Ecohorror in the Anthropocene'. In *Fear and Nature: Ecohorror in the Anthropocene*, edited by Carter Soles and Christy Tidwell, 1–4. Pennsylvania: The Pennsylvania State University Press.

Vartan, Starre. 2019. 'How Wildlife Bridges over Highways Make Animals – and People – Safer'. *National Geographic*. Last Modified 17 April 2019. https://www.nationalgeographic.com/animals/article/wildlife-overpasses-underpasses-make-animals-people-safer.

Vinney, Cynthia. 2022. 'Why Do We Enjoy Horror Movies?' Verywellmind. Last Modified 8 April 2022. https://www.verywellmind.com/why-do-people-like-horror-movies-5224447.

Walsh, Enda, director. 2022. *The House*. Netflix.

INDEX

Milton Keynes UK
Ingram Content Group UK Ltd.
UKHW021911190524
442833UK00004B/46